SOVIET

FOREIGN PROPAGANDA

BY FREDERICK C. BARGHOORN

PRINCETON, NEW JERSEY

PRINCETON UNIVERSITY PRESS

1964

Publication of this book has been aided
by the Ford Foundation program
to support publication, through university presses,
of works in the humanities
and social sciences.

Printed in the United States
of America

Second Printing 1966

TO THE MEMORY OF

JOHN FITZGERALD KENNEDY

◈ ﹥ PREFACE

ALTHOUGH by now a truly vast literature on the Soviet
Union has been produced by scholars, many significant aspects of Soviet policy still remain relatively unexplored. Perhaps one of the most important of these neglected areas is
the international political communication program of the
USSR. In this study I have attempted to trace the historical
development of the unprecedentedly systematic effort made
since 1917 by the Soviet communists to shape world opinion.
I have also sought to analyze the major themes and to describe
the organization and techniques of the international propaganda activity centered in Moscow.

Perhaps an attempt to deal with such a vast subject between two covers smacks of rashness. I hope, nevertheless,
that this book will not only contribute to knowledge of a
significant instrument of Soviet foreign policy but will also
stimulate other scholars to seek to widen and deepen our understanding of the role of the manipulation of symbols on the
international scene as a factor in Soviet world policy.

Whatever the limitations of this study may be, they would
certainly have been much more serious had I not benefitted
by a great deal of invaluable advice and assistance from a wide
variety of sources. I owe a continuing debt to those pioneers
in the analysis of the political uses of communication, Hadley Cantril, Mark A. May, and Harold D. Lasswell, for friendly
counsel and stimulating example. Of course, neither they nor
the many other persons in academic or official positions who
generously offered bibliographical or interpretive suggestions
bear any responsibility for the use or misuse I may have made
of their help.

My work on this book, like that on my somewhat related
study, *The Soviet Cultural Offensive,* was facilitated in a
variety of ways by my association with The Inter-University
Committee on Travel Grants. I should like to express my

appreciation to colleagues on the Committee and especially to its indefatigable Deputy Director, Mr. Stephen B. Viederman, for sharing insights and information. Data on Soviet secrecy practices cited in the study were assembled partly in connection with a RAND Corporation project directed by Dr. Fred C. Iklé. A number of officials of the Department of State and the United States Information Agency called my attention to or made available unclassified but relatively inaccessible materials useful in my research.

My attention was called to certain aspects of Soviet propaganda activity in Japan by Professor Rodger Swearingen. Professor Boris Meissner called my attention to an important published document on communist propaganda in the German Federal Republic. Professor Saul N. Silverman and Mr. Franklyn J. C. Griffiths made useful bibliographical suggestions regarding Soviet peace propaganda.

This book could probably not have been written without the stimulation derived from working with undergraduate and graduate students at Yale University and with graduate students at the Russian Institute of Columbia University. I owe a great deal to the conscientiousness and ingenuity of Miss Joelle Schroeder, Mrs. Denis Mickiewicz, and Messrs. George Vojta, Allen Sinel and Frank Letcher, who assisted me in assembling some of the material upon which this work is based.

The cheerful efficiency of Miss Veronica O'Neill, the highly competent secretary of the Yale Political Science Department, and the exceptional patience and skill of Mrs. Hazel O'Donnell, who saw the numerous drafts of the manuscript through their typings, contributed greatly to the completion of the monograph.

A particularly vital contribution to the production of the book was made by Messrs. Gordon Hubel and David C. Harrop of the Princeton University Press. Their editorial advice was characterized by a singularly felicitous combination of firmness and fairness.

I take particular pleasure in once again expressing my appreciation to all of my colleagues and administrative superiors at Yale whose friendly assistance did so much to make possible the researching and writing of this book. Financial assistance from the Stimson Fund of Yale University played an essential facilitative role. Even more important, however, was the continued assurance of an appropriate setting for research.

After completing this study, I made another trip to the USSR and was arrested and detained by Soviet State Security police from October 31, 1963, until November 16. This action adds a new dimension to the Soviet propaganda techniques discussed in Chapter VII. Among its probable motives was a desire to lend some semblance of credibility, however contrived, to the increasingly frequent Soviet charges that American Sovietologists are really "spies" in disguise. This charge, made by many speakers at the Kremlin ideological conference in December 1961—its proceedings were published in 1962 in the important book *XXII sezd KPSS i voprosy ideologicheskoi raboty* (*The Twenty Second Congress of the CPSU and Problems of Ideological Work*)—in turn reflects Kremlin concern over the growth of skepticism and other "harmful" attitudes toward the official creed of Marxism-Leninism among some strata of Soviet intellectuals and students. To deal with such attitudes and discredit the west, Soviet propagandists in recent years have demanded the application of "offensive" tactics. My experience may have resulted from an unusually vigorous manifestation of "offensive" Soviet propaganda in action. It is to be hoped that Soviet behavior in this episode represented a deviation from a trend toward easier and freer international communication rather than a violent expression of a strategy designed to prevent objective investigation of Soviet reality by foreign scholars.

FREDERICK C. BARGHOORN

December 2, 1963

 CONTENTS

 SOVIET FOREIGN PROPAGANDA

CHAPTER I

SOVIET DOCTRINE ON THE ROLE OF PROPAGANDA

WORDS and pictures have played a more continuous, and perhaps a more vital role than bullets or rubles in Moscow's struggle to undermine the social order of capitalism and to reconstruct society on "Marxist-Leninist" foundations. Lenin and his followers were convinced that they had an historic mission to transform human relations and ultimately shape a "new" communist man. The conviction that only they are privy to the "truth" has given communists confidence in the righteousness of their cause. It has not, however, rendered them at all indifferent to the necessity of exercising the utmost skill in shaping the outlook and firing the imagination of their audiences. Communists know it is their duty to master the legacy of Lenin, who, like other successful propagandists, taught that the success of a social movement depended as much on use of the art and strategy of persuasion as on firmness of convictions. Communist propaganda is formidable because it combines crusading zeal with professional skill. Today, to these sources of strength it adds the material achievements of the "socialist camp," most spectacularly manifested in the feats of Russian astronauts. Selected aspects of Soviet achievements are highlighted by Moscow as proof of the success of socialism.

Understanding of the contemporary significance of propaganda as an instrument of Soviet foreign policy requires some acquaintance with the writings of V. I. Lenin on the instrumentalities of politics. Perhaps the salient characteristic of Lenin's version of Marxism, especially of his conception of the disciplined hierarchical revolutionary organization out of which grew the bolshevik party, the Soviet state, and the international communist movement, was his emphasis upon the power of political communication. It is noteworthy that in his central contribution to the bolshevik theory of strategy and tactics, *What Is To Be Done?*, Lenin paid close attention to urging the establishment of an all-Russian political newspaper. Its staff was to act as his agents in propaganda, intelligence, and organizational work.[1] In this work, Lenin exhorted his followers to "go to all classes of the population" in the capacity of "theoreticians, propagandists, agitators and organizers." Lenin thus stressed the political significance of communication.

Also, like Trotski and other left-wing Russian Social Democrats, Lenin defined, in terms broader than those which western European Marxists had usually used, the social targets for his party's revolutionary mission. In this way he helped to provide a basis for rationalizing what was to become the bolshevik predilection for various forms of limited collaboration between Leninists and other political groups. Lenin's emphasis on the breadth of his movement's short-run goals reflected his realization that bolshevism could not gain power in a backward and still largely agrarian society unless the "party of the proletariat" won over to its side at least substantial portions of the peasantry, and the still weak but rapidly developing middle classes. Most important for our interests in this study is the fact that Lenin established a tradition within which bolshevik "professional revolutionaries" and, later, specially trained functionaries of the Soviet state and of foreign communist parties, have systematically employed modern communications techniques in a continuing effort to bring about "the radical transformation of the conditions of life of all of mankind."[2]

Obviously, the present leadership of the Soviet Union shares

[1] V. I. Lenin, *Izbrannye proizvedeniya v dvukh tomakh*, Vol. I (Moscow, 1943), pp. 157, 176, 186.
[2] *Ibid.*, p. 252.

Lenin's concern regarding the significance of propaganda as a political instrument. Indeed, an intensification of emphasis on the role of political communication has been a conspicuous feature of the post-Stalin era. Continuous reissuing of Lenin's complete works—a fifth edition is now in process of publication—is one of many indications of continuity in outlook between Lenin and those who proudly proclaim themselves his pupils and successors. Such "classics" of Leninism as *What Is To Be Done?* are studied and re-studied in both the general educational and the special political training institutions which shape the outlook of Soviet citizens, especially those aspiring to elite status.[8]

The major addresses delivered at congresses of the Communist Party of the Soviet Union by Lenin, Stalin, Khrushchev, and other important leaders, or at special meetings of the ruling CPSU devoted to problems of propaganda and political education, have always emphasized that the party regards agitation, propaganda, and other forms of "ideological work" as one of its central tasks. Such ideological work is also deemed a significant function of the subordinate "mass organizations," such as the Young Communist League, the Soviet trade unions, and others. This concern with mass communication was emphasized in an article published in a Soviet

---

[8] See, for example, Alex Inkeles, *Public Opinion in Soviet Russia* (Cambridge, Mass., 1951), Part 1; John A. Armstrong, *The Soviet Bureaucratic Elite* (New York, 1959), Chaps. 3 and 7; *Programma po kursu zhurnalistiki*, published by the Higher Party School of the CPSU central committee (Moscow, 1958); *Aspirantura, spravochnik dlya postupayushchikh v aspiranturu i soiskatelei uchenykh stepenei* (Moscow, 1960). The latter indicates the works of Lenin, Stalin, Marx, Khrushchev, etc., which must be studied in the political courses taken by Soviet graduate students. See also *Lenin-zhurnalist i redaktor* (Moscow, 1960), in which Lenin's activities and techniques as political journalist and editor are held up as models for present-day Soviet practitioners in these fields; and *Lenin o propagande i agitatsii* (2nd edition, Moscow, 1962); a handbook of selected statements by Lenin on propaganda. E. Adamov, in his pamphlet, *O masterstve rechi propagandista* (Moscow, 1962), quotes Lenin frequently—but quotes Khrushchev even more frequently, perhaps.

reference work in 1939, which stated that "the problem of propaganda has always been the center of attention of all party congresses and conferences."[4]

A particularly interesting indication of the importance attached to propaganda by the CPSU leadership in the post-Stalin era was contained in a speech given by Leonid F. Ilichev (now, next to Khrushchev, perhaps the leading Soviet policymaker in all fields of political communication) at a conference held in Moscow in September 1960. As quoted in *Pravda* for September 14, 1960, Ilichev stated that the CPSU had "now raised ideological work and the communist education of the working people to the level of the central task of the party, the trade unions, the Young Communist League and other public organizations." Continuing, Ilichev asserted that "the need to step up ideological-educational work derives from the present-day domestic and international situation and is objectively dictated by the laws of socialist construction." He stated further that the building of communism in the USSR was not merely an internal Soviet affair. It was also a decisive factor in the competition of two social systems in the world. The Soviet people, he went on to say, looked upon their struggle to build communism as an obligation to the working people of the whole world. Ilichev thus stressed two major themes which have normally been prominent in Soviet statements regarding political communication, and which, since the death of Stalin, have been vigorously reemphasized. One theme, as already indicated, is that the success and very survival of communism as a movement depend largely upon the energy and skill of communists as communicators. Secondly, Ilichev's references to the international situation and

---

[4] *Malaya sovetskaya entsiklopediya*, 2nd ed., Vol. 8 (Moscow, 1939), cols. 726-731. The article also briefly summarized Lenin's activities as a propagandist, referring, for example, to the school for training party propagandists organized by Lenin in Paris, in 1911, Lenin's sloganeering during World War I, and his role after the bolshevik revolution of 1917 in helping to establish the Soviet network of propaganda agencies.

the struggle of "two systems" reminded his audience that to-day, despite the changes in—some would say, the degeneration of—Russian Marxism since the period when Lenin first demanded the establishment of a party of professional revolutionaries, communist propaganda is devoted, ultimately, to a political-ideological mission. This mission is overthrowing "capitalism" and first establishing "socialism," and, eventually, "communism" throughout the world.

Contemporary Soviet doctrine reaffirms a well-established pattern by also emphasizing the foreign propaganda significance of the internal economic development of the USSR. A resolution passed by the Twentieth CPSU Congress, in 1956, called for "a closer link between propaganda and agitation and the task of establishing the material-productive base of communism."[5] It is clear from the context of this and later similar statements that they relate to foreign as well as to domestic Soviet policy.

Since this study is concerned primarily with the role of propaganda as an instrument of the foreign policy of the Soviet state, it may be well at the outset to remind ourselves that Moscow's appreciation of the political significance of propaganda does not imply any underestimation of the role of other instruments of domestic and international politics. Harold D. Lasswell has cogently observed that the aim of Soviet propaganda has been "to economize the material cost of world dominance."[6] However, Moscow—not to mention Peking—has never explicitly repudiated Lenin's dictum that great political problems are decided, in the last analysis, by force.[7] It is clear, however, that in our era of super-weapons the Soviet communists prefer more than ever before to achieve

[5] *XX sezd kommunisticheskoi partii sovetskogo soyuza, stenograficheski otchet*, Vol. II (Moscow, 1956), p. 426. This resolution was also referred to in *Politicheski slovar* (Moscow, 1958), p. 456.

[6] Harold D. Lasswell, "The Strategy of Soviet Propaganda," in Wilbur Schramm, ed., *The Process and Effects of Mass Communication* (Urbana, Ill., 1954), p. 538.

[7] Lenin, *Izbrannye proizvedeniya*, Vol. I, p. 436.

their ends by persuasion rather than by force, and that they share, to a high degree, the fear of the consequences of nuclear war which bulks so large in the policy calculations of Washington and London.

In a period of "competitive coexistence" the significance of propaganda may be great indeed. Professor Henry L. Roberts of Columbia University a few years ago raised the question whether under conditions of a military stalemate "of sorts," the "whole weight . . . of these two tremendous political and ideological systems will be brought to bear on one of the few areas of relative mobility and change—the realm of ideas and of cultural activities."[8] Professor Roberts' question seems as pertinent today as in 1958. Indeed, it may be more pertinent if the conclusion of a partial nuclear test ban treaty in 1963, while mitigating weapons competition, puts an even greater premium upon skill in persuasion.

The Soviet communists are, then, dedicated to an energetic, systematic, and persistent propaganda effort, both at home and abroad. How does the Soviet approach to foreign propaganda compare with the "western" approach? What have been the major elements of continuity and of change in the perception by the Soviet leadership of the functions of propaganda as an instrument of foreign policy? Before seeking answers to these questions in major Soviet writings and statements, it might be useful for us to establish a basis for comparison by examining some non-Soviet interpretations of the nature and functions of political propaganda. Robert T. Holt and Robert W. van de Velde note that there are almost as many definitions of propaganda as there are writers on the subject, but they identify it as "the attempt to influence behavior . . . by affecting, through the use of mass media of communications, the manner in which a mass audience perceives and ascribes meaning to the material world." Lasswell, in a study already

[8] *Columbia University Forum*, Spring, 1958, p. 29. See also Abraham Brumberg, "New Formula for Soviet Propaganda," *New Leader*, August 15-22, 1960.

8

referred to, describes political propaganda as "the management of mass communications for power purposes," while E. H. Carr, stressing Soviet success in the use of mass communications for foreign policy ends, defines propaganda as "a process organized and carried out by officials . . . as part of the normal conduct of foreign policy." Lindley Fraser traces the use of propaganda in political and religious struggles to the Old Testament, observing, however, that the American Civil War was the first important struggle during which propagandists "regarded it as a major part of their task to persuade outsiders—in particular, Great Britain—that their cause was good and would prevail. . . ."[9]

The above definitions tend to emphasize the elements of manipulation, or even of deception, in propaganda. They reflect the generally suspicious attitude toward the manipulation of symbols for political ends which has been typical of modern western political thought. Western students of politics, and especially of mass communications, are inclined, on the whole, to agree with Dovring's negative characterization of propaganda as "biased communication." Democratic governments, except perhaps in periods of acutely felt international crisis, are more inhibited than are totalitarian states from the employment of propaganda as a major instrument of foreign policy. The high degree of voluntary consensus that prevails in prosperous democracies fosters tolerance and skepticism. The lack of continuity of office and policy characteristic of democracy, especially in the United States, also militates

[9] Robert T. Holt and Robert W. van de Velde, *Strategic Psychological Operations and American Foreign Policy* (Chicago, 1960), pp. 26-27; E. H. Carr, *The Soviet Impact on the Western World* (New York, 1947), p. 69; Lasswell, *op.cit.*, p. 538; Lindley Fraser, *Propaganda* (London, 1957), p. 30. Other studies which provide particularly valuable insights or concepts useful in the analysis of Soviet propaganda include the following: Gabriel A. Almond, *The Appeals of Communism* (Princeton, 1954); Frank S. Meyer, *The Moulding of Communists* (New York, 1961); Neal Wood, *Communism and British Intellectuals* (London, 1959); Karin Dovring, *Road of Propaganda* (New York, 1959); and Murray Dyer, *The Weapon on the Wall* (Johns Hopkins Press, 1959).

against a systematic government-organized foreign propaganda program of the kind that seems to be a logical concomitant of totalitarianism.

However, the propaganda weaknesses of a democracy are more apparent than real. The unwillingness to attempt to impose its values and organizational patterns on the world that characterizes the government of a mature democratic society bespeaks a broad basis of agreement on fundamental values that is lacking in the outwardly confident but perhaps inwardly seething totalitarian regime. Still, the vigorous propaganda of totalitarianism, with its air of certitude regarding values and goals, has often proved persuasive to disillusioned, alienated, or politically unsophisticated audiences. The communists are at least partly correct in assuming—as they so evidently do—that facts will speak for themselves only if those who communicate them perform their function forcefully and competently.

By way of contrast with western usage, Soviet writers, nurtured in a tradition of what one might call political messianism, have tended to use the term "propaganda" in a highly positive sense, as more or less equivalent to education. Their approval, of course, is restricted to communist propaganda—that disseminated by the "international bourgeoisie" is invariably denounced as the essence of mendacity. Soviet communicators are generally unwilling to admit, except implicitly and infrequently, that they employ propaganda in the sense in which the term is pejoratively used in the west. Moreover, they are vague and usually reticent regarding the foreign propaganda activity of the Soviet state. This reticence has gradually replaced the frank exhortations to political missionary activity of the first few years of the bolshevik regime, and has tended to complicate the task of government officials and scholars seeking clues to Kremlin objectives and tactics in overt Soviet communications.

· Reticence, even extreme secretiveness, was Moscow's response from the early post-revolutionary years, to the often exaggerated but not unjustified accusations in foreign countries that Soviet Russia was seeking, by propaganda, to subvert the established social order wherever it saw any possibility of so doing. Almost from the inception of the Soviet regime, foreign governments began to be frustrated and exasperated by what George F. Kennan has called "that ambiguity and contradictoriness of Soviet policy which has endured to the present day: the combination of the doctrine of co-existence—the claim, that is, to the right to have normal outward relations with capitalist countries—with the most determined effort behind the scenes to destroy the western governments and the social and political systems supporting them."[10] Yet, there have also been many occasions when foreign communists, and some Soviet communists, have felt that Moscow was not doing everything in its power to support the cause of social revolution.[11]

Lenin and his followers were acutely aware of the impossibility of inducing more than a tiny fraction of even that most "advanced" social class, the proletariat, to understand, assimilate, and, above all, act in accordance with the complex Marxist system of beliefs and values to which they subscribed. After all, a central tenet of bolshevism always has been that the workers, peasants, and other underprivileged strata of "bourgeois" society, given the influence exerted on their thinking by the machinery of propaganda in the hands of the bourgeois "ruling class," could never elevate their understanding of political and social forces above the level of mere "labor union consciousness" without the guidance of full-time "professional" revolutionaries.[12] The articles on propaganda and

[10] George F. Kennan, *Russia and the West under Lenin and Stalin* (Boston & Toronto, 1960, 1961), p. 166.
[11] See Alexander Dallin, "The Use of International Movements," in Ivo J. Lederer, ed., *Russian Foreign Policy* (New Haven & London, 1962), Chap. 10.
[12] Lenin, *Izbrannye proizvedeniya*, pp. 175, 186.

11

related topics in Soviet encyclopedias and other authoritative sources over a period of some forty years have continued to quote and paraphrase Lenin's prescriptions for overcoming the influence of "bourgeois" propaganda on the "masses" and for awakening the victims of "capitalism" to an awareness of their true interests.[13] According to the Leninist theory of opinion formation a few intelligent and dedicated individuals, drawn from all social classes, could be converted by means of propaganda to the "correct" Marxist, or Marxist-Leninist, point of view, and eventually some of these individuals might become fully trained party leaders. However, most people, including most members of the "working class," could best be influenced, and even then usually only temporarily, by what in Leninist doctrine is known as "agitation." In Lenin's original conception, agitation consisted of simple, concrete, forceful illustrations of the general principles of Marxism. In one example given by Lenin an agitator discussing the problem of economic crises took as a starting point the death from starvation of a worker's family. This illustration could be used to drive home the idea of "the senseless contradiction between the increase of wealth and the increase of poverty." A more complete explanation, according to Lenin, should be left to the propagandists.[14]

With the passage of time, and particularly since the consolidation of power in Russia by the bolsheviks after 1917, the concrete, agitational element in Soviet political communication has tended to overshadow the more abstract theoretical or propagandistic element. Also, agitation has tended to become more and more demagogic. As Alfred G. Meyer has

[13] See, for example, *Malaya sovetskaya entsiklopediya*, 1st ed., Vol. 1 (Moscow, 1928), col. 103; *ibid.*, Vol. 6 (Moscow, 1930), cols. 931-932; *Bolshaya sovetskaya entsiklopediya*, Vol. 24 (Moscow, 1953), pp. 495-496; 2nd ed., Vol. 35 (Moscow, 1955), pp. 30-33; *Politicheski slovar* (Moscow, 1958), p. 456.

[14] Inkeles, *op.cit.*, p. 39. A full understanding of Lenin's distinction between "propaganda" and "agitation" requires the study of a number of Lenin's works, especially *What Is To Be Done?*.

observed, agitation rather early became largely synonymous with the activity of inciting the masses to action by playing on their instincts and passions.[15]

It will be useful now to examine some typical Soviet statements on the subject of agitation, especially since, as Inkeles was the first to point out, this form of Soviet political communication has been relatively unstudied in the west. The 1928 article in the *Small Soviet Encyclopedia* on the work of the party in the fields of agitation and propaganda asserted that its basis was the inculcation of "the idea of revolutionary internationalism and the task of strengthening the Communist International as the leader of the revolutionary struggle on a world scale." This article, however, also stated that since 1921 the main content of domestic agitation had been defined by tasks connected with the reconstruction of the Russian national economy.[16] The 1937 article on agitation, in the second edition of the same source, asserted that the "bolshevist organization of agitation requires that all the working people be subjected to ideological influence," but it quoted both Lenin and Stalin concerning the necessity of tying agitation closely to the current policies of the party. Interestingly, the article also pointed out that the success of agitation was dependent upon its adaptation to the particular social stratum to which it was addressed.[17] These statements reflected the increasingly pragmatic spirit of the Soviet approach to political communication, especially after the consolidation of Stalin's totalitarian rule.

The 1949 article on agitation contained in the second edition of the *Large Soviet Encyclopedia* defined it as political activity designed to influence by dissemination of ideas and slogans the "consciousness and mood" of the "broad masses." It added that agitation was an important instrument in the

[15] Alfred G. Meyer, *Leninism* (Cambridge, Mass., 1957), p. 50. Meyer strongly emphasizes the manipulative element, even in early Leninism.

[16] *Malaya sovetskaya entsiklopediya*, Vol. i, col. 103.

[17] *Malaya sovetskaya entsiklopediya*, 2nd ed., Vol. i, (Moscow, 1937), cols. 126-127.

struggle of classes and parties, conducted by means of press, radio, speech, posters, leaflets, cartoons, and the like. Regarding the international aspects of agitation, this article declared that agitation conducted by communist parties in capitalist countries was directed toward "the revolutionary training of the working class, and the working people generally, in the spirit of Marxism-Leninism." Such agitation, besides exposing "fascists and warmongers," played an important role in consolidating the ranks of the international labor movement, combatting Titoists, and exposing lies and slander about the USSR.[18]

It is interesting to compare this 1949 article with an article published in 1955 in the same encyclopedia—after a considerable change of the Soviet political "line." This article asserted that the communists of all countries successfully utilized the experience of the USSR "in the struggle for peace, democracy, and socialism." Indicating the determination of the post-Stalin leaders to exploit nationalist, anti-colonialist, sentiments, it declared that "bourgeois" propaganda not only sought to shake the faith of the working people in the possibility of achieving socialism, but, in its efforts to keep the masses in the capitalist countries enslaved, such propaganda also preached the "dogma of the domination of certain peoples over others." In contrast, the communists, the article stated, disseminated the concept of "proletarian internationalism," as well as "the ideology of the friendship of peoples and real patriotism," and, of course, "the struggle for peace in the whole world."[19]

It is probably sensible to assume that from the Kremlin's standpoint most Soviet messages addressed to non-communist foreign audiences, including speeches and interviews by Khrushchev and other top leaders, and statements made by Soviet representatives at the United Nations, fall within the

[18] *Bolshaya sovetskaya entsiklopediya*, 2nd ed., Vol. I (Moscow, 1949), pp. 295-301.
[19] *Bolshaya sovetskaya entsiklopediya*, 2nd ed. Vol. 35 (Moscow, 1955), p. 73.

category of agitation. On the other hand, literature for Marxist-Leninist "study groups," which were found by Royal Commissions in Canada in 1946 and in Australia in 1954 to have been among the instruments for recruitment of susceptible intellectuals into communist "cells," might reasonably be classified as propaganda in the Leninist usage.

We should point out, at this stage of our discussion, that Soviet political communication—hereafter, we will usually use the term propaganda to cover all aspects of such communication—presents both an ideological aspect and a manipulative aspect. By the ideological element in Soviet communication we refer to indications of the faith of Soviet communists that their system of beliefs and their way of life represent an appealing, convincing, model for all of mankind, which will eventually, if its virtues are effectively disseminated, become universal. They can contribute to the adoption of communism by humanity in general by means of exhortation, persuasion, pressure, and, if need be, by violence. Despite the obvious—to a "bourgeois" outsider at least—weaknesses and vulnerabilities of Soviet communism, and also despite the growth of the pragmatic, expediential element in Soviet strategy and tactics, this ideological, almost "religious," but somewhat ritualistic aspect, has never disappeared from the content of Soviet propaganda. Indeed, the persistence of the phraseology of political messianism over a period of more than sixty years in the official documents of Russian Marxism is rather impressive. Looking backward, we find that the first manifesto of the Russian Social-Democratic Labor Party, adopted in 1898, referred to "the great historical mission of the proletariat," namely, the establishment of "a social order in which there will be no place for the exploitation of man by man."[20]

The program adopted sixty-three years later by the CPSU,

[20] *KPSS v rezolyutsiyak i resheniyakh. Tizdanie sedmoe* (Moscow, 1953), Vol. I, p. 13.

at its Twenty-second Congress in October 1961, boasted that one-third of mankind was "building a new life under the banner of scientific communism" and it made bold to claim that "The socialist world is expanding; the capitalist world is shrinking." In these ways the program buttressed its position that "communism accomplishes the historic mission of delivering all men from social inequality, from every form of oppression and exploitation." Thus, in remarkably similar language, it echoed the messianic claim of 1898.[21]

The vision of the glorious society of the future, free of coercion and exploitation, which is allegedly being built in the Soviet Union, has normally played a conspicuous role in Soviet propaganda. This "utopian" aspect of communism bulks large in the Soviet form of what Dyer has called the propaganda of "conversion"—which he contrasts to general propaganda, which seeks "relevant political action."[22] The process of ideological conversion, in turn, "produces revolutionaries and makes possible both the party and its hope for eventual success."[23]

Even in the communist propaganda of conversion and political recruitment, manipulative as well as purely ideological elements are present. As Almond points out, "The process of recruitment into the communist movement has at least two stages. The first is that of attraction to one of the many agitational representations. The second stage, that of training and testing in action screens out those elements who have suitable qualities and potentialities." And, as Almond further notes,

[21] The 1961 program is available in a number of good English translations, of which perhaps the most useful is that edited by Jan F. Triska, under the title *Soviet Communism, Programs and Rules* (San Francisco, 1962). Above material on pp. 24-25. The original Russian text of the program, as adopted, appeared in *Pravda* for November 2, 1961, while a slightly different "Draft" was published in *Pravda* for July 31, 1961; the differences are indicated by Triska.

[22] Dyer, *op.cit.*, p. 14.

[23] Lucian W. Pye, *Guerrilla Communism in Malaya* (Princeton, 1956), p. 40.

recruits "at the point of admission into the movement," perceive only dimly the "inner doctrine and practice of the party."[24] Certainly there is a wide gulf between communist demonology as presented in such mass media as the British *Daily Worker* or the French communist newspaper *L'Humanité*, and the power calculus set forth—though not fully systematized or explicated—in the "classics" of Leninism. Individuals are recruited into communist parties through appeals to personal, ethnic, class, or national aspirations and frustrations. Once under party discipline, they are given the political education and the ideological indoctrination that the party leadership regards as appropriate at a particular historical stage.

The utopian-ritualistic aspects of Soviet propaganda are still important. Like the sacred tenets of any belief system, these aspects bolster the sense of righteousness of those who profess to believe in them. They also serve to rationalize the policies of the communist leadership. However, this facet of Soviet propaganda is probably far less important in terms of both domestic and foreign policy than is the manipulative aspect.

By the manipulative aspect of Soviet propaganda we mean the practice of associating, either explicitly or implicitly, the goals and policies of the CPSU and the Soviet state with noncommunist symbols and sentiments in order to secure for Soviet policies the maximum possible support of noncommunists. Often those influenced by this process of manipulation are unaware of the motives or even the identity of the manipulators. Of course, the tactical flexibility and capacity for manipulation, even of Soviet propaganda, is not and never has been unlimited. To be sure, Soviet propaganda, particularly since about 1934, has been characterized by a high degree of what Lasswell and Blumenstock refer to as "adaptiveness," or

[24] Almond, *op.cit.*, pp. 5 and 93.

the association of key symbols with the aspirations, grievances, and prejudices of the audience to which propaganda is directed. However, as the same authors point out, effective propaganda always requires an element of "distinctiveness." Certain symbols must be "distinctive in meaning and style; otherwise the propagandist will not be able to keep control of the attitudes which he fosters."[25]

Even during World War II, when the Soviet leadership sought to maximize military cooperation with the "capitalist" United States and Great Britain against Nazi Germany, *Pravda* continued to carry on its masthead the traditional appeal, "Proletarians of all countries, unite!" Of course, *Pravda* was not widely available outside the Soviet Union, and what was being said in Russian to Soviet communists was balanced during the period of the "Anglo-Soviet-American Coalition" by soothing assurances, in messages intended for non-communist audiences, of a community of interests and goals between the Soviet Union and the western democracies.

While demanding the exercise of adaptiveness in the interests of effective propaganda, Soviet leaders have usually been alert to the risks of flexibility. Lenin's warning in *What Is To Be Done?* that any deviation from "socialist ideology" signifies a strengthening of "bourgeois ideology" has been cited again and again by his successors whenever they felt it necessary to warn that the limits of flexibility in political strategy and propaganda were being approached.[26] Communists are frequently urged to combine ideological consistency with flexibility, as in Stalin's formula of "the greatest adhesion to principle (not to be confused with sectarianism) with a maxi-

[25] Harold D. Lasswell and Dorothy Blumenstock, *World Revolutionary Propaganda* (New York, 1939). See especially pp. 247-358 and also comment in David D. Truman, *The Governmental Process* (New York, 1951), p. 229.

[26] A recent example of such warnings is contained in the preface to the sixth volume of the fifth edition of the complete works of Lenin. See V. I. Lenin, *Polnoe sobranie sochinenii*, Vol. 6 (Moscow, 1959), ix.

mum of contacts and connections with the masses (not to be confused with 'tailism'!)."[27]

The insistence upon purity of principle in Soviet doctrine has reflected a fear that "alien ideas" might penetrate communist ranks, and that temporary allies might use communists for their purposes instead of serving as instruments of communist purposes. Efforts at maintenance of doctrinal purity have been supplemented throughout the history of the Soviet regime by measures of isolation, censorship, and counter-propaganda designed to combat the influence of the external "capitalist environment" as well as of "survivals of capitalism" inside the Soviet Union. Even in the post-Stalin period, Soviet advocacy of cultural exchange, for example, has never implied dismantling the Iron Curtain, or abandoning the ideological struggle between "socialism" and "capitalism." "Show trials" such as those of the 1920's and 1930's or that of U-2 pilot Francis Gary Powers in 1960 have had as one of their purposes the overcoming of the harmful effects on the Soviet masses and (more to be feared) even on party members, of the influence of "bourgeois" ideas, against which Khrushchev, like Stalin before him, has warned in many major statements.

At the Twenty-first Party CPSU Congress in 1959 Khrushchev asserted that "bourgeois" influences constituted a major obstacle to the fulfillment by Soviet youth of its lofty mission of building communism. He criticized party workers who, he said, underestimated the extent of bourgeois influences on Soviet youth on the ground that "the bourgeoisie was far away" and did not have access to Soviet young people. Khrushchev's warning, besides revealing doubt regarding the ideological stability of Soviet young people, suggested the reservations he must have had in mind when he assured the

[27] Quoted by Georgi Dimitroff in the *Communist International*, Nos. 17-18, 1935 (New York: Workers' Library Publishers, September 20, 1935), p. 1207, from an article by Stalin in *Pravda* for February 3, 1925.

world that his government sincerely desired reciprocity and mutuality in cultural exchanges.[28]

Despite the factors discussed above, however, the dominant, although by no means uninterrupted, trend in the development of Soviet propaganda strategy and tactics has been toward increasing flexibility and adaptiveness. Such adaptiveness is, as we have already indicated, rooted in Leninism, particularly in Lenin's vision of the revolutionary party as a unity, whose mission was to go to "all classes of the population." It can further be seen in Lenin's constantly reiterated emphasis upon the necessity for communists to form temporary alliances with such non-proletarian social forces as the peasantry and even with various segments of the bourgeoisie, or with bourgeois, even bourgeois-nationalistic, political parties. This aspect of Lenin's strategic doctrine received expression in a number of his early writings, in which he urged his followers to "make use of" liberals and liberal parties. The "class point of view," he wrote, required that the proletariat must "push forward" all "democratic" movements, including "bourgeois" democratic movements, and, not remaining content with the limited aims of these movements, turn them to the advantage of the forces of revolutionary socialism.[29]

This basic concept, which has from the ideological inception of bolshevism played a role both in over-all political strategy and in propaganda operations, was officially adopted as doctrine by the Second Congress of the Russian Social Democratic Labor Party—predecessor of the Russian Communist Party and of the present-day CPSU—in 1903. A resolution of this congress sanctioned, under conditions to be prescribed by the party's "central institutions," what were described as "temporary agreements with liberals or with liberal-democratic tendencies." The resolution stipulated that such agreements

[28] *Vneocherednoi XXI sezd kommunisticheskoi partii sovetskoga soyuza*, 2 vols. (Moscow, 1959), Vol. I, p. 58.
[29] V. I. Lenin, *Polnoe sobranie sochinenii*, 5th ed., Vol. 6, pp. 268-270.

should not be of such a character as to result in "confusing" the working class. It was on the basis of such principles that bolshevik propaganda and agitation, including participation in elections and in the activity of legislative bodies in the Russian Empire, was conducted during what Lenin was later to describe as the "preparatory period" of 1903-1917.[30]

It was not until 1920, however, that Lenin, in his important tract, *Left Wing Communism, An Infantile Disorder*, fully elaborated his precepts regarding propaganda flexibility. In this work, Lenin poured scorn on western European communists whose "sectarian" zeal blinded them to the stern necessities of patience, conspiracy, and temporary, expediential cooperation with socialists, non-communist trade unionists, and other non-communists or even anti-communists, against the main "imperialist" enemy. In *Left Wing Communism*, Lenin made his famous statement to the effect that it was necessary to combine "the strictest devotion to the ideals of communism" with the ability to undertake all necessary practical "compromises, maneuvers, agreements, zig-zags, retreats, etc. . . . ," in order, as he put it, to accelerate the "political bankruptcy" of the "bulwarks of private property," to "smash" them, and ultimately to conquer political power.[31]

Lenin described in this work the bolshevik exploitation of the opportunities offered for propaganda by the establishment of the Russian State Duma (Parliament) after 1907, and by the elections in 1917 to the short-lived Constituent Assembly, which was dissolved by the bolsheviks in January 1918. He demanded that communists in solving their "single international task" take into account the "national peculiarities" of each country, and he warned against the dangers both of "right opportunism" and "left sectarianism." Undoubtedly these descriptions and exhortations left a lasting imprint on Soviet and international communist thinking.

[30] *KPSS v rezolyutsiyakh*, Vol. I, p. 49.
[31] Lenin, *Izbrannye proizvedeniya*, Vol. II, p. 570.

Left Wing Communism was published at a time when prospects for revolution in Europe, especially Germany—to which country the bolsheviks tended to look with particularly exaggerated hopes—still appeared to be bright. Also, during this period of revolutionary ferment the concept of the revolutionary potential of an alliance between the socialist-led industrial working class of Europe, and the revolutionary, or "progressive" segments of the "bourgeoisie" of underdeveloped countries, was becoming increasingly prominent in the policy statements of Lenin and some other Soviet leaders. Lenin had already begun to devote attention to this concept before the First World War, in connection with, for example, the Persian Revolution of 1906 and the Chinese Revolution of 1911. At the Second Congress of the Comintern, in July and August 1920, Lenin spelled out in detail the revolutionary possibilities inherent in an alliance between Soviet Russia and the economically backward "oppressed nations," against the industrialized "imperialist nations,"—such powers as Britain, France, the United States, and Japan.[32]

The Tenth Party Congress in 1921 adopted a resolution containing the following statement: "The party of revolutionary Marxism radically rejects the search for forms of organization or methods of work absolutely correct and suitable for all stages of the revolutionary process. On the contrary, the forms of organization and the methods of work are on the whole determined by the peculiarities of the given, concrete historical situation and by the tasks that flow directly from this situation."[33]

This formula, frequently republished, was eventually interpreted so flexibly as almost to allow the Soviet communists to regard as "Marxist" any policy which they considered to be appropriate. The capability of the Kremlin to employ maxi-

[32] *Vtoroi kongress kominterna* (Moscow, 1934), Vol. viii, pp. 98-161, 554.
[33] *KPSS v rezolyutsiyakh*, Vol. i, p. 516.

mum flexibility in its domestic and foreign propaganda was fostered by the development of a totalitarian political system in which the Soviet political leadership reserved a monopoly of the right of interpretation of the official ideology, and a monopoly of control of the communications network.

By the 1930's, a pattern had developed in the Soviet Union, according to which, as Inkeles puts it, "the average party member was no longer expected to master Marxism; it was enough that he understood the party's program and policies and worked to secure their attainment."[34] Inkeles' observation applies, one may add, not only to the internal communications practices of the Soviet communist party, but also to the international communist movement. The development of this pattern, and the accompanying process of "bolshevization" of foreign communist parties, by which these parties were largely converted into administrative agencies of the Kremlin, was paralleled by increasing secrecy in Soviet decision-making. More and more, especially after Stalin's victory over his rivals in the struggle for power within the ruling Soviet party, tactics of secrecy and deception were applied not only to Soviet non-communists and to "bourgeois" foreigners, but also to the rank and file communists, both in Russia and abroad. Under Stalin, propaganda, like other aspects of public policy, was permeated by conspiracy. As early as 1921-1923, long before he achieved supreme power, Stalin formulated a highly conspiratorial approach to propaganda and agitation. Characteristically, portions of the writings in which he set forth his strategic propaganda doctrine remained unpublished until 1947. In two articles, one drafted in 1921 but not published at the time, and the other published in *Pravda* in 1923, Stalin distinguished between "action" slogans and "agitational" slogans. The former were, he wrote, "definite orders" to the party, while the latter were designed to influence the attitudes

[34] Inkeles, *op.cit.*, p. 63.

and moods of various social groups, but did not commit the party to action.[35]

Concomitant with these trends there was a tendency, as Frank Meyer has pointed out, toward "the attrition of open propaganda," which "has, in the years since the mid-thirties, ceased to be periodic and become a permanent aspect of the Party's practice."[36] This tendency, of course, was part and parcel of the elitist, demagogic Soviet approach to opinion control which reached its fullest development in the late Stalin era, and to which Khrushchev is also attuned despite his flexibility and superficial candor.

Throughout most of the 1920's and during the first three or four years of the following decade, unfavorable world conditions tended to restrict the scope and sweep of Soviet foreign propaganda activity. The Soviet Union itself was exhausted by war and revolution and was preoccupied with problems of internal reconstruction and consolidation of the new regime. The USSR was, moreover, wracked until about 1929 by a largely concealed but intensely bitter internal power struggle. In western Europe and the United States, only relatively unstable and alienated intellectuals and a minority of the industrial workers supported or sympathized with the communist parties or responded to what were then still largely unsupported Soviet claims of economic and social achievements.

Most of the underdeveloped countries of the world were, in that period, still held firmly within the sphere of European or American economic, political, and ideological influence. Moreover, the communists' demand for total power, and the complicated and unfamiliar ideology in which it continued to be expressed, compounded the difficulties to be faced in the struggle for access to and impact upon the world audience.

[35] J. V. Stalin, *Sochineniya*, Vol. v (Moscow, 1947), pp. 62-87 and 160-180.

[36] Frank Meyer, *op.cit.*, p. 94.

It is probably also true that the conspiratorial Stalin, given more to the use of physical force than to the arts of persuasion, was considerably inferior both to Lenin and to Khrushchev as a propagandist.

However, both by constructing the power base for every type of Soviet pressure on the non-Soviet world, and by developing certain techniques in the field of international communications, Stalin laid the groundwork for many of the achievements of his successors. Although with rather limited results, Stalin carried on Lenin's tactics of seeking to associate the communist movement both with those few socialist leaders who would cooperate, and with such "bourgeois nationalist" movements as the Kuomintang in China. The latter association proved to be a disastrous one for Moscow and almost led to the destruction of the communist movement in China. Stalin systematically attempted to exploit exchanges of persons for propaganda purposes. He told the Fourteenth Congress of the Russian Communist Party in 1925, for example, that sojourns of "delegations of workers" from the west and visits by Indian, Egyptian, and Chinese groups constituted "the best, most forceful, and active propaganda for the Soviet system against the capitalist system."[37] It was Stalin, also, who pioneered in the use of interviews with foreign correspondents as an instrument of Soviet propaganda. By skillful timing and parsimony in granting interviews, Stalin often succeeded in dominating the headlines of newspapers in London, Paris, and New York.

It was only, however, after the rise of the Nazis to power in Germany, and the deadly threat posed by the Hitler regime to the security of the Soviet Union and the west that Stalin succeeded in achieving substantial impact as a propagandist abroad. The instrument chosen by Stalin to deal with the Nazi—and the lesser but also deadly Japanese threat—was that of the "popular front." Unlike the earlier, Leninist tactic

[37] J. V. Stalin, *Sochineniya*, Vol. VII (Moscow, 1947), pp. 291-292.

of the "united front," the popular front permitted alliances between communist parties or communist-controlled organizations, and "bourgeois" parties. In France, where the strategy of the popular front achieved its greatest success, as indicated by growth of party membership and election of communist or communist-influenced candidates to public office, the communist party for a time cooperated, in elections and otherwise, not only with the Socialist Party but with the rather conservative Radical Socialist Party.

Kermit E. McKenzie has pointed out that the reformulation in Soviet foreign policy strategy of the late 1930's was not only valid for the period 1935-1939, but also in a broad sense is applicable today. The traditional messianic concept of international communism, he emphasized, had involved a revolutionary reconstruction of society by the communist-led "working class." However, during the late 1930's, the communist mission was expanded to include the salvation of "bourgeois democracy," as well as of bourgeois culture, in the form of a somewhat socialized democracy, to which the term "new democracy" was applied.[38] Perhaps the richest and most convenient source for the study of this relatively flexible strategy is the proceedings of the Seventh—and last—World Congress of the Communist International, held in 1935.[39]

At this congress, Georgi Dimitroff, who had acquired a world reputation by defying the Nazis at the famous Reichstag fire trial, and who was at the time the General Secretary of the Comintern, urged that communists adopt the tactics of the "Trojan horse." He criticized the "sluggish" reaction of the communists to the demagogy of the fascists. He pleaded for a united front with socialist parties and socialist-led trade unions, but emphasized that the united front must be controlled by the

[38] Kermit E. McKenzie, "The Messianic Concept in the Third International," in E. J. Simmons, ed., *Continuity and Change in Russian and Soviet Thought* (Cambridge, Mass., 1955), pp. 516-530.
[39] *The Communist International*, Nos. 17-18.

communists. Particularly interesting, in view of later communist tactics, were Dimitroff's statements regarding nationalism. He stated: "Mussolini makes every effort to capitalize on the heroic figure of Garibaldi. The French fascists bring to the fore as their heroine Joan of Arc. The American fascists appeal to the traditions of Washington and Lincoln."[40]

Dimitroff asserted that the communists must prove to the peoples of their respective countries that they were the custodians of national, social, and cultural freedom and that only under communist leadership could the colonial peoples and the oppressed national minorities throughout the world achieve freedom.[41] Sensibly enough, he pointed out that "the broad masses cannot assimilate our decisions unless we learn to speak the language which the masses understand."[42]

The Stalin-Dimitroff propaganda tactics led the American Communist Party to adopt the slogan, "Communism is twentieth century Americanism." Earl Browder, prewar and wartime leader of the American communist movement, was perhaps carried away a bit by his effort to learn to speak "the language of the masses." Interestingly enough, in view of the propaganda use made, even under Stalin, of the concept of "coexistence," Browder in 1945 was to be criticized for allegedly advocating coexistence. Jacques Duclos, second-in-command of the French Communist Party, undoubtedly with the approval of Stalin, wrote that Browder had "declared, in effect, that at Teheran capitalism and socialism had begun to find the means of peaceful coexistence and collaboration in the framework of one and the same world." For this heresy, Browder was replaced as leader of American communism by the late William Z. Foster. The Duclos attack, as Robert V. Daniels has pointed out, signaled the revival of militance throughout the international communist movement.[43]

[40] *Ibid.*, p. 1218.   [41] *Ibid.*, pp. 1217-1221.
[42] *Ibid.*, p. 1239.
[43] Robert V. Daniels, *A Documentary History of Communism* (New York, 1960), Book II, p. 139.

In connection with the foregoing, it is not without interest that a textbook published during World War II for the instruction of Red Army political officers contained the following statement: "Led by the wise Stalin, the Soviet government, carrying out the instructions of Lenin, made use of the contradictions among the capitalist countries in the interests of the Soviet state, in the interests of peace, in the interests of smashing the fascist usurpers."[44]

On the whole, the last eight years of Stalin's rule were a period of consolidation of the territorial and other power gains achieved by the Soviet Union as a result of its military operations in eastern Europe and the power vacuum created in Europe and Asia by the collapse of Germany and Japan. These were not years of notable success for Soviet propaganda, although, as we shall bring out in some detail in the next chapter, the last two or three years of Stalin's life were marked by the beginnings of a departure from the rigidity and sterility which on the whole characterized the international communications practices of the late Stalin era.

Following the death of Stalin, the "neo-Maoist" strategy, in which the communists attempt to appeal directly to all "anti-imperialist" and especially anti-American elements, rather than—as in the period of the "popular front"—through formal alliances "from above" with socialist and other political parties, became the dominant and unprecedentedly successful Soviet propaganda strategy.[45] Under Khrushchev, Soviet foreign policy achieved greater flexibility than ever before in its choice of allies and associates, among which were now included some of the most backward regimes in the world, such as that of Yemen. Correspondingly, Soviet foreign propaganda achieved

[44] Professor G. A. Deborin, *Mezhdunarodnye otnosheniya i vneshnyaya politika sssr, 1929-1941, gg.* (Moscow, 1943), p. 152.

[45] On the nature and development of the "neo-Maoist" strategy, see John H. Kautsky, *Political Change in Underdeveloped Countries* (New York, 1962), pp. 73-89. See also Kautsky's study, *Moscow and the Communist Party of India* (New York, 1956).

hitherto unknown semantic adaptiveness. As Kautsky notes: "But though words lag behind action or, to use Marxist terminology, the ideological superstructure is transformed more slowly than the material base, in communist propaganda and theoretical writings, the 'peoples masses' and 'all peace-loving people'—and, most broadly, simply 'the peoples'—are more and more replacing the 'proletariat' and the 'working class,' fighting now not the 'class struggle' for 'class interests' and for the 'socialist revolution,' but in the 'national interest' for 'national independence.' "[46]

The post-Stalin flexibility in choice of propaganda targets and of language undoubtedly facilitated Soviet exploitation of nationalism, anti-colonialism and other major social forces of our time. However, this further development of the expediential, manipulative element in Soviet political discourse seems to be accompanied by tendencies toward ideological stagnation, and perhaps even reflects the partial decay of Soviet Marxism as a theoretical system. Unable to develop significant new concepts relevant to the modern world, or at least to that part of it which enjoys the blessings and copes with the problems of the "affluent society," Soviet theoreticians and propagandists have operated on what appear to be two related, but increasingly disconnected, levels. One level is that of obsolete, ritualistic formulas concerning such alleged but unproved conditions as the "increasing impoverishment" of the working class in the "capitalist" countries. The other is that of an often effective, but theoretically crude, pragmatism, seen particularly in the form of exploitation of the anti-western attitudes of the peoples of states recently established that formerly were under colonial rule. The frequently noted striking inferiority of Khrushchev to Lenin, and even to Stalin, as a theorist—perhaps more than balanced, however, at least in comparison with Stalin, by agitational talent of a high order—is illustrative

[46] *Ibid.*, p. 79.

of the further overshadowing of the ideological by the manipulative aspects of Soviet political communication in the post-Stalin era. It is interesting in this connection that Khrushchev, in the section of his report to the Twentieth CPSU Congress, in 1956, entitled "Problems of Ideological Work," emphasized that propaganda must not be overly concerned with "studying and lecturing on the principles of communism," but must be "practical." In this same report, Khrushchev used the word propaganda almost in the sense in which communist writers had traditionally used the term agitation. A few years later, Leonid Ilichev was to write that "in our era the boundaries between propaganda and agitation become more and more relative and conditional."[47]

The attenuation, admitted by Khrushchev and Ilichev, of the ideological element in Soviet propaganda seems to mark a further stage in its transformation from an instrument of a fanatical but vital political religion into a gigantic totalitarian public relations program. Today, this is a formidably effective program. Yet one may question whether its effectiveness may not gradually diminish if the problems of the underdeveloped countries become less acute and if the ideological *élan* of Soviet communism continues to fade.

In this chapter we have outlined the development of Soviet propaganda doctrine. In the next, we shall seek to deepen our understanding of the motives and strategy of Soviet propaganda by broadly describing its content, particularly since about 1950, as embodied in such typical forms as political slogans.

[47] *Kommunist*, No. 14, 1960, p. 35.

CHAPTER II

DEVELOPMENT OF THE PROPAGANDA

LINE

IN THIS CHAPTER we examine a series of Soviet propaganda messages which reflect Kremlin expectations regarding both threats, which were usually stressed in Soviet communications, and opportunities, which resulted, so the Soviet leaders felt, from the play of forces in the "capitalist environment" with which Moscow has been forced to cope, pending the revolution by which it is to be dismantled and then reshaped to communist specifications.

Since the CPSU's "general line," formulated and reiterated with appropriate modifications in certain key statements, sets the ideological and semantic framework to which Soviet propaganda must conform, a survey of a series of these propaganda directives may furnish a background useful for understanding the major propaganda themes to be treated in detail in subsequent chapters.

The communications examined have policy as well as propaganda aspects. It should be noted here that in Soviet political communication it is unusually difficult, and sometimes nearly impossible, to distinguish clearly between the elements of policy and propaganda. One can, of course, seek to infer policy from action. In reading Soviet mass media, however, it is difficult to separate analysis and directive, on the one hand, from demagogy and even deception, on the other. A heavy component of propaganda is built into most published Soviet statements, especially those intended for distribution outside of a relatively narrow circle of heavily indoctrinated, experienced communist party insiders. The party leaders, as is indicated by the Soviet propaganda doctrine analyzed in the preceding chapter, tend to view even most communists as objects of propaganda manipulation. Moreover, difficulties arise because they are impelled to resort to guarded, esoteric communication patterns that reflect both the influence of the elitist, conspiratorial political structure in which they operate and probably also the inadequacy of Marxist-Leninist terminology as a political language.[1]

Of course, the student of Soviet political prose learns to distinguish between statements intended primarily as policy directives for party executives and propaganda specialists, for example, and agitational statements designed to play upon the emotions of rank and file communists and of non-communists. Thus, an analysis in a CPSU theoretical journal such as *Kommunist*, most of the readers of which belong to the Soviet political elite, of the "political essence" of the "national bourgeoisie" can be classified as primarily a policy document. Still, such an article may be permeated with propaganda connotations of a more or less covert nature. It may be intended, in part, to convey to Soviet and foreign communist functionaries instructions regarding tactics to be applied in dealing with, for example, Indian, Indonesian, or Brazilian "bourgeois" statesmen. By contrast, when Khrushchev openly and insistently advocates "universal and complete disarmament" but dodges the issues of control and inspection, he is dispensing propaganda, but of course within the framework of the policy line controlling Soviet behavior in the given period.

Many Soviet statements, perhaps particularly those concerned with professed values and long-range goals, offer a

---

[1] Aspects of the "exoteric-esoteric" dichotomy in Soviet political communication have been perceptively analyzed by Almond, *op.cit.*, especially in chap. 3, and by Nathan Leites, in *A Study of Bolshevism* (Glencoe, Ill., 1953); see also Myron Rush, *The Rise of Khrushchev* (Washington, D.C., 1958) and Robert Conquest, *Power and Policy in the U.S.S.R.* (New York, 1961). Rush and Conquest are concerned primarily with Soviet domestic politics but their techniques of analysis have relevance also for the study of Soviet foreign policy statements.

rather confusing mixture of propaganda and policy content. Such a characterization would appear to be applicable to the statement taken from the 1961 CPSU program, and quoted by *Pravda*, for December 3, 1961 that "Communism fulfills the historic mission of rescuing all people from social inequality, from all forms of oppression and exploitation, from the horrors of war and establishes in the world peace, labor, freedom, equality, fraternity and the happiness of all peoples." Such a statement embodies both long-range policy and short-run agitational content. It also contains an element of myth and the reader's evaluation of it depends upon his fundamental political philosophy and his level of intellectual sophistication.

Understanding of Soviet propaganda strategy is facilitated by familiarity with certain kinds of statements, or indicators, such as the slogans issued by the party central committee in connection with the May Day and November 6 revolutionary holidays, or the documents emanating from congresses and other important meetings of the CPSU and the international communist movement. As a rule, the instructions, demands, and perspectives contained in slogans and other influence-seeking messages remain valid indicators of the Kremlin's outlook until they are altered or superseded by new communications that reflect new analyses and new decisions. Of course, these indicators have their imperfections. Even the leaders of various national communist parties often have difficulty in deciphering their full meaning for their particular situations. Nevertheless, acquaintance with those sequences of statements in which the semantically flexible but attitudinally rigid international policy line of Soviet communism have been embodied over time is essential to an understanding of Soviet foreign propaganda. Let us begin with a survey of the international implications of Soviet slogans.

A systematic analysis by Lasswell and Yakobson of trends in Soviet May Day slogans for the period 1918-1943 yielded significant results.[2] The central finding of the study, which covered a period, it should be noted, when Moscow was usually on the defensive, was a pronounced diminution in "universal-revolutionary" symbols.[3] This was attributed to "changed expectations regarding the imminence of world revolution, and the resulting change in the relationship of the ruling elite to the world balance of power."[4] During the dangerous year 1940 even the term "international proletariat" disappeared from the May Day slogans. It was in that year that the threat of "imperialist encirclement" seemed to the Soviet leaders to become more acute than ever before. In 1940 and again in the early months of 1941, the slogans reflected a desire "not to affect adversely, by any hasty or unfriendly word, the established understanding with Berlin."[5]

In 1942, during the first year of the Soviet-Nazi war, the slogans called upon the "proletarians" of all countries to fight against German-fascist aggression. The Nazis were referred to as "Hitlerite imperialist bandits," an expression calculated to mobilize both traditional Russian patriotic hatred of an invading enemy and the newer "Soviet patriotism" based upon devotion to Marxist-Leninist ideology and upon identification with Soviet institutions and achievements. The 1942 slogans significantly failed even to mention the Communist International. Its name was thus dropped well in advance of its official liquidation in 1943—"either by reason of obsolescence or in an effort to appease the new democratic allies."[6] Beginning in 1943, such words as "proletariat" and "proletarian" were no longer used in the slogans. From that year on, the slogans themselves began to be referred to as "appeals." The

[2] Harold D. Lasswell, Nathan Leites, and associates, *Language of Politics* (New York, 1949). The article on slogans, by Lasswell and Sergius Yakobson, entitled "Trend: May Day Slogans in Soviet Russia, 1918-1943," is on pp. 233-298.
[3] *Ibid.*, p. 242.   [4] *Ibid.*, p. 245.
[5] *Ibid.*, p. 279.   [6] *Ibid.*, p. 281.

1942 and 1943 slogans contained cautiously friendly references to Great Britain and the United States.

In the late 1920's and in the 1930's, a theme gradually emerged which is vital in Khrushchevian propaganda, and which like so many of Khrushchev's propaganda lines owed its inception to initiatives taken by Stalin. This theme was the superiority of the Soviet model for industrialization of a previously backward society, and it took on increasing significance during the period of the great depression in the west, in the early 1930's. By 1939, the slogans declared that the "immediate task" facing the Soviet people was that of "overtaking and surpassing" the economically progressive capitalist countries.[7] Even at this early stage, "the Soviet economy was ambitious to lead the world."[8] Of course, the introduction of the industrialization motif did not distract attention from urgent concerns connected with the difficulty of surviving in what Moscow correctly appraised as an exceedingly threatening world situation. The slogans, reflecting the bitter struggle of the Soviet leadership against external enemies and their real or fancied internal supporters, were dominated by warnings of impending dangers.

From the perspective of our times, however, it is significant that these slogans contained so many expressions of confidence about the future world role of the Soviet Union and of the communist movement in general. Despite the lesser prominence in the slogans and other contemporary communications of the general theme of "world revolution," this objective was, of course, not repudiated. For example, the famous "Short Course" on the history of the CPSU, published in 1938, stated in its introduction that the study of the history of the CPSU inspired confidence in the final victory of communism in the whole world.

World War II, while setting the stage for the second great

[7] *Ibid.*, p. 277.
[8] Lasswell and Yakobson, *loc.cit.*

35

period of expansion of world communism, also temporarily weakened the Soviet Union. In this complex and contradictory situation the Kremlin seized and, in the aftermath of the war, consolidated its control of as much territory as it could in eastern Europe and in Asia. Reflecting alarm at western resistance to Soviet expansion, the slogans, beginning in 1947, denounced the "warmongers" of the west. The May Day slogans, 1947-1952 inclusive, placed toward the beginning of the list such exhortations as "Workers of all countries: Struggle for a firm peace against the warmongers!"[9]

These slogans reflected Kremlin strategy in the period of military-political consolidation of the gains resulting from World War II.

May Day and November 6 slogans from 1953 on suggested only the broad outlines of the new world-wide propaganda strategy. Nevertheless, they furnished clues both to Soviet estimates of developing susceptibilities in various audiences and to the capability of the USSR to take advantage of them. In particular, they reflected Khrushchev's decision, from 1955 on, to exploit anti-western sentiments in Asia, Africa, and Latin America.

The most striking over-all difference between the post-Stalin slogans and those of the late Stalin period was the reappearance and growing frequency of "internationalist" symbols. This trend was signaled by the May Day slogans in 1953 which were issued about six weeks after the death of Stalin. The very first slogan contained the exhortation, "Raise higher the banner of proletarian internationalism!"[10] In every subsequent year following the death of Stalin this exhortation was repeated. Until 1962 it was contained either in the first slogan or in one of the first three, sometimes as part of one of the

[9] *Pravda*, April 26, 1947. The above was slogan No. 2. Slogan No. 3 urged the "workers of all countries" to "expose the aggressive plans of the imperialists! Tear the mask from the inciters of a new war!"
[10] *Pravda*, April 22, 1953, p. 1.

slogans and sometimes as a separate slogan. However, in 1962, it dropped to seventh place in the listing, perhaps reflecting a certain disillusionment in Moscow with the results of cultivating the foreign "internationalist" audience—though the clue may be too minor a one to serve as a basis for interpretation.

It is possible to distinguish between two kinds of "internationalism" in Soviet propaganda since Stalin. There is the traditional kind of communist internationalism, which is directed toward some group assumed to be favorable to the USSR—such as "peace partisans" or "workers"—or which revives such symbols of international communism as "proletarian internationalism." There is also a "great power" internationalism, in which the Soviet Union or other great powers appeal to world audiences without regard to class or ideological considerations. The relative weight of both of these kinds of international or "foreign" appeals increased in Soviet slogans and in the total Soviet propaganda output after the death of Stalin. The increase in slogans with "ideological internationalist" connotations was particularly pronounced after 1957. This type of appeal was, however, played down in 1955, the year of the "Geneva spirit" and the high point of the post-Stalin campaign for "relaxation of international tensions."

An analysis of Soviet slogans since Stalin's death revealed trends of interest for the study of Soviet foreign propaganda.[11] There was a substantial rise in the percentage of attention devoted to "foreign" as against "domestic" problems. The total number of slogans and especially the number devoted to foreign countries increased. The slogans reflected the fact that Soviet concern with and attention to the external world increasingly flowed outward from the Soviet-Chinese heart-

[11] These observations are based largely on two quantitative studies, respectively, of May Day and November 6 slogans for the period May 1950-November 1958, by Mr. Arend Lijphart, and of November 6 slogans for the period 1954-1960, inclusive, by Mr. George J. Vojta.

land into areas to which previously little attention had been given. The area of Soviet attention broadened to include more and more countries in the "neutralist" world. For example, India has been addressed by a whole slogan since May Day, 1954, and in 1958 Indonesia began to appear. The 1958 May Day slogan addressed to Indonesia praised it for "defending its freedom and independence in the struggle against foreign imperialists." Particularly after 1957, the content of the slogans indicated revival of belief in the power of symbols of communist internationalism to further the extension of Soviet influence.

Thematic analysis of the November 6 slogans during the 1954-1960 period indicated that international problems of war, peace, disarmament, etc., were salient for the Kremlin. In 1957, however, intra-bloc troubles, reflecting the Polish and Hungarian upheavals of October-November 1956, overshadowed world problems and were faithfully reflected in the slogans. Although the percentage of total slogans which could be placed under the rubric of "ideological internationalism" was on the increase throughout the entire period, reaching a height in 1959, it dipped in 1960, perhaps reflecting concern with the crises in Laos, the Congo, and Cuba. As crises in the relations between the Soviet bloc and the western great powers flared up or subsided, attention was called in the slogans to particular "peoples" or countries.

Not surprising, perhaps, but worthy of note is the fact that, in terms both of persistence of mention in slogans and rank order in their respective groups—"socialist" or "imperialist"— West Germany, the United States, Britain, and China received preponderant attention.

Another indication of the role of slogans, both as indicators of Kremlin calculations and as instruments for exploiting the developing predispositions of propaganda targets, was the appearance of statements on Soviet space achievements in the 1958-1962 May Day slogans. Slogan No. 67 of the 87

1958 May Day slogans hailed Soviet scientists, engineers, technicians, and workingmen for making possible the first flights in history of artificial earth satellites, and "blazing a trail toward the mastery of cosmic space."[12]

Slogans numbered 79—out of 96, in 1959; and again 79—of 97, in 1960; 81—of 99, in 1961; 87—of 104, in 1962, and 84—of 102, in 1963 broadcast to the world a message of Soviet priority in this epoch-making chapter of man's struggle for mastery over natural forces. The 1962 and 1963 slogans followed the exploits in April and August 1961 of Yuri Gagarin and Gherman Titov, and the "group flight" of Andriyan Nikolaev and Pavel Popovich in August 1962. The 1962 and 1963 slogans both referred to the "heroic Soviet Cosmonauts." One is inclined to be surprised at the relatively low priority given by the slogans to Soviet space spectaculars, but this treatment is consistent with the political realism which pervades Soviet propaganda. Moscow realizes that, important as it is, the conquest of space does not lead immediately to victory on earth.

The slogans issued to the world by the CPSU following Stalin's death indicated a revival of confidence that the forces of world social revolution were once again on the move, especially in the underdeveloped countries. At the same time, they also reflected acute awarenesss in the Kremlin of the enormous dangers involved in the confrontation of Soviet bloc and western military power. Finally, unlike those issued during the first few years of the bolshevik regime, the post-Stalin slogans suggested that the leaders of world communism regarded Soviet state power rather than the international proletariat as the chief instrument for remaking the world.

It will now be useful to briefly survey and compare the vitally significant and revealing communiqués issued by the two world communist summit meetings of 1957 and 1960. The 1957 document was endorsed by the CPSU and eleven other

[12] *Pravda*, April 13, 1958.

ruling "communist and workers' parties." The 1960 document was subscribed to by eighty-one communist parties.[13] In essence, both of the communiqués heralded a revival of the international communist movement particularly with reference to the underdeveloped countries. With the internal situation in the Soviet bloc once again under tight control late in 1957, the Soviet and other communist leaders apparently felt that the time was ripe for the resumption of the international propaganda and psychological warfare offensive. The very beginning of the 1957 communiqué asserted that the "fundamental content of our epoch" was the "transition from capitalism to socialism, begun by the Great October Socialist Revolution in Russia." It went on to assert that the most important consequence of the increase in the influence of the "forces of socialism" was that it had "stimulated the rapid extension of the anti-imperialist national liberation movement in the post-war period." It listed various countries that had "shaken off the colonial yoke and established national independent states." It hailed the struggle of the peoples of "the colonial and dependent countries" for "national liberation."

Both communiqués depicted the capitalist countries as fighting to preserve a deteriorating position of world power. The 1960 communiqué, officially entitled Statement of the Conference of Representatives of Communist and Workers' Parties, referred to the contemporary historical period as a time of "socialist revolutions . . . nationalist revolutions . . . a time of the breakdown of imperialism . . . the abolition of colonialism . . . of transition of more peoples to socialism and communism on a world-wide scale." Both communiqués described the world socialist movement and the "national liberation

[13] For the text of the 1957 document, see *Programmnye dokumenty borby za mir, demokratiyu i sotsializm* (Moscow, 1^61), pp. 4-21. The text of the 1960 communiqué was published in *Pravda* and other central Soviet newspapers for December 7, 1960, and is available in English in the *Current Digest of the Soviet Press*, for January 4, 1961.

movement" as natural allies in a bitter struggle to destroy capitalism. Both presented the "socialist camp" as the only possible model for economic and social development. Both also branded the United States as the leading exponent of reactionary policies and portrayed that country as the leader of a monopolistic, capitalist-imperialist bloc.

The two communiqués both set forth similar strategical concepts. One was that of the non-inevitability of war between the capitalist and socialist blocs and the other was the doctrine of the "anti-imperialist" coalition. Both communiqués expressed the conviction that the victory of socialism could be achieved without an all-out war. Such a war would be unprofitable for socialism. It was, however, necessary to keep socialist military strength stronger than that of the adversary in order to discourage a resort to war by the capitalist bloc. Perhaps because of the Chinese challenge to the thesis of the non-inevitability of all-out war, the 1960 communiqué dealt at much greater length than that of 1957 with the problem of peaceful coexistence. The 1960 communiqué held that peaceful coexistence was "the only correct and reasonable principle of international relations" and that this policy was "an ally of socialism." It certainly did not, however, imply a cessation of the class struggle or any reconciliation of socialist and bourgeois ideologies. On the contrary, it demanded an intensification of "the struggle for the triumph of socialist ideas."

With regard to the "anti-imperialist coalition," the 1960 communiqué defined it as "the world socialist movement, the international working class, the national liberation movement, and the countries opposing war, and all peace-loving forces."

The language of the two communiqués indicated that the leaders of the international communist movement were confident that the socialist bloc could win the adherence of all the underdeveloped countries of Asia, Africa and Latin America

41

to their general line of policy and leadership. In addition, they counted on gaining the support of neutral countries and of all factions in the western world that were opposed to war and to the use of nuclear weapons. Finally, they could rely on foreign communist parties to facilitate their efforts. By marshaling these political and social forces they expected to bring about, systematically and rapidly, the progressive isolation of the western democracies from any influence outside the North American continent and western Europe.

In keeping with this strategic analysis, the two communiqués contained directives for propaganda tactics. They urged the defense of "peace." The 1960 communiqué demanded "an end to nuclear testing in the arms race, of foreign bases, foreign occupation, the disbanding of all military blocs, a peace treaty with Germany, the demilitarization of Berlin, and the prevention of the revival of militarism in Germany and Japan."

Secondly, the communist parties were urged to fight in defense of the "national and democratic interests" of the peoples of all countries. The 1960 communiqué was more radical, however, than the 1957 communiqué with respect to the "national liberation struggle." It foresaw as the immediate objective of this struggle the establishment of the "independent national-democratic state," or "national democracy."

The 1960 communiqué defined an independent national-democratic state as: "A state that consistently defends its political and economic independence, struggles against imperialism and its military blocs, against military bases on its territory; a state that struggles against new forms of colonialism and the penetration of imperialist capital; a state in which the people are assured broad democratic rights and freedoms (freedom of speech, press, assembly, demonstrations, and establishment of political parties and political organizations) and the opportunity to work for agrarian reform and the satisfaction of other demands in the sphere of democratic and social transformations and for participation in the determination of state policy."[14]

It would seem, then, that a central criterion for the establishment of "national democracy" is the elimination of "imperialist," or in other words western economic, political and cultural influence. Further characteristics of the national-democratic state also appear from the above definition to include nationalization of the major sectors of the economy, a radical program of agrarian reforms, and freedom of action for the local communist party. It is expected that the national-democratic state will be established through the unification of all "progressive" forces "vitally interested in abolishing the domination of the monopolies," these forces being the working class, peasantry, intelligentsia, and urban, petty, and middle bourgeoisie.[15] It seems clear from the 1960 communiqué and from the resolutions of the Twenty-second Congress of the CPSU that the stage of "national democracy" is regarded as one of preparation for the transition to socialism. This is evident from the 1960 communiqué, which stated that: "The participation in the struggle for democratic transformations by the broad strata of the population convinces them of the necessity of unity of action with the working class and helps to increase their political activeness. . . . In the process of this struggle they continually strengthen their ties with the masses, raise the level of the masses' political consciousness and bring them to understand the tasks of socialist revolution and the necessity of achieving it. . . . Marxists-Leninists are firmly convinced that the peoples of the capitalist countries will in the course of their day to day struggle come to understand that socialism alone is the real way out for them."[16]

Soviet foreign policy and foreign propaganda efforts continue to be linked to the objective of fostering and accelerating

[14] *Current Digest of the Soviet Press*, January 4, 1961, p. 4.
[15] *Ibid.*, p. 5. [16] *Ibid.*, p. 5.

world-wide social revolution. And, as we pointed out in the preceding chapter, Khrushchev and other Soviet leaders continue to urge adherence to another Leninist policy, namely, that of making maximum possible use for communist purposes of temporary class allies such as the "national bourgeoisie" or various other non-proletarian strata and groups. The communists, of course, reserve to themselves the right of defining these groups and of deciding when they cease to be useful and should be attacked or destroyed. However, while recommending cooperation with non-proletarian and non-Marxist groups and organizations whenever it is expedient, the 1960 communiqué and other current Soviet documents make it clear that the communists are prepared to resort to violence, or at least to threaten its use, to prevent the loss of any gains that may have accrued to them as a result of their exploitation of the national liberation movement and other contemporary social forces. In this connection it is significant that the 1960 communiqué also declared that it was the duty of all communists to oppose the "export of counter-revolution." This doctrine has assumed a particularly ominous significance since 1961 in connection with the Cuban problem and Khrushchev's ambiguous but nevertheless threatening statements that United States military action against the Castro government would mean war.

The main lines of the 1960 communiqué were reiterated in Khrushchev's speech of January 5, 1961 to a gathering of Soviet communists in Moscow, entitled, significantly, "For New Victories of the World Communist Movement," as well as the 1961 program of the CPSU. For example, the program indicated that although there could be differences in the "forms and tempo" of social revolution, revolution remained the only means and the dictatorship of the proletariat (declared by the program to be superseded inside the Soviet Union by the "state of the entire people") the inevitable outcome of the struggle still underway in the non-communist world.[17]

The above doctrines, reflected in Soviet strategy *vis-à-vis* such countries as Guinea, Laos, and Cuba, indicated Khrushchev's determination to achieve Leninist aspirations for world revolution even in the conditions of the nuclear age. Among many ominous manifestations of the post-Stalin rededication to the export of violent revolution, certain little-noticed Korean developments are worth mentioning. The Fourth Congress of the North Korean Workers (Communist) Party, in September 1961, called for establishment in South Korea of a "revolutionary Marxist-Leninist party," to fight against US "imperialist occupation," and carry out an "anti-imperialist" program.

Secretary of State Dean Rusk in an address on July 10, 1961 noted that in Soviet policy, "the very language of international intercourse became distorted and contrived." "Peace" had, he observed, become a word to describe whatever condition would promote the communist world revolution. "Aggression" was whatever stood in the way of this revolution. He thus reminded the world of a communist practice, first applied on a global scale in the mid-1930's, of employing traditional symbols of democracy and liberalism for communist purposes. Of course, such terms as peace, negotiation, freedom, democracy, progress, etc., mean different things to communists than to western democrats, liberals, and non-communist socialists. The importance of what Lindley Fraser in his excellent study *Propaganda* called "double talk" is that very often the non-communist targets of the use of these terms by communists are not fully aware or perhaps not aware at all that, for example, as Fraser puts it, "world peace will be for the first time achieved when the world as a whole is converted to communism."[18]

[17] *Pravda*, November 2, 1961, p. 3. See also Triska, *op.cit.*, pp. 29-34.
[18] Lindley Fraser, *op.cit.*, p. 144.

The doctrines, directives, and messages which we have surveyed reflect the dominant and persisting influence exercised in Soviet propaganda strategy by what Brzezinski calls the "dichotomic" Soviet vision of the nature of international politics. The data examined would appear to support Brzezinski's contention that the Soviet international outlook has been shaped by "the notion that social developments throughout the world operate on the basis of a sharply definable dichotomy—a dichotomy that is proof per se of an unbridgeable hostility between the emerging socialist state (later a system of socialist states) and the rest of the world."[19]

But, as we have also observed, the dichotomic orientation permits and indeed requires the exercise of strategic and tactical flexibility. It is probably true, as Robert C. Tucker impressively but perhaps a little too forcefully argued in 1957 in his article "The Psychology of Soviet Foreign Policy," that Stalin in the last few years of his life was so obsessed with physical control over territory and people that he was, in contrast to his successors, unable to employ propaganda effectively as an instrument of foreign policy.[20] While there is much truth in such an interpretation of Soviet policy during the late Stalin era, it tends to exaggerate the differences between the policies of Stalin and those of his successors. During the last three years of Stalin's lifetime some essential elements of the strategy which has paid considerable political dividends to Khrushchev were worked out at least in preliminary form. The truth may be that Stalin, or some of his

[19] Zbigniew K. Brzezinski, *Ideology and Power in Soviet Politics* (New York, 1962), chap. IV. Quoted material on p. 101.

[20] Robert C. Tucker, "The Psychology of Soviet Foreign Policy," in Alexander Dallin, ed., *Soviet Conduct in World Affairs* (New York, 1960), pp. 228-243. In this brilliant article Tucker argues that Stalin's neurotic concern for physical control made it impossible for him to seek to exercise mere influence, for which the logical means would have been persuasion, and that Soviet foreign propaganda came to be devoted mainly to preserving an "official illusion about Russia and the world" required by Stalin personally for psychological reasons.

46

lieutenants, perceived the need for more flexibility in Soviet foreign policy and for a more persuasive manner of presenting it. But it is possible that the dictator was temperamentally incapable of adjusting fully to the challenges and opportunities which the emerging international constellation offered for the extension of Soviet influence.

Nevertheless, as Marshall D. Shulman has convincingly argued, Stalin adopted, in 1949-1952, a policy designed to disintegrate the unity and mobilization achieved by the western powers in their efforts to counter the Berlin blockade, communist aggression in Korea and other communist actions. Stalin turned to "the use of nationalism, the peace issue, neutralism, trade, and other forms of collaboration with elements of the bourgeoisie."[21] Among the major propaganda operations in which the Soviet policy shift after 1949 were reflected, the Moscow International Economic Conference of April 1952, and a stepped-up "peace" campaign were perhaps the most conspicuous. Although with less enthusiasm and skill than Khrushchev was later to display, Stalin nevertheless attempted to convince foreign businessmen that it was profitable to trade with communist Russia. Shulman compares the late Stalin "right-wing policy" with other temporary Soviet retreats, succeeded, as was that of 1949-1952, by renewed advances. He arrives at an interpretation which may seem reassuring because it differs from theories that emphasize neurotic compulsions in the personality of leaders as driving forces in Soviet policy, but should also serve as a warning against underestimating the effectiveness of that policy. Shulman sees in Soviet policy—and this writer agrees with his finding—a "largely rational responsiveness to changes in the world environment, particularly to changes in world power relationships." What may be an irrationally intense urge for power

[21] Marshall D. Shulman, "Some Implications of Changes in Soviet Policy Toward the West: 1949-1952," the *Slavic Review*, Vol. xx, No. 4 (December, 1961), pp. 630-640. See especially pp. 631-632.

is associated with sensitivity to many dimensions of social and political reality, including some often neglected by non-communists, and with a formidable, coordinated program to shape the future of mankind in conformity with the Marxist-Leninist vision. If to these strengths one adds the energy displayed by Soviet communicators, and the resourcefulness they so clearly possess, it becomes possible to better understand the magnitude of the challenge posed by their urgent and persistent appeals to world audiences.

CHAPTER III

THE IMAGE OF THE ADVERSARY

SOVIET propaganda, even in the post-Stalin era, continues to present a polarized, dichotomic image of world politics. This simplistic "two world" imagery is consistent with the pattern described in the preceding chapters, which evidently shapes Soviet communicators' perception of the international environment. Marxist theory, in the name of which Soviet propaganda operates, could, if interpreted with understanding and sophistication, be a subtle tool of analysis. However, most Soviet propaganda is couched in terms of crude contrasts between the stereotypes applied by Soviet communicators to "socialism" and "capitalism." Theodore Kruglak, for example, found in a survey of communications transmitted to Moscow from the United States in October and November 1959 by the Soviet news agency TASS, a picture of east-west and especially of Soviet-American relations which features a struggle of the "good guys against the bad guys."[1] Regarding "images of East and West in TASS," Kruglak writes that: "The impression to be gained from an examination of the TASS World Service reports and the Moscow press is that there is unanimity among the countries of the Soviet bloc, discord and strife in the western bloc, and friendship toward the USSR among the neutral nations. An examination of the *New York Times* for the same period gives no clear-cut impression of anything remotely resembling a world behavior pattern based on political loyalties."[2]

The focusing of propaganda hostility upon the United States since the end of World War II thus reflects not merely the

[1] Theodore E. Kruglak, *The Two Faces of TASS* (Minneapolis, 1962), p. 170.
[2] *Ibid.*, p. 147.

structure of contemporary world power relationships but also traditional Soviet political attitudes and imagery. The world of capitalism has normally been portrayed in terms of a "camp" or conspiracy, which, though torn by "contradictions" of various kinds, is nevertheless under the control of one or more powerful and ruthless command centers. This vision, in turn, is probably a projection upon the non-communist adversary of the Soviet leaders' own crisis-nurtured, power-oriented mentality—but, of course, no acknowledgment of such a projection has occurred. International conduct is not evaluated with reference to absolute moral or legal norms, but relativistically, in terms of characteristics of political actors which are, by official definition, ultimately derived from class origin. "Imperialists," no matter how decent they may be as human beings, are "objectively" evil—unless their behavior at a given moment happens to facilitate Soviet goals. In such cases, they may be temporarily tolerated—or even guardedly described, as Franklin D. Roosevelt was up to about 1948, and again has been since the death of Stalin, as "far-sighted" statesmen. Fundamentally, however, actors in the Marxist-Leninist political dramaturgy play out the roles assigned to them by the "laws of history"—but only as these laws and roles are interpreted by those in power in the Kremlin. Thus, in the final analysis, the Marxist-Leninist "science" by which roles are assigned to historical actors may turn out to be a system of largely subjective judgments by holders of power professing to be Marxists.

In any case, in each of the more or less distinctive periods into which the Soviet leadership divides history, Soviet propagandists must perform the task of applying to the current policy categories that are compatible with official doctrine. This rule applies to the depiction of events in the capitalist world as a whole, and especially to the dissemination of a designedly revolting and infuriating image of the particular "imperialists" regarded as most dangerous at the moment. In each period, the ideological-political adversary is exemplified by one or more political movements, states, or group of states.

Of course, the emphasis can and does shift. For example, for a time following World War II, the expression "Anglo-American Imperialists" was used frequently to describe the western adversary. With the sharpening of Soviet-American tensions, however, especially after 1947, and with the shift of the center of western defensive power more and more to the United States, Soviet foreign propaganda focused more narrowly on the American target. During recent years, anti-American propaganda has at times been reinforced by associating the image of "American imperialism" with that of "revenge-seeking German militarism."

Incidentally, surprising as it may seem to some readers today, France was, before the rise of Hitler to power in Germany, denounced—for example, at the Sixteenth CPSU Congress in 1930—as the most aggressive of all imperialist powers. Even in 1940, French "ruling circles" were, according to the Soviet *Political Dictionary* waging a struggle "for world domination."[3] In a contrast reflecting intervening changes in the world power configuration, the second (1958) edition of this reference work for Soviet officials stated that France, because it had allowed itself to be drawn into "economic and military-political alliances," had suffered a deterioration in power relative to "more powerful imperialist competitors." This deterioration was attributed to the "expansionist policy of the American monopolies." This example suggests how by "zeroing-in" on a primary target Soviet propagandists hope to increase the chances of driving wedges in the "imperialist camp." This practice conforms to Leninist doctrine, which stresses simultaneously the "internationalism" of capitalism and the irreconcilability of its "contradictions." In the future, if the European Common Market is successful in achieving its goals, there will probably be a partial shift of Soviet propa-

[3] *Politicheski slovar* (Moscow, 1940), p. 611.

ganda animus from the United States to this new embodiment of "imperialist" power.

To some degree this shift has already occurred, although Soviet attacks on the Common Market movement usually characterize it as an instrument not only of Western European but also of United States "imperialism." The "Theses" on "Imperialist Integration in Western Europe," published in *Pravda* for August 26, 1962 and in *New Times* for September 5, 1962 declared, in their final introductory paragraph, that "leaders of the imperialist powers" were trying to make the Common Market a new "Holy Alliance," directed against the "working class, national-liberation and general-democratic movements"—in order to strengthen NATO in Europe. However, Moscow also points frequently to friction between Britain and the continental countries, and to US-European stresses allegedly caused by the economic integration movement.

Once the main propaganda target has been selected, instructions are issued to the Soviet and world communist communications networks to direct their fire against it. A CPSU decree, first published in 1961, which criticized, and issued instructions to, the Soviet government's main newspaper, *Izvestiya*, shed some light on the nature of such instructions. Its foreign policy section stated that: "In the exposition of international life and foreign policy the newspaper must constantly conduct propaganda for the foreign policy actions of the Soviet government, the struggle of the USSR for peace and the relaxation of international tension, and must expose and uncover the imperialistic character of the foreign policy of the capitalist states and in particular of the United States of America. The most important obligation of the newspaper consists in convincingly conducting propaganda for the idea of peaceful coexistence of states with different social-economic systems, and of the struggle of the USSR for the prevention of a new war and the adjustment of disputed international issues by negotiations, and the exposure of the plans of the capitalist states, directed against the USSR and the countries of peoples democracy and against the peoples fighting for liberation from colonialism."[4]

While this declaration is entirely compatible with what we know of Soviet propaganda methods, it is, nevertheless, rather startling. It constituted, in effect, an order from the executive organ of the ruling Communist Party of the Soviet Union to the staff of the second most important newspaper in that country to do everything in its power to blacken the image of the United States. It simply assumed, of course, that the characteristics of the political actors whose behavior was to be "reported" were known in advance.

A level of closed-mindedness similar to that reflected in the above quotation is also displayed in the USSR in the fields of philosophy and social science. An announcement in *Pravda* for February 7, 1961 revealed that one of the areas of specialization open to students of the CPSU central committee's Academy of Social Sciences is "criticism of contemporary bourgeois philosophy and sociology."

An important aspect of the process by which Soviet propaganda agencies seek to undermine the influence of the United States consists in systematic attacks on the credibility of statements made by American officials. The sixty-page brochure, *Words and Deeds* (*Slova i dela*) published in 1960 by the Publishing House of the Soviet Institute of International Relations—an agency of the USSR Ministry of Foreign Affairs—contains many such attacks. This pamphlet was devoted mainly to "debunking" the American political system. It surprises the reader not so much by its hostility—particularly its virulent attack on Dwight D. Eisenhower—praised by Khrushchev in 1955 and 1959 as a "man of peace"—as by its monotonous repetition of Leninist clichés. For example, the brochure asserts that the government of the USA is a "trusted commit-

---

[4] *Voprosy ideologicheskoi raboty*, pp. 278-279.

tee of monopolists," and it repeats as if nothing had changed for a century, standard Marxist and Leninist assertions regarding the allegedly increasing impoverishment of the working people of the United States.

Since 1946, the world scapegoat and symbol of capitalism, imperialism, and evil has usually been the United States. Illustrative of the post-war shift in the main Soviet propaganda onslaught from Germany and Japan to the United States was a statement made by Georgi Malenkov in his speech on November 6, 1949, in honor of the thirty-second anniversary of the October Revolution. Malenkov accused the United States of seeking "by force and new wars" to establish "an American world empire" which would be bigger than all previous empires.

He asked, "in what way do the delirious plans for such an 'Americanization' of all countries and continents differ from the mad plans of Hitler and Goering for the Germanization, first of Europe and then of the whole world?" He answered that the only difference between the imperialist plans of the Germans—and the Japanese, and those of the Americans, was that the American program of aggression was on a scale larger than that of the Germans and the Japanese combined.[5] The horrifying image of an American threat to the life, liberty, and happiness of mankind furnished a convenient background for Soviet "peace" campaigns and for other, more "positive" aspects of Soviet propaganda. Communist promises could look all the more attractive against the backdrop of the menace from which, according to Moscow and its allies, mankind needed to be rescued.

After Stalin's death the tactics of anti-American and anti-western propaganda were somewhat modified. The effort, begun as has already been pointed out, in 1949-1952, to win as much support as possible for Soviet policies among the

[5] Text in *Bolshevik*, No. 21 (November, 1947), pp. 1-17; quotation on p. 10.

more wavering and unstable segments of the *bourgeoisie* set a framework in which blandishments replaced, or at least supplemented, zoological phrases such as "fascist hyena," "running dogs of imperialism," and the like in Moscow's statements about Washington and its works. Also, even in propaganda intended mainly for Americans, including that emanating from the Communist Party of the United States, a wider net was cast, with the evident intention of building the broadest possible united front against the "monopolists." Finally, the repudiation by Khrushchev of the repulsive characteristics associated with the person of Stalin facilitated efforts, begun immediately after the dread dictator's death, to appeal to western conservatives who yearned for a detente in the east-west conflict and to western liberals and socialists anxious to see in the "new" Soviet Union a trend toward "liberalization."

The main features of Stalinist anti-Americanism have already been described elsewhere.[6] Consequently, we here emphasize the post-Stalin period. Also, since Soviet propaganda regarding alleged American intentions to plan or wage war against the Soviet Union and other countries is discussed in detail in Chapter IV, problems of war and peace will be treated only incidentally in this chapter. The main aspects of contemporary Soviet anti-Americanism dealt with here are those concerned with the impact of American foreign policy on the peoples of the world, the Soviet characterization of the American economic and political system, and, finally, Moscow's attack on American civilization and culture. Soviet propaganda regarding these three main aspects of America's role in the world reflected determination to weaken American influence abroad. It was actuated also by a desire to sap the faith of Americans themselves in their leadership and institutions. Finally, of course, Soviet anti-Americanism, like all

[6] See, for example, Frederick C. Barghoorn, *The Soviet Image of the United States* (New York, 1950).

Soviet propaganda, continued to have as one of its purposes the strengthening of the power of the communist regime inside Russia itself.

Because the fanning of anti-American feelings for Soviet internal propaganda purposes has merely tangential relevance for this study, we touch but briefly upon it before turning to foreign propaganda. Illustrative of the scapegoat role of the United States in Soviet domestic propaganda was the tendency, still very much in evidence after the Twenty-second CPSU Congress, to blame the United States, directly or by implication, for what were, essentially, internal failures of the Soviet system. Thus, when in June 1962 the prices of meat and butter were substantially increased in the USSR, the decree announcing this unwelcome news attributed the action by obvious implication to alleged American initiative in stepping up the international arms race.[7] In September 1962 Moscow announced postponement of scheduled income tax cuts which were part of a program, begun in 1960, of abolition of income taxes. Despite the relatively minor role of this form of taxation in the Soviet economy tax cuts had been the subject of much propaganda fanfare. Again, this disappointing action was blamed on "the aggressive schemes of imperialism."

Turning now to the main concerns of our inquiry, we find that immediately after the death of Stalin the Kremlin began a propaganda campaign designed to force the United States to settle major international problems, such as the German question, on Soviet terms. However, instead of being depicted, as it had been since 1947, as a nation led by militant warmongers, the United States was now cast in the role of a somewhat fumbling but still dangerous obstructor of progress toward the solution of the great problems of our time. Because it was less shrill in tone than the Stalinist line, the new presentation was probably more acceptable to a conflict-weary

[7] The text of the decree is available in *Kommunist*, No. 8, May, 1962, and in other publications.

world propaganda audience. Neatly turning the propaganda tables, Moscow, with the odious figure of Stalin out of the way, posed as the champion of "normalization" of international relations.

For example, the May Day slogans for 1954, published in *Pravda* on April 21, contained an assertion that there was no question that could not be settled by negotiation. Soviet spokesmen, particularly when talking to foreign businessmen, now attempted to create the impression that ideological differences were not important. Simple good will, they averred, could solve the most difficult international problems. At the same time, epithets, such as "cannibal," or "bloodsucker," which abounded prominently in the vocabulary of Soviet foreign propaganda in the late Stalin period, virtually disappeared from 1953 on. One is impressed by the change of tone between Malenkov's speech of October 5, 1952, to the Nineteenth Party Congress, to take a conspicuous example, and the same speaker's major address to the Supreme Soviet of the USSR on August 8, 1953.[8] Also, the new air of normalcy was rendered more plausible by the partial reopening of Russia to foreign visitors, beginning in 1954-1955, and by the sending of Soviet intellectuals, scientists, and even "tourists," on visits to foreign countries.

Soviet efforts to pin the onus on the United States for refusal to cooperate in relaxing international tensions were facilitated by the difficulties confronting Washington in its efforts to achieve consensus, both at home and throughout the free world, regarding which policies to adopt to counter Soviet expansionism. American wares and ways became all too visibly involved in the daily life of the peoples of many nations. A comical but symptomatic reflection of this involvement was the uproar in western Europe in the early "cold war" period over the allegedly sinister role of Coca-Cola as an instrument of United States cultural imperialism, to which

[8] See *Pravda*, October 6, 1952 and August 9, 1953.

E. A. Kahn devotes some amusing pages in his book *The Big Drink*. American foreign economic programs, efforts to build a coalition of democratic states to oppose communist pressures, and the very nature of the market economy created myriad targets for Soviet propaganda. Moscow, of course, with its communist agents operating throughout the world, had to contend with anxieties and hostilities aroused by the subversive activities which it promoted. However, communists, being usually natives of the countries in which they operated, could at least partly conceal their foreign sponsorship—something which local branches of American corporations, for example, found it rather more difficult to do.

Stalin's successors, taking shrewd note of growing American involvement throughout the world, and the frictions which often resulted therefrom, worked to render more plausible the traditional communist propaganda charge that United States policy sought the economic exploitation, for the benefit of "Wall Street," of all countries where American business operated or American capital was invested. Particularly but not exclusively, in the developing areas the Soviet image of American exploitation and "neo-colonialism" reinforced local demands for the curtailment or elimination of American business and the substitution for American and other western commercial ties of links with the Soviet bloc. One interesting concurrent aspect of Soviet propaganda on the subject of American foreign economic policy was the charge that United States business enterprises intended to displace the European powers in their colonial empires. This theme can be traced at least as far back as the San Francisco Conference in 1945, at which Soviet representatives energetically reasserted their traditional interest in the "colonial problem." Insinuations and charges of this nature were calculated to play on the fears of the developing countries as well as to sow dissension among the western allies.

Soviet accusations were often far from subtle. For example, *New Times* for March 2, 1949 published an article which stated that the Arabian-American Oil Company punished recalcitrant Arab exployees by cutting off their hands with a cleaver kept in the Aramco hospital, after which American surgeons sewed up the stumps.[9]

Especially after the beginning of the Korean War in June 1950, Soviet propaganda frequently attacked American foreign economic aid, and particularly the Point Four Program inaugurated in 1949. American aid programs were pictured as devices for penetrating into colonial and semi-colonial countries and seizing control of them.[10] When Secretary of State John Foster Dulles made his tour of the Near East in the spring of 1953, Soviet propaganda expressed the opinion that one of the purposes of his trip was to push American plans for "liquidating" the economic interests of Great Britain in that part of the world.[11] Even the modest American-supported village community development program in India was attacked in 1952 as an effort to enslave the Indian people.[12] As early as 1954 Staley observed that Soviet propaganda to discredit America in the less industrialized lands was reverberating around the world in publications, in local communist agitation, and, to a disquieting extent, in non-communist media. Among the latter he mentioned the Peronista press of Argentina and various nationalist periodicals in Asia and the Middle East. Wrote Staley, "Sometimes communists have picked up popular prejudices useful to their propaganda and given them further circulation. In other cases ideas originally of communist manufacture have caught on and spread."[13] The significance and impact of this aspect of Soviet propaganda grew steadily during the post-Stalin period, espe-

[9] Cited in Eugene Staley, *The Future of Underdeveloped Countries* (New York, 1954).

[10] See, for example, article by I. Lemin, "Colonial Expansion of the U.S.A.," *Trud*, May 22, 1952.

[11] *Pravda*, June 5, 1953 and July 15, 1953.

[12] Staley, *op.cit.*, p. 152.   [13] *Ibid.*, p. 147.

cially with the launching in 1954 and 1955 of a Soviet bloc program of foreign economic aid and technical assistance that was intended in part to counter American efforts in these fields.

It was Nikita Khrushchev, beginning on the trip that he made with Nikolai Bulganin, then Chairman of the Council of Ministers of the USSR, to India, Burma, and Afghanistan in 1955, who most effectively disseminated the twin themes of the American threat to the economic development of other lands and Soviet promises of economic assistance. The persuasiveness of Khrushchev's propaganda in this context was enhanced by the fact that he had by this time modified Stalin's tactless thesis that the governments of such countries as India, Egypt, and others were merely "lackeys" of British and American capitalism. This modification of tactics in turn reflected Khrushchev's shrewd appraisal of the upsurge of anti-imperialist movements throughout Asia and Africa, vividly reflected in such events as the Asian-African Conference held at Bandung, Indonesia, in April 1955. For a time, following Bandung and the Suez crisis of 1956, the Soviet Union seemed to be riding the crest of a wave of nationalism.[14]

In this connection, it is significant that beginning in 1956 the Higher Party School and other Soviet institutions for the training of party cadres have offered courses on the "history of the international labor and national-liberation movement." Although Moscow was to find that there were certain obstacles in the path of capturing the nationalist movements in the developing countries, propaganda directed against western economic influence in these areas remained prominent. It has not diminished in virulence.

[14] An excellent analysis of Khrushchev's attempts to take advantage of this situation was contained in an unpublished paper, entitled "Changes and Variations in Soviet Policies Toward the Underdeveloped Areas," presented by David T. Cattell to the Conference on Soviet and Communist Studies, American Political Science Association, September 9, 1961.

Bulganin and Khrushchev in their speeches in India in 1955 largely confined themselves to insinuation and innuendo. They emphasized the necessity for India to develop her own national industry, stressing that industry develops better under native leadership than under foreign supervision. The implication was that the west was trying to hold back the economic development of India.[15] A much more forceful attack on western economic influence in the underdeveloped world was made by Khrushchev on October 3, 1958. Replying to a question put by a Brazilian journalist as to why, in a joint communiqué signed by the Soviet government and that of Communist China, direct reference was made, for the first time, to Latin America, Khrushchev said: "A great historical transformation is taking place before our eyes: more and more nations are taking the path of just struggle against colonialism and against exploitation by foreign monopolies. It is not only the peoples of the colonies and dependent countries of Asia and Africa who are taking this path: so, too, are the peoples of Latin America. This is, of course, understandable. For many decades American, British and other foreign monopolies have like giant leeches attached themselves to the living body of Latin America and are draining her natural wealth, ruthlessly exploiting her peoples and distorting the economies of the Latin American countries, and thus obstructing their independent development. Can the peoples of Latin America accept such a state of affairs?"[16] The above quotation was part of a statement given wide circulation throughout the world in the Soviet magazine *International Affairs*, which is published in numerous languages, both western and Oriental.

Many similar statements about alleged United States intentions and activities in Latin America appeared, subsequently, in Soviet newspapers and magazines, including those intended

[15] See, for example, *Pravda*, November 19, 20, 22, 1955.
[16] Nikita S. Khrushchev, *For Victory in Peaceful Competition with Capitalism* (New York, 1960), pp. 673-674.

for Soviet readers as well as those with extensive foreign distribution.[17] Such Soviet propaganda might have had little effect, of course, if conditions and attitudes in Latin America were not favorable to its reception. A startling indication of passionate anti-Americanism in Latin-American intellectual circles was furnished by publication late in 1961 of a book with the suggestive title, *The Shark and the Sardines*. According to a full-page advertisement of this book in the *New York Times* for November 25, 1961, millions of Latin Americans perceive the United States as a "striped shark with a star-eye."

The author of this book was Dr. Juan Jose Arevalo, a former president of Guatemala. Under his administration the communists were allowed to infiltrate into the Guatemalan labor unions, but Dr. Arevalo was apparently not a communist. He was described by Robert J. Alexander, in his authoritative study, *Communism in Latin America,* as a "rather fuzzy thinker who, though aware of the nature of communists, was more interested in avoiding trouble than in having a showdown with them." When well-meaning but perhaps naive intellectuals in underdeveloped countries irrationally blame all the woes of their unfortunate countries on the United States, the success of Soviet propaganda is of course facilitated. It is also facilitated by the equally irrational tendency of some conservative North Americans to condemn all Latin American, Asian and African social reformers as "Reds."

The victory of Castro in Cuba furnished added impetus to Soviet anti-American propaganda by allowing Moscow to pose as the defender of Cuban liberty against the threat from the imperialist colossus. The Soviet press lost little time in claiming that Castro's victory and the continued existence of his

[17] See, for example, the article by G. Andreyev, "U.S. Imperialism: Exploitation of Latin America," in *International Affairs*, No. 1, 1961, or the article in *New Times* for March, 1961, entitled "Puerto Rico Rediscovered," alleging that because of United States policy the Puerto Ricans both in their native island and in the United States are "horribly exploited."

regime were largely the result of the support of the Cuban Communists and of the Soviet Union. The intensity of this theme reached its zenith after the Cuban crisis of October 1962. In fact, in his speech to the Supreme Soviet on December 12, 1962, Khrushchev asserted that the main achievement of the foreign policy of the USSR and of "all peace-loving forces" in 1962 was prevention of the attack on Cuba "prepared by the aggressive imperialist circles of the United States."[18]

Beginning with the November 6 slogans of 1960, individual greetings were extended to "Heroic Cuba," whose effort to "build socialism" began to be applauded in 1962. The May Day 1963 slogan asserted that Cuba was already "building socialism." The special Cuban slogan supplemented a general Latin American one, which since 1958 has hailed the "struggle against imperialism" and for "independence" of the "peoples" of that continent. Subsequently, Moscow pointed to Cuba as the model for emulation by Latin American and other peoples who had not yet achieved "national liberation." A significant feature of Soviet anti-American propaganda with respect to Latin America was the attempt—which was also made in other parts of the world—to link the denunciation of American economic influence with the Soviet thesis that only Soviet policies could prevent war. For example, the Soviet Army newspaper *Red Star* for September 8, 1959 charged that the United States was using its economic and political pressure to convert Latin America into a range for nuclear weapons. *Red Star* quoted the Brazilian newspapers *Ultima Hora* and *Journal do Brazil* in accusations against the alleged effects of a United States nuclear test conducted in 1958 off the shores of South America under the code name "Project Argus."

An interesting aspect of the Soviet propaganda drive against the influence of the United States and other western nations

[18] See, for example, article by M. Kremnyov, "Revolt in Cuba," *New Times*, No. 1, 1959. See also the text of Khrushchev's speech in *Pravda*, December 13, 1962. Material cited on page 1.

in Asia, Africa, and Latin America is the concept of "collective colonialism." This term was widely used in connection with Khrushchev's trip in February 1960 to Indonesia, India, Burma, and Afghanistan.[19] However, its origin antedated Khrushchev's second swing through southeast Asia. A booklet by E. D. Modrzhinskaya released for publication by the Soviet censors in November 1959 used the term in attacking alleged efforts of right-wing western European socialists to defend colonialism. Modrzhinskaya referred to an article in a French socialist magazine published in 1957 which asserted that Europe needed Africa and Africa needed Europe. The French socialists had argued, cogently but tactlessly, that "premature" independence for some of the African countries would be contrary to the ideals of internationalism. Countering this contention, the Soviet pamphleteer stated that the French socialists in reality championed not internationalism but various kinds of collective colonialism. She then proceeded to attack both European socialists and "the reactionary circles of the United States" for favoring such projects as "Eurafrica."[20] One obvious objective of this attack was to tar the United States with the brush of European colonialism. Another, of course, was to set Americans against Europeans. Perhaps the most important purpose was to weaken the faith of Africans and Asians in American anti-colonialism.

The Soviet attack on United States "colonialism," and in particular Khrushchev's personal role in it, rose to a crescendo in 1960. Among the climactic events involved wewre Khrushchev's trip to southeast Asia, already mentioned, the visit of First Minister Djuanda of Indonesia to the Soviet Union in July, the political explosion in the Congo, and Khrushchev's agitational activity at the Fourteenth General Assembly of the United Nations, particularly his introduction of a Soviet decla-

---

[19] See, for example, *Kommunist*, No. 4, March, 1960, p. 5.

[20] E. D. Modrzhinskaya, *Ideologiya sovremennogo kolonializma* (Moscow, 1959), pp. 31-32.

ration demanding speedy independence for colonial countries.

The spring and summer of 1960, in fact, witnessed one of the sharpest switches in the kaleidoscopic history of Soviet propaganda and apparently ushered in a new and somber phase of tension. Having met with resistance from the western political leaders he had been sedulously wooing, Khrushchev jettisoned the "spirit of Camp David" which had reigned for a few months following his 1959 visit to the United States. He took a course in favor of exploiting what must have seemed irresistibly tempting opportunities to harass the west in Asia, Africa and Latin America.

In 1959, Khrushchev had offered the shadow of universal and complete disarmament without the substance of effective inspection and controls. In 1960, he focused his attention mainly on western "colonialism."[21] In addition to attacking colonialism, Khrushchev at the 1960 session of the UN General Assembly launched an assault on the institution of the General Secretariat of the UN. This was part of a continuing effort to eliminate obstacles to the political exploitation by the Soviet Union, aided by local communists, of the situation created by the establishment of independent, but often poor and unstable, new governments in Asia and Africa. Khrushchev in 1960 proposed that the headquarters of the United Nations be removed from New York. In this connection, he charged that the representatives of the young African and Asiatic states were subjected in the United States not only to racial discrimination but also to "bandit attacks."

Our attention thus far has been directed mainly to the official Soviet image of American and general western imperialism and colonialism, and especially its alleged economic effects. This is probably the most important single theme of current Soviet foreign propaganda, with the exception of that

[21] See *Pravda*, September 24, 1960 for Khrushchev's main speech, in which he introduced the declaration regarding independence for colonial countries and peoples.

which is concerned with the war danger. However, the attack on American foreign policy is not confined, of course, to allegations of economic imperialism and neocolonialism. The United States has, in fact, been accused of responsibility for virtually every one of the social and political ills of each and every nation of the world. In Europe for example, American leadership of NATO, which after all developed as a defensive alliance against communist expansion, furnished a pretext for Moscow to associate the United States with the specter of a revival of German fascism and aggression. It is a fact, however, that the Soviet Union armed communist East Germany long before a military force was established in the German Federal Republic. In North Africa, particularly of course in Algeria, Soviet propaganda for years sought to blacken the image of the United States by linking American policy with that of France. In India, the attempt was made to turn Indian resentment regarding the Kashmir dispute with Pakistan, or differences with Portugal over Goa, against America. In Indonesia, Moscow has pictured the United States as the heir of Dutch imperialism. In the Congo, the Kremlin's attack was directed against "the Belgian and American colonizers." In Japan, particularly concerned about the effects of radiation and other consequences of the testing or even the carrying—on Polaris submarines, for example—of nuclear weapons, Soviet propaganda has sought to create the impression that the United States is irresponsible and callous in its attitude toward the handling of such weapons.

The speech delivered by Frol R. Kozlov, perhaps already at the time second only to Khrushchev in the CPSU hierarchy, on November 6, 1960, presented a typical Soviet rationalization of the policy of instigating and exacerbating conflict. Kozlov stated: "The imperialist policy is undergoing a deep crisis. The moral-political isolation of American imperialism—the bulwark of militarism and colonialism, hated by the peoples, is intensifying with every passing day. This is confirmed by the overthrow of the bloody Syngman Rhee regime in South Korea, by the fall of the openly pro-American regime of Bayar and Menderes in Turkey, by the indignation of the Japanese people against the American-Japanese Military Alliance, by the upsurge of national-liberation movements of the peoples of Africa. The struggle of the peoples of Latin America, who have been inspired by the example of heroic Cuba, is broadening."[22]

This image of a reactionary, greedy, and aggressive American foreign policy has continued since the death of Stalin to be accompanied in world-wide Soviet propaganda by the traditional Soviet picture of American morality, daily life, and culture. The United States is accused not only of seeking to frustrate the legitimate political and economic aspirations of the workers, farmers, small businessmen, and progressive intellectuals of the world, but also of wishing to corrupt them by imposing upon them a decadent civilization. The Soviet image of the American domestic scene presumably serves a number of purposes. One is to hearten the enemies and to discourage the friends of American democracy by demonstrating its weaknesses, or in Leninist jargon, its irreconcilable "contradictions." Another is to destroy the attractiveness of the political, ideological, and cultural freedom of choice offered to the individual by the American system, with the argument that this freedom is only a sham. Still another motive is to establish bonds of sympathy with those foreign intellectuals who are repelled by what they regard as the "materialism" of American culture. Another very important purpose, to which constant attention is directed, is to arouse indignation against the United States for practicing racial discrimination. Finally, Soviet propaganda continues to present an ideologically determined image of the situation of the American working man as the slave of capital.

[22] *Pravda*, November 7, 1960.

The post-Stalin image of the American domestic scene was not as lurid as the one broadcast to the world in the late Stalin era. For one thing, in its effort to woo at least some sections of American public opinion, Soviet propaganda acknowledged that there were some sober and sensible elements even in the ranks of American business. Also, cultural exchanges partially cracked the Iron Curtain and permitted a trickle of uncensored Soviet-American communication. Perhaps the biggest breach in Soviet communications control took place in 1959 when some three million Soviet citizens visited the American National Exhibition in Moscow. Such events presented problems. At home, they posed the danger that the official image of America might be shaken as far as Soviet citizens were concerned. Abroad, they may perhaps have tended to blur somewhat the image traditionally disseminated by Moscow of a world struggle between two bitterly hostile and irreconcilable forces.

To deal with these problems Soviet propaganda emphasized that coexistence among governments did not in any way diminish the intensity of the ideological struggle between socialism and capitalism. It also resorted to a wide variety of other devices. For example, it persistently accused the United States of seeking to turn cultural exchanges into a political instrument. It denied the representativeness or the authenticity of American cultural exports. A textbook for the teaching of English published in the Soviet Union in 1959, for example, published a purported "Message from American Cultural Workers," which illustrates this point. The "message" stated that "the poetry and music our State Department broadcasts to Europe, to impress everybody with the riches of imperialist culture, are the work of men neglected and scorned throughout their lives by hypocrites who now pretend to honor them."[23]

[23] Quoted by Stephen Viederman in article entitled "Co-existence English," in *Columbia University Forum*, Fall, 1960, p. 45.

A central thesis of Marxist-Leninist doctrine on international relations asserts that the foreign policy of "imperialism" flows inevitably from forces generated by the international anarchy of competing economic interests battling fiercely for markets and sources of raw materials. There has been no significant deviation from this Stalinist image of international relations in the post-Stalin period comparable to that which was contained in Eugene Varga's notable book, *Changes in the Economy of Capitalism as a Result of the Second World War.* This book was, of course, repudiated in the course of the Stalinist ideological reconversion following World War II. Varga had suggested that the capitalist countries could, on a modest scale, utilize economic planning measures to partially solve some of the social and economic problems of capitalism. The post-Stalin interpretation of western capitalism is even less sophisticated than that achieved by Varga in 1945.[24] However, perhaps one element of realism in Soviet propaganda about the American economy was the partial acknowledgment after Stalin's death of the high degree of prosperity enjoyed by the American people as a whole.

An important Soviet reference book entitled *The United States of America*, released for publication by the Soviet censors in November 1960, presented one of several frequently used Soviet explanations for American prosperity—to the limited degree that the Soviets are willing to acknowledge its existence. This work, edited by a committee of influential Soviet officials, including M. A. Kharlamov, then chief of the Press Department of the Soviet Ministry of Foreign Affairs, attributed the rapid economic development of the United States to such factors as the slave labor of Negroes, the abundance of immigrants from Europe, the expropriation of the Indians, the plundering of neighboring states and islands, the availability of European capital, and the wealth of natural

[24] Varga himself corrected his heretical views in a revised version of his book, published in 1953.

resources available in North America.[25] The article in this handbook on "American Capitalism" presented this remarkable view of American economic development and went on to criticize "American bourgeois economists and reformers" for allegedly seeking to explain the rapidity of American economic development by reference to the exceptional nature of American capitalism. The handbook, of course, denied that American capitalism differed from capitalism elsewhere. Capitalism in the United States, it insisted, was founded, like capitalism everywhere, on exploitation and was characterized by class conflict and crisis. Just as world capitalism as a whole, the American form had entered its period of incurable "general crisis" as a result of the first World War and the October Revolution in Russia. Linking its analysis of the internal structure of the American economy with United States foreign policy, the article attributed to the "ruling circles of the U.S.A." a policy of struggling for a redivision of the world in their favor. It further asserted that the United States was "the greatest colonial power" and that it had developed new forms of colonial oppression in the form of military alliances.

As might be expected, the article laid great stress on the alleged economic exploitation of American workers, and asserted that under the pressure of a falling standard of living, and of unemployment, the workers were turning increasingly to strikes and other forms of resistance to economic oppression. It added that social conflicts in the United States not only pitted the *bourgeoisie* against the working class but also involved a struggle between the "monopolistic *bourgeoisie*" and all other strata of the people, including the proletariat, the masses of the farmers, the intellectuals, the tradespeople, and other groups.[26] The foregoing brief summary of one representative article in this six-hundred-page book suggests the massive barriers to international understanding interposed by

[25] *Soedinennye shtaty ameriki* (Moscow, 1960), pp. 89-95.
[26] *Ibid.*, pp. 93-94.

Leninist demonology between the Soviet world and the constitutional democracies.

One interesting aspect of Soviet and international communist propaganda concerning the American economy is concerned with strikes. Strikes are presented as evidence of the exploitation of the workers. On the other hand, the communist rulers usually devote relatively less attention to strikes in countries such as the United States than one might expect. Perhaps some light is shed on the relative caution and the high level of distortion with which the Soviet press usually reports strikes in America by a conversation reported to the author in Leningrad in the summer of 1959 between a Russian and an American. The Russian asked the American why the steelworkers in the United States were on strike. The latter replied, "Because they want more money." When the American, in turn, asked the Russian "What do the workers do in your country when they want more money?" the Russian failed to reply. In this connection it is perhaps worth recalling that Khrushchev experienced considerable embarrassment in his conversations during his September 1959 American trip with several prominent labor leaders. Following Khrushchev's return to the Soviet Union, the Soviet press heaped vituperation upon Walter Reuther.

Even the most skeptical of American political scientists would presumably agree that political competition for public office through free elections is close to the heart of western constitutional democracy. However, the Soviet press has continued to present the traditional Leninist view according to which the American system of elections "is intended to assure the political domination of monopolistic capital in the United States."[27] It may be interesting to examine briefly how this formula was applied to the United States presidential elections of 1952, 1956, and 1960. (We include 1952 in order to furnish

[27] *Soedinennye shtaty ameriki, op.cit.*, p. 122.

a basis of comparison with the Stalin era.)[28] From the point of view of a non-communist American political scientist, the Soviet presentation of all three of these elections was shaped by a combination of ideological prejudice and deliberate falsification. The element of falsification was greater in publications such as *Trud, Pravda,* or *Izvestiya,* than in the magazine *New Times,* which is intended for foreign distribution and is published in many languages.

This fact perhaps reflected Soviet appreciation of the relative difficulty of falsifying the nature of the American election system to foreign audiences not subject to Soviet controls on communication. Somewhat encouraging was the fact that the reporting of the American presidential elections in Soviet publications was more accurate in 1956 and 1960 than in 1952. For example, the charges made in 1952 that the American elections took place in an atmosphere of violence and "police terror" were absent in 1956 and 1960.[29] Even *New Times* in its 1952 reporting of the Philadelphia mayoralty election had reported that it was conducted in an atmosphere of "bribery and corruption, blackmail and violence."[30] From this account, it would have been impossible to draw the conclusion, in fact correct, that the election was marked by the victory of a reform ticket.

In their reporting of the 1956 and 1960 elections, Soviet publications contained interesting indications of awareness that there were differences not only between the Democratic and Republican parties, but also within them. However, the main line which they followed was the traditional one that the policy and the purposes of the two parties were identical. Khrushchev himself stated the Soviet position at an industrial exhibition in Hungary in August 1960 when he said that both

[28] The material here on United States presidential elections is drawn in part from a study made by Michael Moss.
[29] See, for example, *Pravda,* November 15, 1952.
[30] *New Times,* No. 8, February 20, 1952, p. 31.

Kennedy and Nixon were "servants of monopoly capital, so there is no choice for us here."[31] Interestingly enough, Stevenson, who had been treated in 1952 and 1956 as a typical representative of monopoly capitalism, was presented in 1960 as a relatively desirable possibility for the Democratic nomination, apparently because of his expressed attitudes toward international issues.[32]

Thus the Soviet interpretation of this central aspect of the American political system continued to be shaped by traditional Leninist orthodoxy. At the same time, however, it also reflected some increase of knowledge of the facts of American political life and, at the same time, an irresistible desire to fit these facts into whatever was the Kremlin's propaganda preoccupation of the moment.

Perhaps something should be said here about the Soviet propaganda treatment of the first few months of the Kennedy administration.[33] A systematic study of Soviet short-wave radio broadcasts in English from Moscow to eastern North America, the United Kingdom, and Europe from the period November 8, 1960 to May 3, 1961 revealed an interesting pattern. The Soviet radio interpreted the victory of Mr. Kennedy as an expression of the dissatisfaction of the American people with the Eisenhower administration. The keynote of the early attitude toward President Kennedy was struck by Khrushchev in his telegram to Mr. Kennedy on November 9, 1960, expressing the hope that relations between the USSR and the USA would return to the line along which they were developing in the days of Franklin D. Roosevelt. This gambit, combined with a "wait and see" attitude toward Kennedy, was apparently designed to project to the peoples of the world the

[31] *Pravda*, August 31, 1960.
[32] S. Menshikov, "Who Will Be America's Next President?" *New Times*, July, 1960, p. 14.
[33] The paragraphs dealing with Soviet attitudes toward the early stages of the Kennedy administration are based mainly on a study made by Mr. Frank Letcher.

73

Soviet desire for a fresh start in international affairs and, at the same time, to throw the onus of failure to achieve this, if need be, on the United States and the American president. Significant was a broadcast on November 17, which stated that cooperation was necessary for progress in negotiations with the Soviet Union, but warned that there were individuals in the leadership of the Democratic Party who did not stick to the "realistic course" which Roosevelt followed toward the Soviet Union.

Also significant was the fact that while the broadcasts to Europe contained much criticism of the American government, those to eastern North America were virtually free of such criticism, except for continuous attacks on Eisenhower. However, as early as December 11, 1960, one broadcast to eastern North America charged the Central Intelligence Agency with plotting an attack on Cuba. Also, numerous broadcasts attempted to create the impression that the United States and its western European allies were continuously becoming less trustful of one another. Beginning in April, and especially after the abortive anti-Castro landing in Cuba, the Soviet radio began to attack the Kennedy administration and the president himself.

While attacking the American "ruling circles" and, less frequently, Presidents Truman, Eisenhower, and Kennedy, Soviet propaganda has continued its effort to persuade both the Soviet people and the other peoples of the world that the "simple people" of America, and also some of the more sensible elements of the American elite, would like to respond favorably to Soviet overtures for a relaxation of international tensions. In fact, many of Khrushchev's most important speeches have contained sections suggesting, in effect, a "deal" between Russia and America. For example, in his speech to the Twentieth Congress of the CPSU in 1956 Khrushchev devoted several paragraphs to the attractive prospects which would be opened up by the "establishment of firm, friendly relations

74

between the two greatest powers of the world, the Soviet Union and the United States of America."[34] One way of lending credence to this professed objective, especially in contacts with businessmen, is to suggest that better political relations will lead to profitable trade. Another is to attempt to cultivate cordial personal relations with individual businessmen, labor leaders, and professionals. Soviet diplomacy and propaganda devoted considerable attention to these objectives in the post-Stalin period, although the results were probably modest.

The generally negative image of the United States that we have been briefly sketching here is extended into the past by Soviet historians. An interesting and widely circulated example of the rewriting of American history to suit the purposes of post-Stalin foreign policy is contained in the section on American history of *The Great Soviet Encyclopedia*, which was published in an annotated translation in 1960 by the State Historical Society of Wisconsin.[35] Unlike the relatively objective 1945 Soviet encyclopedia article on the same subject, this one stressed American "imperialistic expansionism" and racial, social, and economic unrest. Rather interesting, in view of Khrushchev's attempt to manipulate the Roosevelt symbol in world affairs, was the unfavorable characterization of Roosevelt's policies—not quite as unfavorable, however, as that accorded the policies of other American presidents.[36]

The massive two-volume work on United States history edited by Grigori Sevostianov, published in 1960 by the Institute of History of the Academy of Sciences of the USSR was also informative.[37] The preface to the second volume of the work is particularly interesting. It stresses such themes as

[34] *XX sezd kommunisticheskoi partii sovetskogo soyuza*, Vol. II, p. 31.
[35] *A Soviet View of the American Past* (Madison, Wis., 1960). This is a translation of material published in Vol. 39 of the *Bolshaya sovetskaya entsiklopediya* in 1956, pp. 557-654.
[36] See, for example, statement on p. 47 of the above translation regarding the alleged sharp increase in profits of the "monopolies" during Roosevelt's presidency.
[37] *Ocherki novoi i noveishei istorii S Sh A* (2 vols., Moscow, 1960).

alleged American leadership of the intervention against the Soviet government in 1918-1919, the hope of the American "imperialists" that with the aid of the atomic bomb they could achieve world domination, and the "unprecedented terror" to which the Communist Party was subjected in the United States. A significant thesis, which is at least implied in this and other Soviet works on American history, is that not only the "ruling classes" of America but also to some degree the people as a whole have been the beneficiaries of privileges to which they were not entitled. Perhaps it would not be too fanciful to speculate that in Soviet eyes one of the missions of the "world labor movement" is to put an end to these unjustified privileges.

Of course the Kremlin regards Soviet-American relations not only as a power struggle but also as a competition between two cultures, or two civilizations, with Moscow representing the socialist camp and Washington representing capitalism. A somewhat similar view is widely held in the western world. Moscow professes to believe that socialist institutions and culture are destined to spread throughout the world until all of humanity will live under a socialist and eventually a communist system. Perhaps the most systematic Soviet treatment of the Soviet design for a world socialist culture was a book published in 1954 by G. G. Karpov, who asserted that after the destruction of bourgeois culture throughout the world a "truly unified and universal human culture" would be established "under conditions of socialism."[38] In spite of the fact that there has been an increased access to non-communist books, films, and other cultural materials in the Soviet Union since 1953, there has been no indication that Moscow has abandoned the pretensions to universal cultural dominion of which Karpov's book was one expression.

While working for and waiting for the world cultural revo-

[38] G. G. Karpov, *O sovetskoi kulture i kulturnoi revolyutsii v s.s.s.r.* (Moscow, 1954), p. 3.

76

lution the Kremlin continued its campaign against western culture, and in particular against those aspects of modern culture most attractive to adventurous minds in the Soviet Union itself, such as abstract art or "progressive" jazz. Typical was the statement that "the New York Museum of Modern Art, founded in 1929 by the magnates of capital, has become the avenue for disseminating formalistic, abstract art as the official art of the United States."[39] The long and critical article on American motion pictures in the already-cited official Soviet Handbook on the United States concludes with the following statement: "The situation which developed in the post war years in American film art serves as a clear reflection of the general crisis of bourgeois culture, of the capitalist society and social system."[40]

As Melville J. Ruggles found, after surveying a vast array of Russian translations of American literature, "The America that the Russian knows from the American literature available to him is a land of Simon Legree, the coonskin cap, the heroic sled dog, the sharecropper, the sweatshop, the dispirited, defeated, and depraved, the frivolous, the bloated billionaire, the regimented traveler in space."[41]

While depreciating the dominant "bourgeois" American culture and its exponents, the Soviet and international communist press extols as examples of "progressive" American culture a handful of almost unknown communist or procommunist writers, scholars, cinema directors, and artists such as Albert Maltz, Michael Gold, Herbert Aptheker, Rockwell Kent, and a few others. It should be noted, however, that at least in the handbook to which we have several times referred,

[39] This and similar statements were contained in an article by P. Fedoseev entitled "Socialist Humanism and Culture," published in *Sovetskaya kultura* for November 5, 1957.

[40] *Soedinennye shtaty ameriki*, p. 377.

[41] Melville J. Ruggles, "American Books in Soviet Publishing," *Slavic Review*, Vol. xx, No. 3, Ocotber, 1961, pp. 419-435. Quotation on pp. 431-432.

the attitude taken toward American music was relatively friendly and objective, perhaps partly because so many leading American composers or performers are of Russian origin. Prominence is given in Soviet sources, as we might expect, to evidence of the popularity of Soviet music in the United States.

In view of the generally hostile and fearful Soviet attitude toward modern American culture described above, it is easy to understand why the Kremlin unleashed a press campaign against the American Exhibition in Moscow in 1959. The Soviet leadership was apparently particularly annoyed because the Exhibition featured, not heavy machinery, but consumer goods and cultural achievements. The official criticism was that failure to show more heavy machinery was in effect an insult to the Soviet people. For weeks before the Exhibition opened, and during the five weeks while it was on display, Soviet newspapers and magazines instructed their readers in the attitude that the authorities expected viewers to take. Measures were also taken to restrict the viewers, insofar as possible, to party members and other well-indoctrinated persons.

Along the same lines, Khrushchev returned from the United States in 1959 with criticisms of American cultural decadence. And, whatever their private opinions may have been, Soviet visitors to America, including the very few among the Soviet participants in American-Soviet academic exchanges who published statements about their experience in the citadel of capitalism, echoed the official line. In spite of this, there was reason to believe that even the relatively limited contact between Russians and Americans after 1953 constituted one of the most hopeful aspects of the total world situation. In considerable part, the official Soviet negative image of America was a defensive measure designed to shield impressionable Russians from what the Kremlin regarded as harmful influences.

Still, Soviet anti-Americanism continues to give much cause for concern. It aggravates international tensions and renders very difficult the achievement of stability and tranquility in a troubled world. It is, ultimately, an instrument of the communist program for world conquest. It goes hand in hand with the statements of Khrushchev and other communist leaders and propagandists to the effect that the United States is destined to be defeated, first in the battle of production and then in the world political struggle. Since 1956 Soviet propaganda has been increasingly bold in suggesting that henceforth not Russia but America would face the prospect of encirclement. The pattern was set in an important article published by A. Sobolev in *Kommunist*, No. 14, 1956, which predicted that eventually the United States would be "surrounded" by a "friendly socialist environment." It would then be easy to elect a "government of a new type." It was clear that however figuratively he may have been speaking, Khrushchev was in deadly earnest in his well-known promise to "bury" capitalism.

CHAPTER IV

PEACE AND WAR

PROPAGANDA designed to associate the policies of the USSR with the aspirations of the peoples of the world for relief from the fear and suffering of war has probably been the most powerful psychological instrument of world communism since the bolsheviks came to power in 1917. Contemporary Soviet doctrine on international relations, implicitly acknowledging this, continues to assert that the Soviet regime from its inception has pursued policies which embody the desire of all peoples for a just and democratic peace. For example, a recent university level textbook published by the Central Committee of the CPSU declares at the outset that "The foreign policy program of the Great October socialist revolution was set forth in the decree on peace, adopted by the second all-Russian congress of Soviets on November 8, 1917 on the basis of a report by V. I. Lenin."[1] Thus, asserts Moscow, its intentions have always been peaceful, and have always conformed to the prescriptions laid down by Lenin.

One might sum up the "dialectical" Soviet attitude toward peace and war in the words, "peace through struggle." From Lenin through Khrushchev a favorite phrase of Soviet propagandists has, indeed, been "the struggle for peace" (*borba za mir*). The paradox, perhaps, makes some sense, in terms of the tortuous logic of Marxism-Leninism. As Brzezinski observes, in his article referred to in the last chapter, Soviet communists have professed to believe that human society was inevitably moving toward "socialism" and hence that war was an effort, on the part of the bourgeoisie, to delay progress toward this

[1] *Mezhdunarodnye otnosheniya i vneshnyaya politika SSSR* (Moscow, 1961), p. 6.

goal. If this is so, Brzezinski appears to argue, communists must believe they are always peaceful, since obviously they, with "history" on their side, could not fight against "progress." Certainly, despite an increase in Soviet fear of the possible consequences of war, and increased stress in Soviet doctrine on the possibility of "peaceful coexistence" of states with different social systems, sponsored by Khrushchev since 1955, world revolution remains the ultimate acknowledged objective of Soviet policy. Means change, but the goal of a world revolution presided over by Moscow has never been abandoned. However, it seems increasingly clear, as British Foreign Secretary Lord Home pointed out in a speech on October 1, 1962, that Moscow, like the western powers, recognizes the inappropriateness of nuclear war as a means for achieving political goals. Exceptionally forceful re-statements of this position were contained in Khrushchev's speech to the Supreme Soviet on December 12, 1962, and in a declaration published in *Pravda* for January 7, 1963. In a slashing attack on the Albanian-Chinese faction of international communism, the declaration in *Pravda* flatly asserted that the only alternatives facing mankind were "peaceful coexistence among states with different social systems or devastating war." The declaration went on to say that the socialist countries did not "need" war, since their victory in economic competition with capitalism would have "exceptional significance" in causing all peoples to choose socialism in preference to capitalism.

Lenin, Stalin, and Khrushchev shared the belief that the ambitious objectives of Soviet communism could not be realized without a fierce struggle. At the same time, the Soviet leaders have been adept in exploiting mankind's longing for peace in an era of wars and revolutions. They have proclaimed their own desire for peace eloquently, insistently, and with endless repetition. They have sought ceaselessly to implant the idea in world public opinion that capitalism, particularly in its modern "imperialist" stage of development, is a social system dedicated to conflict. In support of this thesis they have cited various arguments of Marx and Lenin, especially those deriving from Lenin's *Imperialism.*

According to the formula developed by Lenin and ritualistically echoed by his successors, the "monopolists" who dominate the foreign policy of the non-communist states are engaged in a never-ending struggle for the "redivision of the world." This struggle leads to conflicts among the capitalist powers. The capitalist "ruling classes" and the governments they control are, however, in agreement on one crucial point. They hate and fear "socialism," the anti-capitalist movements of the "proletariat" of advanced industrial countries, and the "struggle for national liberation" of the peoples of underdeveloped countries who seek, according to this doctrine, to throw off the political, economic, and cultural yoke imposed upon them by the imperialists.

Marxism-Leninism, Stalinism, and, if one may coin a term, Khrushchevism, have been in essential agreement on the cardinal doctrine that only by the elimination of capitalism, including what most Americans describe as constitutional democracy, could a stable and just peace be achieved. As we shall learn by examining typical statements by Lenin, Stalin and Khrushchev, the Soviet leaders have been remarkably frank in proclaiming their dedication to the concept of revolutionary class struggle which has always been the doctrinal justification for their approach to problems of peace and war. At the same time, however, in their propaganda to non-communists, especially to non-communist governments, the Soviet leaders have minimized or concealed their belief in the inevitability of conflict. In dealing with foreign governments and with non-communist world opinion, the Soviet government has generally taken the line that "normal" international relations could be achieved if only non-communist governments would approach the Soviet Union in a spirit of good will. Soviet propaganda has obscured the fact, obvious from authoritative Soviet sources and also easily inferred from Soviet behavior, that coexistence has normally been regarded as a transient, though perhaps long-lasting, pattern of relations between the socialist and capitalist worlds. And it is one to be terminated whenever the forces of revolution feel free to resume their forward march toward world communism.

There is an obvious component of disingenuousness in the Soviet approach to peace and war. This does not, however, mean that the Soviet leaders do not fear war. Theirs is an expansionist doctrine. It has not usually, however, been a traditional military expansionist doctrine. It is founded upon professed belief in the inevitability and desirability of world revolution, as interpreted and applied by the "vanguard" of the working classes, the self-chosen communist elite. This doctrine asserts not only that the weakness and disunity of non-communist societies make revolution inevitable, but that it is the duty of revolutionaries to accelerate revolutionary social change as much as they are able.

The doctrine also recognizes the fact that the social order which the communists seek to undermine will struggle to survive. The character and degree of resistance depend on circumstances, including social and political conditions and the state of weaponry. And yet, it is clear that adherents of the social conflict doctrine we are describing can be as sincere as their opponents in desiring peace and fearing war. Both communists and anti-communists desire peace on their own terms. However, communists have normally been far more pessimistic about the prospects for peace than have non-communists. This is indicated, for example, by the sharply contrasting articles on peace and war in Soviet and western encyclopedias. The *Encyclopaedia Britannica* gives prominence to the views of Kant on the irrationality of war, while the *Bolshaya sovetskaya entsiklopedia,* in volume 27 of its current edition, asserts flatly that the "ruling classes" of capitalist countries resort to violence whenever they cannot achieve their objectives by other means.

This pessimism is combined with an extremely self-centered world outlook, which views any accretion of strength to a rival power as a grave threat to Soviet security. Such attitudes impel Moscow to be ever hunting for anti-Soviet plots and they foster the recurrent Soviet tendency to launch virulent propaganda campaigns against alleged imperialist "warmongers."

It is safe to say that neither the Soviet leadership nor that of the western democracies has valued conflict for its own sake, although some statements of Lenin and other Soviet leaders and certain actions of the Soviet government, such as its attempt to establish communism in Poland in 1920 by military invasion, have at times indicated a tendency to welcome war and military operations as an instrument of or as an inspiration to revolution. In this connection it is interesting that Lenin, while characterizing war as "a great disaster" also expressed the opinion that a war which served the "interests of the proletariat," represented "progress," regardless of the suffering it entailed.[2] During and after the Polish-Soviet war of 1920 the brilliant strategist Tukhachevski proclaimed the doctrine, which the Chinese communists seem to echo in our era, that military invasion can be a highly desirable instrument for bringing socialism to the workers and peasants of non-communist nations.

During the period since the establishment of Soviet power in 1917, the capitalist governments, with the important exceptions of Nazi Germany, Fascist Italy, and Japan, have seldom acted as if they thought that large-scale war was a useful instrument for the expansion of political influence. However, military intervention on the side of the anti-bolshevik forces during the Russian Revolution, limited and unsuccessful though it was, tended to confirm Soviet suspicions that the capitalist powers would destroy Soviet socialism if they could.

[2] Cited in T. A. Taracouzio, *War and Peace in Soviet Diplomacy* (New York, 1940), p. 53.

Certainly military intervention by "bourgeois" governments and their subsequent hostile acts and statements facilitated the tasks of Soviet propagandists. A half-true impression was created that "bourgeois" governments were working feverishly to do maximum harm to the Soviet Union. Foreign general staffs and intelligence services have been accused of a wide range of hostile intentions and actions. The most serious of these charges revolved around alleged plots to make war against the Soviet Union and accusations that foreign intelligence services were planning counter-revolutionary movements inside Russia. Often such accusations were made in times of internal crisis in the USSR. For example, the accused in the political trials of 1936-1938 were charged with acting as agents of British, French, Japanese and other intelligence services. *Pravda* for December 17, 1953 accused Lavrenti Beria, who had faithfully served Stalin for many years in the Soviet security organs, of using his official position "in the interests of foreign capital, striving in its perfidious schemes to set the Ministry of Internal Affairs above the party and government in order to seize power and liquidate the Soviet worker-peasant system for the purpose of restoring capitalism and the domination of the bourgeoisie." The same accusation contained a charge that Beria had begun to work for British Intelligence as far back as 1919.[3] The state of mind reflected in such charges has prevailed in the Soviet Union from the earliest days of the regime. It is interesting in this connection to recall that *Pravda* for March 3, 1921 charged that the French Intelligence Service had instigated the rebellion of the Kronstadt sailors against the Soviet authorities.

The relatively high level of anxiety about war in the Soviet Union has probably facilitated the success of Soviet peace propaganda, both domestic and foreign. The intensity of

[3] An English translation of the text of the announcement on the case of Beria is contained in Robert Conquest's book, *Power and Policy in the USSR*, pp. 440-444.

Soviet feelings on the subject of war and peace has lent to Soviet spokesmen a convincing air of sincerity which has often impressed even the most conservative foreign leaders. This anxiety has also of course spurred Soviet personnel to work with exceptional energy in the dissemination of peace propaganda. Anxiety, reflecting the harsh struggle of the Soviet regime to survive against both domestic and foreign enemies, has often caused the Soviet leadership to fantastically exaggerate foreign hostility. This anxiety, reflected in domestic propaganda about war dangers, has made the Soviet population more conscious of problems of war and peace than the peoples of the western democracies usually have been. This, in turn, has facilitated the impact of Soviet peace propaganda. Foreign visitors have often returned from the Soviet Union, particularly in the period of increased international communication since 1953, deeply impressed by the apparent sincerity of the desire of the Soviet man in the street for peace.

Soviet concern about the danger of war and determination to exploit the world's longing for peace as a propaganda weapon has been reflected in myriad ways. The peace theme is injected into almost every aspect of Soviet propaganda. For this reason, it is difficult to deal with it as a separate feature of Soviet propaganda. However, it will be useful to treat propaganda statements about peace and war as a special aspect of Soviet international communications, provided that we bear in mind the interconnections between the peace theme and other aspects of international propaganda. By linking other aspects of propaganda with that of peace and war Soviet propaganda has often succeeded in reaching audiences that would otherwise have been inaccessible or indifferent.

In order to deal with a subject as vast as Soviet peace propaganda it is necessary to focus on a few of its most significant aspects. We shall deal here with three important instruments of Soviet peace propaganda, namely theoretical, or ostensibly theoretical statements, diplomatic negotiations, particularly disarmament negotiations, and, finally, attempts to organize or exploit mass peace propaganda campaigns.

It is, of course, extremely difficult to distinguish clearly in Soviet communications between theoretical and doctrinal statements on the one hand and propagandistic and agitational statements on the other. Even in western political discourse, with its tradition of relative candor, the identification of motives is difficult. The manipulative character of communist political communication greatly increases the difficulties. When we refer in this chapter to theoretical and doctrinal statements, therefore, we assume that when these statements are employed in Soviet mass media intended both for domestic and foreign audiences they serve not only indoctrinational but also propagandistic and agitational purposes.

Soviet doctrinal statements about peace can conveniently be divided into two main categories. The first category, to which the familiar Soviet expression, "the struggle for peace," may be applied, consists of statements regarding the hostile, aggressive, warlike, and militaristic nature of capitalism. The charge that capitalism and the capitalist governments threaten the peace is designed to appeal primarily to communists, potential communists, and other persons or groups prepared to support Soviet and communist foreign policies. The struggle for peace is regarded as an instrument for mobilizing pro-Soviet elements. It also serves to inhibit defense measures by non-communist governments against Soviet pressures. It may even, in certain cases, become a sufficiently powerful pressure to intimidate foreign governments.

The second major category of Soviet statements pertaining to peace is symbolized by the term "coexistence." Often other terms, such as "normalization" or "relaxation of international tensions" are used. These terms, and the promises and propositions connected with them, are designed to appeal mainly to neutral and even to anti-communists. Beginning in 1955, particularly while traveling with Bulganin in

India, Burma, and Afghanistan, Khrushchev gave world-wide currency to the expression "peaceful coexistence." He also asserted that what he described as the Soviet foreign policy of peaceful coexistence was a direct continuation of the policy of Lenin. This assertion, of course, was false, as the historian Sergei Pushkarev demonstrated with an abundance of documentation in the New York Russian-language newspaper *Novoe Russkoe Slovo*, for January 22, 1956.[4] Despite the weakness of their case in terms of discoverable historical evidence, Soviet propagandists have to this day continued to assert that Lenin not only desired, but believed in the feasibility of "peaceful coexistence." For example, Otto Kuusinen, in a speech on April 22, 1960, attempted—without furnishing any relevant evidence—to prove an identity between Lenin's denunciation of war and the Khrushchevian advocacy of coexistence. Also N. Inozemtsev, in *Pravda* for January 17, 1962 attacked Molotov for having asserted—correctly—that Lenin never spoke about the possibility of peaceful coexistence of states with different social systems.[5]

The fact is that Khrushchev substantially revised the view of Lenin and of Stalin that an all-out military clash between the Soviet Union and the capitalist countries was sooner or later inevitable. At the same time, although Khrushchev's revision of Leninism represented a substantial shift of emphasis in Soviet thinking, it did not involve abandonment of the basic Soviet belief in the inevitability of the ultimate imposition of the Soviet pattern of culture and civilization on the whole world. Rather it represented recognition of the danger of large-scale violence in a period of super-weapons. It reflected a developing confidence that an economically

[4] See also L. Pistrak, "Mirnoe sosushchestvovanie po leninu," *Sotsialisticheski Vestnik*, November, 1959, pp. 212-215.

[5] For bringing to my attention this and an abundance of other data proving conclusively, at least in my opinion, the falsity of Soviet propaganda regarding the continuity of Khrushchev's coexistence doctrine with the views of Lenin, I am indebted to Mr. Saul N. Silverman.

powerful Soviet Union could undermine the western powers by means short of all-out war.[6]

If it was Khrushchev who placed the main emphasis in Soviet peace propaganda on the concept and tactics of co-existence, this does not mean that this tactic was never employed by Lenin and Stalin. Nor does it mean that Khrushchev abandoned the traditional Leninist thesis that capitalism was the sole cause of war and the source of the war danger. Under Lenin, Stalin, and Khrushchev Soviet expressions of an ardent love of peace, as well as propaganda against "imperialist warmongers," have been combined with attempts to convince "capitalists" that they could line their pockets by doing business with communists. All of these themes have played major roles in Soviet peace strategy and propaganda.

Let us now analyze the tactics of Soviet peace propaganda, which in its most candid form attempts to convince Soviet citizens and foreigners alike that the elimination of capitalism is the only reliable means of assuring lasting peace in the world. Lenin often said as much. One of the most vivid of his statements was his assertion in 1918 that either victorious imperialism or Soviet power could exist in the world, but that no middle ground existed. Still more striking was his prediction in 1920 that a funeral dirge would be sung either over the Soviet republic or over world capitalism.[7] Lenin's preoccupation with the threat to Russian communism and the Soviet state from the continued existence of capitalism was indicated by the fact that in his last significant article, published on March 2, 1923, he expressed confidence in the

---

[6] On the post-Stalin tendency to substitute economic competition for military force as the major instrument for Soviet expansion, see Milton Kovner, *The Challenge of Co-existence* (Washington, D.C., 1961). See also J. M. Mackintosh, *Strategy and Tactics of Soviet Foreign Policy* (London, 1962), chaps. xxi and xxii.

[7] Cited by Pushkarev in the above article. See also the collection of Lenin's statements on international relations and the world revolution in the pamphlet "Peaceful Co-existence, What It Means to Khrushchev," distributed by American Committee for Liberation, New York, 1960.

final victory of socialism but added that what was most important was tactics which would assure Soviet survival and "prevent the Western-European counter-revolutionary states from crushing us." Interestingly enough, in this article Lenin saw the problem in terms of assuring the existence of the Soviet Union until "the last military clash between the counter-revolutionary imperialistic West and the revolutionary and nationalistic East."[8]

It is sometimes argued that the Lenin-Stalin view regarding the inevitability of war between socialist and capitalist states resulted from the experience of Soviet Russia during the Civil War and intervention. The fact is that Lenin's belief in the impossibility, over the long run, of preventing total war between Soviet Russia and the non-communist states was one of his central tenets. It long antedated the accession of Lenin's party to power. Bolshevik attitudes and policies after 1917 were a logical continuation of attitudes formed around the turn of the twentieth century. As far back as 1902, in the most important of all of his writings, *What Is To Be Done?*, Lenin emphasized the special role of the Russian proletariat in the world-wide struggle between the forces of socialism and those of capitalism. With the outbreak of World War I Lenin proclaimed his slogan of the "transformation of the present imperialist war into a civil war" and he followed this up by his efforts to found a Third International, which was established in March, 1919.[9] When Khrushchev claimed, from 1955 on, that he was pursuing the "Leninist policy of peaceful coexistence," he was either distorting Lenin, or else peaceful coexistence did not mean what Khrushchev said it meant, namely, "a renunciation of interference in the internal affairs of other countries with the object of altering their

[8] V. I. Lenin, *Kommunisticheski internatsional*, Vol. II (Moscow, 1934), pp. 584-585.

[9] See, for example, Robert V. Daniels, *A Documentary History of Communism*, pp. 68-86.

system of government or mode of life or for any other motives."[10]

It is true, of course, that Lenin in the last three or four years of his life was forced to recognize that the Soviet state would have to exist for some time in a largely capitalist world. Lenin, the realist, began to refer to the "breathing spell" gained by the young Soviet state, and also to use such terms as coexistence and even peaceful coexistence—for example, he sometimes used the Russian expression "mirnoe sozhitel-stvo," meaning literally peaceful cohabitation. Apparently, however, the first conspicuous use of the formula of peaceful coexistence was made by the arch-revolutionary Leon Trotski. "Our peace program," said Trotski on November 23, 1917, "formulates the burning aspirations of millions. We desire the speediest peace on principles of honorable coexistence and cooperation of peoples. We desire the speediest possible overthrow of the domination of capital."[11] Very interesting to the student of propaganda is another of Trotski's statements, also made in November, 1917, that "All governments are under pressure from the peoples, and our policy is the force that increases that pressure." This pressure was the sole guarantee, Trotski continued, that there could be coexistence between Soviet Russia and the peoples of western Europe.[12] As indicated by the above and similar statements of Trotski and Lenin, early Soviet manipulation of the coexistence symbol was mainly within the context of revolutionary agitation. However, by 1920, Soviet Foreign Affairs Commissar Chicherin was referring to establishment of peace with Estonia as "the first experiment in peaceful coexistence with bourgeois states."[13]

[10] Nikita S. Khrushchev, "On Peaceful Co-existence," *Foreign Affairs*, October, 1959, Vol. 38, No. 1, pp. 1-18; quotation on p. 3.

[11] Quoted by Bertram D. Wolfe in Tamiment Institute Pamphlet entitled "Is Co-existence Possible" (New York, 1955), p. 14.

[12] L. Trotski, *Sochineniya*, Vol. III, Part 2, p. 163.

[13] Louis Fischer, *The Soviets in World Affairs*, 2 Vols. (Princeton, N.J., 1951), I, p. 254.

Lenin, in 1922, began to take the position that some form of temporary coexistence was possible between the Soviet Union and the capitalist states. For example, in November, 1922, he declared that the Soviet Union desired peaceful coexistence in its foreign relations.[14] It was Stalin, however, who further developed the concept of long-term coexistence, but always with the implication that this was an armed truce which might be terminated by an imperialist attack on the Soviet Union, or, with sufficient growth in the military strength of the USSR, by Soviet assistance to social or nationalist revolutions in the non-Soviet world.

As Historicus, in his article "Stalin on Revolution," noted, Stalin's most important doctrinal work was his article, "On the Foundations of Leninism."[15] This work, which first appeared in 1924 was republished again and again throughout Stalin's lifetime. In it Stalin, discussing the concept of the dictatorship of the proletariat, stated that this dictatorship could not arise on the basis of a peaceful development of bourgeois society and of bourgeois democracy, but could only result from the smashing of the bourgeois state machine, the bourgeois army, and police, etc. Stalin followed Lenin who had written in 1917 that Marx's belief that countries such as England and America might achieve socialism without a violent revolution was no longer valid because these countries had become police states. Stalin declared that the "law of violent revolution" applied to all of "the imperialistic countries of the world." Stalin added, however, that in the distant future, if the proletariat were victorious in the most important capitalist countries and the "present capitalist encirclement" were to be replaced by a "socialist encirclement," then a "peaceful" path of development might become possible for

[14] V. I. Lenin, *Sochineniya*, 4th ed., Vol. xxx, p. 352.
[15] See Historicus, "Stalin on Revolution," reprinted in Alexander Dallin, ed., *Soviet Conduct in World Affairs* (New York, 1960), especially pp. 167-169.

certain capitalist countries. The capitalists of those countries would find themselves in an unfavorable international situation and would consider it expedient to "voluntarily" make "serious concessions" to the proletariat.[16]

Like most of Stalin's ideological and propaganda formulas, his conception of the possibility of a peaceful transition to socialism in one or more capitalist countries was borrowed from Lenin. Lenin had envisaged that in "some small country," the capitalists might surrender power peacefully to "save their (capitalist) heads." The situation that Lenin had in mind was one in which the communist revolution had been victorious in neighboring countries.[17]

The foregoing views of Lenin and Stalin are of exceptional interest in the light of some of Khrushchev's statements. For example, Khrushchev in his published "Political Report" to the Twentieth Congress of the CPSU in February 1956 asserted that under contemporary conditions, when the "socialist camp" was so much more powerful than in the past, war was no longer "fatalistically inevitable."[18] However, Khrushchev in this same speech reaffirmed the necessity of a "revolutionary transformation of capitalist society into a socialist one." Echoing Stalin thirty-two years before, he optimistically asserted that under favorable circumstances, where the "capitalists" were weak, this revolutionary transfer of power could take place without a civil war. Thus Khrushchev set forth a strategy of a "parliamentary path to communism" and of world revolution by "socialist encirclement," which was actually far less new than it seemed to many observers at the time.

It should be emphasized that all of the Soviet leaders, from

[16] J. Stalin, *Voprosy leninizma*, 11th ed. (Moscow, 1945), pp. 31-32.
[17] John A. Armstrong, *The Politics of Totalitarianism* (New York, 1961), p. 294. Armstrong quotes an article by Oskar Anweiler, "Lenin und der friedliche Uebergang zum Sozialismus," in *Ost-Europa*, Vol. VI (1956), p. 194.
[18] *XX sezd kommunisticheskoi partii sovetskogo soyuza*, Vol. I, p. 37.

Lenin and Trotski through Stalin and Khrushchev, strove in their peace propaganda to appeal both to revolutionaries seeking the overthrow of constitutional democracy and to western businessmen, liberals, pacifists, and the general public whose non-dialectic conception of peace was limited to the simple absence of armed conflict. It remained for Khrushchev, the great apostle of peaceful coexistence, to add to the arsenal of Soviet peace propaganda the now familiar instrument of nuclear blackmail. This was employed during the Suez crisis in 1956, against Turkey in 1957, in the Lebanese crisis of 1958, during the U-2 episode in 1960, etc. The Soviet Union in September 1961 injected into the atmosphere in a period of two months more radioactive fall-out than had been produced by all tests of nuclear weapons from 1945 on, and then threatened that if the United States were to resume testing, the USSR would conduct still further tests. Moscow's production and testing of megaton bombs may have been designed to overcome a relative weakness *vis-à-vis* the United States in nuclear weapons, but at the same time superbombs served as a potent instrument of the Soviet strategy of terror.

In spite of the militaristic sword concealed by Soviet assurances of peaceful intentions, the reassuring statements made by Stalin and Khrushchev have received far greater attention throughout the world than have their dire doctrinal pronouncements, which were intended mainly for communist audiences. Stalin, in 1925 and again in 1927, used the term peaceful coexistence to describe relations between the Soviet Union and the western nations. An indication of the effectiveness of this slogan is furnished by the fact that Louis Fischer wrote in a book published in 1930 that "Moscow today submits the proposition—embodied in a Soviet resolution, for instance, at the International Economic Conference in Geneva in May, 1927— that the capitalist and communist worlds may live side by side in peaceful co-existence."[19] Numerous examples could be

[19] Louis Fischer, *The Soviets in World Affairs*, II, p. 823.

cited of the way in which Stalin and his agents abroad disseminated the concept of peaceful coexistence as if it were the essential basis of Soviet foreign policy.

Stalin's statement to the American newspaper publisher Roy Howard in 1936 that "the export of revolution—that is nonsense," published in *Pravda* for March 5, 1936, quickly became famous throughout the world. As "Historicus" notes, this statement said nothing about ways in which the Soviet Union might aid local revolutions. But despite their sophistry, such statements had a certain soothing effect. It is interesting that in his statement to Howard, Stalin denied that the Soviet Union had ever had any plans for world revolution. And, like Khrushchev when he insists that his policy of peaceful coexistence is a continuation of that of Lenin, Stalin maintained that Soviet policy before him had always been perfectly consistent and had never changed. This insistence on the appearance of consistency is characteristic of all Soviet propaganda.

The dissolution of the Comintern in May 1943, was a gesture designed to lend credence to Soviet coexistence propaganda. In a letter to the Reuters correspondent, King, which received world-wide attention, Stalin said that the dissolution of the Comintern was a correct decision because it exposed the lie of the Hitlerites that Moscow intended to intervene in the life of other states and "bolshevize" them. However, neither the Howard interview nor the letter to King received the kind of lasting, repetitive distribution in the Soviet Union which was given to statements by Stalin indicating his fidelity to the cause of world revolution.[20]

Another Stalin formula that is highly pertinent to propaganda on peace and war, and which Khrushchev has also frequently employed, is that the communist and capitalist systems can cooperate if "both sides desire it." One of the many important occasions when Stalin employed this tactic

[20] "Historicus," in Dallin, *op.cit.*, pp. 168-172.

was his interview with Harold Stassen in 1947. In the course of this interview Stalin was reported by *Pravda* to have declared "There was not a single party congress or plenary session of the Central Committee of the Communist Party at which I said or could have said that cooperation between the two systems was impossible. . . . Could the USSR have cooperated with Germany? Yes, the USSR could have cooperated with Germany but the Germans did not wish to cooperate. Otherwise the USSR could have cooperated with Germany as with any other country."[21] It is clear from Stalin's statement to Stassen about "cooperation" between the Soviet Union and non-communist countries that Stalin drew no essential distinction between capitalist countries such as Great Britain and the United States on the one hand and Fascist Germany on the other.

Against Stalin's assurances that the Soviet Union desired to cooperate with non-communist states in maintaining peace, must be set not only his failure to repudiate Lenin's doctrines regarding the inevitability of war and of violent revolution, but also a number of his own statements addressed to communist audiences. For example, in his election speech of February 9, 1946, Stalin interpreted World War II as an inevitable result of the workings of the capitalist system of world economy. Stalin stated in this speech that such a cataclysm could only have been avoided if it were possible periodically to redivide raw materials and markets among the powers, in accordance with their economic strength. He added, "But it is impossible to achieve this under present capitalist conditions of the development of world economy."[22]

A link between Soviet peace doctrine and subversive movements against non-communist governments was indicated by

---

[21] Quoted in Kovner, *op.cit.*, p. 14.

[22] For discussion of this speech and other Soviet statements on peace and war during the years 1945-1950, see F. C. Barghoorn, *The Soviet Image of the United States*, pp. 125-134.

a widely publicized special interview given by Stalin to a *Pravda* correspondent on February 16, 1951. In this interview, which of course occurred during the Korean war, Stalin said that the United Nations was being turned into an instrument of war, and was thus following the "inglorious path" of the League of Nations. Peace, however, could be preserved if "the people" took the protection of peace into their own hands. This interview was an important step in the world peace campaign then being waged by the communists. This campaign had begun with the organization of the World Peace Council in 1948-1949.

The peace campaign conducted by the "partisans of peace" under the direction of the Soviet Union, acting through the Soviet-controlled World Peace Council (WPC) combined appeals for peace with the most violent accusations against the United States and other western powers. We shall presently discuss some aspects of the activities of the WPC. Let us first complete our survey of Stalin's doctrinal-propagandistic exploitation of the peace theme. Although he clung to the thesis that the "contradictions" between socialism and capitalism were irreconcilable, Stalin, particularly after World War II, appeared to hold out increasing hope that a strong communist bloc could prevent the imperialists from unleashing a new anti-Soviet crusade. For example, in his final major ideological statement, his article entitled "Economic Problems of Socialism in the U.S.S.R." Stalin stated that: "It is most probable of all that the contemporary movement for the maintenance of peace . . . in case of its success, will lead to the prevention of a *given* war, to its temporary postponement, to the temporary maintenance of a *given* peace, to the retirement of a war-like government, and the replacement of it with another government prepared to keep the peace temporarily."[23] At the same time, Stalin declared that Lenin's thesis

[23] Quoted by Aleksander W. Rudzinski, "Soviet Peace Offensives," *International Conciliation* (April, 1953), No. 490, p. 190.

that imperialism gives rise to wars had not become obsolete. Thus Stalin both in doctrine and in propaganda was extremely ambiguous and opportunistic regarding the meanings and uses of peace.

Although the same can be said of Khrushchev there was an important shift of emphasis in Soviet peace propaganda under him. The two concepts of the struggle for peace and of peaceful coexistence remained central to Soviet peace propaganda, but emphasis shifted more and more to the relatively optimistic line that peaceful coexistence—which in effect meant a continuation of world revolution but without all-out military conflict—might become a permanent condition. A great many of Khrushchev's statements on peace, war, and peaceful coexistence are now available in English, and it will not be necessary to review them extensively here.[24]

Stalin's assurances of peaceful intent were balanced by expressions of implacable hostility to capitalism and by policies which led to the Berlin blockade and the Korean War. Khrushchev's similar assurances must be viewed in the light of somber doctrinal pronouncements and alarming expectations regarding recurrent crises in international relations, as well as the use of nuclear blackmail and terroristic testing of nuclear weapons.

Reference has already been made to Khrushchev's attempts to propagate the idea that by peaceful coexistence he meant the kind of normal relations among states to which countries such as the United States or Canada are accustomed. Another sense in which Khrushchev has frequently used this term is as a synonym for ideological struggle. For example, at Novosi-

[24] See, for example, N. H. Mager and Jacques Katel, *Conquest Without War* (New York, 1961), pp. 59-75; see also pamphlet issued by American Committee for Liberation, already referred to; Kovner, *op.cit.*, also presents many of Khrushchev's most important statements regarding these matters; a provocative analysis is presented by Fred Warner Neal in his article "Co-existence and the Kremlin," in *Bulletin of the Atomic Scientists*, Vol. XVI, No. 7, September, 1960, pp. 283-288.

birsk, in Siberia, on October 10, 1959, on his way home from his visit to the United States and to Communist China Khrushchev pointed out that coexistence implied the continuance of the struggle between social systems by peaceful means but that the ideological struggle must continue. He has said the same thing on many occasions, often in extremely militant language. Soviet sources have also frequently linked the concept of peaceful coexistence with class struggle and social revolution. An important lead editorial in *Kommunist* in 1959, which was entitled "Peaceful Coexistence and Ideological Struggle," contained the following significant paragraph: "In reality is the existence together of two systems on one planet fully accounted for by relations among states? No, although these relations by themselves are very important. The existence of two systems has another side. Each system embodies the domination of a class—in the one case of the capitalist class and in other of the working class—between which an irreconcilable struggle continues, and this struggle represents the basic content of our historical period. The struggle of these classes began long before the first Communist Party and it was not discovered by Marx."[25] The editorial went on to say that there could be only one outcome to this struggle, namely, the complete victory of the working class which was connected with the most progressive system of production. This victory would eventually take place throughout the entire world. Such, exulted the editorial, was the "law of history." According to the editorial, the Soviet Union sought to conduct this struggle without war.

As Neal and others have noted, it is the intention of the Soviet Union to conduct revolutionary struggle in the non-communist world, but to exclude all non-communist influence in the portion of the world controlled by the Sino-Soviet bloc. Attempts by non-communist countries to prevent or slow up the process of social revolution and of the anti-colonial

[25] *Kommunist*, No. 16, 1959, p. 7.

struggle, including the various kinds of relatively small-scale local wars which are regarded as justifiable in Khrushchev's doctrine—as they were in those of Lenin and Stalin—have been regularly denounced by Khrushchev and his colleagues as aggression. Thus the Khrushchev doctrine of peace and war remains a most troublesome one for the democratic world. Nevertheless, there is some truth in Neal's statement that "What was for Lenin and Stalin a temporary tactic has become for Khrushchev a basic, strategic doctrine. Both to preserve the Soviet Union and to achieve the Kremlin's clearly stated goals—in the interest of the USSR both as a nation-state and as the center of a world revolutionary movement, 'real co-existence' has become a necessity."[26]

This Khrushchevian doctrine furnished the basis for a very appealing propaganda strategy. There is considerable evidence that the Soviet leaders in the post-Stalin era felt that in the Khrushchev slogan of peaceful coexistence or, as it was sometimes described, peaceful competition, they had a potent instrument for influencing world public opinion. Even the blows to the image of a peace loving Soviet Union struck by such episodes as the suppression of the Hungarian Revolution, did not apparently shake the Kremlin's confidence in the effectiveness of the coexistence propaganda. For example, Boris Ponomarev, addressing himself in part to Chinese critics of Soviet policy, wrote in *Pravda* for August 12, 1960 that the "struggle for coexistence" would help the Soviet Union "to win the masses over to the ideas of socialism." Ponomarev also expressed the opinion that "this campaign would facilitate the consolidation of the socialist camp and erode and weaken the capitalist system." Another typical Soviet statement was in an editorial in *Kommunist*, 1958, No. 11, according to which "if the west accepts the principle of coexistence, negotiations will not be difficult." Also typical of the use made of the coexistence slogan in Soviet peace propaganda was its promi-

[26] Neal, *op.cit.*, p. 286.

nence in the speech given by Khrushchev in honor of the Chief of State of Cambodia in December 1960.[27] On that occasion, *Pravda* devoted most of its foreign news space to an exchange of speeches between Mr. Khrushchev and Norodom Sihanouk, Chief of State of Cambodia, under the headline "At the Basis of Our Policy—the Principles of Peaceful Coexistence."

It is not surprising that Soviet writers sometimes describe peaceful coexistence as the highest form of the class struggle. Yet in spite of numerous reassuring statements in Soviet foreign propaganda about the possibility of a durable peace, there are also such statements as that which Khrushchev made in a letter to Prime Minister Nehru of India published in *Pravda* for September 23, 1961. This letter was written after Khrushchev had again activated the Berlin crisis which he first instigated in November 1958. Khrushchev wrote to Nehru that "during the whole post-war period the danger of war has perhaps never been felt so keenly as at present." Khrushchev in this letter accused certain "circles" of seeking a war and of exerting increasing influence on the "NATO powers." He reverted, at least part way, to an old Lenin-Stalin argument that the imperialist powers, feeling that time was working against them, were redoubling their aggressive efforts in the world arena.

However, the Soviet press continued to issue statements indicative of Moscow's awareness of the grave threat to civilization posed by nuclear war. One of the most powerful was contained in a major article in *Pravda* for January 17, 1962 which acknowledged that the avoidance of such a conflict was the "essential condition for any progress, the most important pre-requisite for the further development of world civilization and the solution of the most important social, political and national problems." A similar statement was made in the

[27] *Pravda*, December 2, 1960.

authoritative central committee magazine, *Kommunist*, No. 8, 1962.

As noted earlier, Soviet propaganda seeks to insinuate the peace theme into messages which deal with a wide range of subjects. For example, Khrushchev in a greeting to the Eleventh General Conference of UNESCO, declared that the present epoch has every possibility of a genuine flowering of mankind and of creating an abundance of material and cultural values for all peoples. But, he continued, the threat of war hangs over the world and many peoples are still living in colonial slavery. Here Khrushchev linked up two of the most potent themes of contemporary Soviet propaganda, namely, peace and anti-colonialism.

Another important use made of peace propaganda by the Soviets, especially since the death of Stalin, has been in support of the Soviet policy of seeking to expand such types of trade and cultural relations as are convenient for their purposes. Often Soviet leaders have charged the western powers of being afraid of peaceful economic competition with the Soviet Union. For example, Anastas Mikoyan charged during his visit to Japan in August 1961 that the western powers were afraid that this kind of competition would mean their destruction, and he urged competition for world welfare. A systematic presentation of this kind of thesis was contained in an article by a top Soviet propagandist, Leonid Ilichev, in *Problemy mira i sotsializma*, No. 11, 1959. The article, entitled "Peaceful Coexistence and the Struggle of Two Ideologies," asserted that western statesmen "fear the development of cultural relations with the countries of socialism on the basis of mutuality."[28] Ilichev stated that communists believe that the victorious system in the competition of ideologies was the one which gave genuine political freedom and satisfied the "healthy demands" of mankind.[29]

[28] *Problemy mira i sotsializma*, No. 11, 1959, p. 9.
[29] *Ibid.*, p. 11.

The ambiguity and deviousness of Soviet peace propaganda is perhaps more than matched in the Kremlin's efforts to convince the world that Moscow favors disarmament. Soviet disarmament propaganda has a long history. In a sense, it can be traced to the policies of the Tsarist Russian regime. The first modern peace conference was convened at The Hague in 1899. A message from Tsar Nicholas II stressed the heavy burden of the arms race which was then proceeding in Europe. The motives of the Russian government in making the disarmament proposals they then put forward were somewhat similar to those which inspired Soviet disarmament proposals at Geneva in the 1920's and the 1930's, and to Soviet "ban the bomb" propaganda in the 1940's. There is a long history of Russian proposals designed to overcome the lead possessed by rival powers in certain aspects of weaponry, without offering anything of substance on the Russian side in return for the concessions demanded from other states. The Soviets, with their self-righteous ideological stance, have been in an exceptionally favorable position to practice this kind of demagogy. Resistance to their disarmament and other peace proposals has been denounced by them as evidence of capitalist iniquity.

Soviet propaganda has been designed to appeal to mass audiences unfamiliar with the technical difficulties involved in such matters as effective inspection and control of either nuclear or conventional disarmament measures. It has therefore often had considerable impact, especially on audiences already predisposed to be receptive because of class, ethnic, or other factors. Perhaps the most dramatic example of worldwide presentation of the appealing but disingenuous Soviet formula of "universal and complete disarmament" was in Khrushchev's address to the UN General Assembly in September 1959. Here, as Soviet representatives had done on many previous occasions in UN matters, Khrushchev proclaimed the willingness of the Soviet Union to accept control over disarmament. But Soviet acceptance of the need for control has seldom been accompanied by convincing evidence of willingness to agree upon practical measures for the kind of systematic and continuous inspection without which control remains nothing but a word. However, there is perhaps now a trend toward Soviet acceptance, at least in principle, of the necessity of inspection. During 1962 and 1963 the zig-zag course of disarmament and test-ban negotiations was marked by a reduction in the number of annual inspections demanded by the Western powers for a test-ban agreement, but not to a level considered low enough by Moscow. A discouraging note was sounded by Soviet delegate Tsarapkin in May 1963 when he declared that the 17-nation Geneva disarmament conference had thus far proved to be a waste of time, because, as he put it, the west refused to engage in serious negotiation.

As in the case of general Soviet peace propaganda, Soviet professions of interest in disarmament are frequently injected into seemingly irrelevant contexts. The purpose of this tactic appears to be to emphasize the Soviet desire to do everything possible to bring the blessings of peace to mankind. Disarmament proposals, whether made at the League of Nations or in the United Nations, or in negotiations beween heads of state and ministers of foreign affairs, lend credence and plausibility to Soviet peace propaganda. A typical example of the injection of the disarmament issue into the general stream of diplomacy was furnished by the fact that Khrushchev in his Kremlin speech of July 9, 1960, welcoming Prime Minister Juanda of Indonesia, stressed not only Soviet solicitude regarding Indonesian national independence, but also the mutual interest of the two countries in the "struggle" for disarmament.[30]

In the fall of 1962, the Soviet UN delegation put on the agenda of the 17th General Assembly a so-called "Economic Program for Disarmament." An article under the same title

[30] *Pravda*, July 10, 1960.

in the widely distributed Soviet magazine *International Affairs*, for December 1962, represented an unusually plausible example of Soviet use of the disarmament issue in conjunction with other propaganda themes. This article simply assumed that the "imperialists" were blocking Moscow's disarmament proposals for selfish, material reasons. If only, it went on, the west would accept the Soviet plan, all of mankind, in particular the underdeveloped countries, would benefit enormously, since the resources of the world economy could immediately be devoted to the rapid development of the economies of the underprivileged lands. The propaganda message of the article is perhaps best summed up in a sentence of its final paragraph, which states "General and complete disarmament, the final abolition of colonialism, the elimination of the economic backwardness of underdeveloped countries in the lifetime of one generation—these three inseparably connected tasks express the common interest of all countries and peoples."

It may be useful here to survey some of the main stages and aspects of Soviet disarmament propaganda.[31] Throughout most of the negotiations and discussions on disarmament the Soviets have combined efforts to stave off possible attacks by foreign powers with clearly agitational tactics. While bargaining shrewdly and tenaciously to preserve advantages and to protect themselves against the consequences of disadvantages, they have for propaganda purposes put forward utopian proposals with the obvious objective of eliciting refusals. They have then denounced those refusing to accept their proposals as obstructionists and even as warmongers. These

[31] For a brief treatment of the initiative taken by Nicholas II, and of Soviet policy at Geneva in the 1920's and 1930's, see Rudzinski, *op.cit.*, pp. 177-181; see also Taracouzio, *op.cit.*, and W. L. Mahaney, *The Soviet Union, the League of Nations and Disarmament, 1917-1935* (Philadelphia, 1940); N. M. Khaitsman, *SSSR i problema razoruzheniya 1918-1940* (Moscow, 1959) and Joseph L. Nogee, *Soviet Policy Towards International Control of Atomic Energy* (Notre Dame, Ind., 1961).

comments are not intended to suggest that such tactics are uniquely Soviet. Similar tactics, though less systematically presented, were employed by the representatives of non-Soviet powers in the disarmament negotiations of the 1920's and 1930's which took place among the powers that emerged victorious from World War I.

Soviet comment on disarmament proposals made by non-communist governments sheds indirect light on the Kremlin's skepticism about disarmament. As Richard Barnet notes, the outstanding Russian historian Eugene Tarle wrote in the official Soviet *History of Diplomacy*, in 1945—at the height of Anglo-Soviet-American cooperation in a common war effort—that "From time immemorial the idea of disarmament has been one of the most popular means of dissimulating the true motives and plans of governments. The explanation of this is very clear. . . . Every proposal for the limitation of armaments can always count on wide popularity and support from world opinion."[32]

As early as July, 1921, Soviet foreign affairs commissar Chicherin telegraphed the governments of Great Britain, France, the USA, China, and Japan that "disarmament can only seem to the Soviet government as worthy of approval."[33] At the Genoa Economic Conference in early 1922 the Soviet delegation created a sensation by unexpectedly introducing a disarmament proposal.

As Franklyn J. C. Griffiths has discovered, the comprehensive peace and disarmament program contained in Chicherin's Genoa proposal had been approved by Lenin as a "magnificent" tactic for "splitting" the *bourgeoisie*, particularly by playing upon the pacifist inclinations of certain western liberal circles. Chicherin's program included such familiar features of later Soviet international tactics as a recommendation

[32] Quoted in Richard J. Barnet, *Who Wants Disarmament?* (Boston, 1960), p. 56.
[33] Elliot R. Goodman, *The Soviet Design for a World State* (New York, 1960), p. 299.

for representation of colonial peoples and labor organizations at international conferences. In many ways, the dozen or so points contained in Chicherin's insidiously plausible project broke ground for the strategy employed by Khrushchev in 1955-1962.[34]

In December, 1922, the Moscow Disarmament Conference further advertised Soviet advocacy of universal disamament, later to be spectacularly pushed by Litvinov in 1927 and again in 1932-1934 at Geneva. As Taracouzio observed, Soviet diplomacy used this gambit at every subsequent conference for the limitation of armaments.[35]

There is no reason to doubt that underlying the disarmament propaganda of Stalin and his successors were the calculations set forth in the Theses and Resolutions of the Sixth Congress of the Communist International in 1928. They stated, *inter alia*, that:

"The disarmament policy of the Soviet government must be utilized for purposes of agitation much more energetically . . . than has been done hitherto; however, it must not be utilized as a pretext for advancing similar demands in the capitalist countries, but as a means (1) for recruiting sympathizers for the Soviet Union, the champion of peace and socialism; (2) for utilizing the results of Soviet disarmament policy and its exposure of the imperialists in the effort to eradicate all pacifist illusions and to carry on propaganda among the masses in support of the only way toward disarmament and abolition of war, viz.: arming of the proletariat, overpowering of the

[34] As Mr. Griffiths pointed out in an essay, entitled "Proposals of Total Disarmament in Soviet Foreign Policy, 1927-32 and 1959-62," submitted to the Russian Institute of Columbia University in 1962, the Soviet government in 1959 saw fit to publish in full Chicherin's letter to Lenin outlining a draft of the Genoa proposal, and Lenin's reply. See *Leninski sbornik*, Vol. xxxvi (Moscow, 1959), pp. 451-455. As Griffiths suggests, Moscow may have been impelled to take this step under pressure, to refute Chinese communist implications that Khrushchev's peaceful coexistence strategy was incompatible with the spirit of Leninism.

[35] Taracouzio, *op.cit.*, pp. 115-117.

bourgeoisie and establishing the proletarian dictatorship."[36]

Also in 1928, the British communist Bell wrote: "It is very important for us to have in mind the tremendous propaganda of the bourgeoisie and the reformists for disarmament that is going on today. At the present moment, this hypocritical propaganda recalls the period of the Hague Peace propaganda of 1912, when they were handing out peace prizes for those who were able to produce the best essays on how to prevent war. In this connection the parties must be able to expose the political significance of this sham disarmament propaganda, and its implications in the preparations for war. The greater the increase in armaments, the louder becomes the 'peace' talk."[37] The quotations illustrate the mixture in Soviet and communist peace propaganda of genuine convictions and disingenuous tactics. They belong, of course, to a period when communists still spoke frankly, at least to one another.

Unclassified Intelligence Information Brief No. 41, released by the Department of State December 2, 1958, presented data indicating how small, in fact, had been the Soviet contribution to solving the problems of disarmament in the period after World War II. The USSR voted affirmatively on disarmament resolutions passed by three sessions of the United Nations General Assembly, namely, the resolutions in 1946 creating the UN Atomic Energy Commission and outlining the principles governing disarmament, and the ninth (1954), and the eleventh (early 1957) procedural resolutions reconvening the UN Disarmament Commissions Subcommittee, established by the eighth General Assembly. The USSR abstained from vote on the resolution creating the Subcommittee and had earlier voted "No" on the establishment of the Disarmament Com-

[36] *International Press Correspondence*, Vol. viii, No. 84, November 28, 1928, p. 1597.
[37] *International Press Correspondence*, English Edition, Special Number, Vol. viii, No. 58, September 1, 1928.

mission. On all other disarmament resolutions, the USSR and the other countries of the Soviet bloc also voted "No." As of early 1963, despite Soviet agreement in principle to on-site inspection to verify a possible disarmament agreement, there still appeared to be no likelihood that an actual agreement could in fact be negotiated, since Moscow refused to agree to a number of inspections considered by the United States and Britain to be the necessary minimum for a safe and workable treaty.

What Nogee has to say about Soviet objectives in atomic energy negotiations is applicable, in general, to Soviet disarmament policy and propaganda generally. According to Nogee, Soviet representatives used the atomic energy negotiations to achieve the following objectives: (1) To reject the American Atomic Energy proposals without appearing to do so; (2) To link Soviet policy with popular aspirations throughout the world; (3) To portray the policies of the western bloc—and the United States in particular—as aggressive; (4) To prevent the United States government from using its atomic superiority to gain political advantages; (5) To stall for time.[38]

An interesting and significant episode connected with disarmament policy and propaganda was the attempt which was begun in 1958 and at times was seemingly on the road to success, but which in 1961 broke down, to achieve agreement on cessation of nuclear weapons tests. As Nogee points out, nuclear testing first became an international issue in March 1954 after explosions carried out by the United States in the Pacific Ocean. India in April 1954, asked the UN Disarmament Commission to consider a "standstill agreement" on testing, "even if arrangements about the discontinuance

[38] Nogee, op.cit., p. 264. The whole of Chapter X of Nogee's book, entitled "The Gamesmanship of International Negotiation" is worth studying for its penetrating and well-documented discussion of the specific strategies employed by the Soviets to achieve the above objectives.

of production and stockpiling must await more substantial agreement. . . ." India's initiative was supported by the Asian-African Conference at Bandung in April 1955. Naturally enough, Japan, the only country which had suffered from the wartime uses of atomic weapons and whose citizens had also been the first serious casualties of their testing, was particularly concerned.

In proposals made in 1955 and 1956, including a letter of Premier Bulganin to President Eisenhower, dated September 11, 1956, the Soviets seized the propaganda initiative, as they so often do. Typical of Soviet disarmament propaganda was Bulganin's statement that "it is a known fact that the discontinuation of such tests does not in itself require any international control agreements, for the present state of science and engineering makes it possible to detect any explosion of an atomic or hydrogen bomb, wherever it may be set off."[39] This patent, but to some perhaps, plausible, oversimplification was rejected by the governments of the United States and Britain. Nevertheless, the campaign conducted by the Soviet worldwide propaganda machine gave the Soviets a certain advantage at least in the earlier stages of the negotiations regarding nuclear testing which began in Geneva in the summer of 1958. According to one expert on India, Russia's declaration that it was discontinuing nuclear tests achieved a striking propaganda advantage over the west in India and other Asian countries.[40]

Even during the series of Soviet nuclear tests launched in 1962 Khrushchev continued to act as if he thought Indian—and world—opinion remained responsive to bland, declaratory Soviet assurances of intention to disarm. According to *Pravda* for October 2, 1962, datelined Ashkhabad, October 1, Khru-

[39] Nogee, *op.cit.*, p. 212.
[40] W. Norman Brown, "Religion and Language as Forces Effecting Unity in Asia," *The Annals of the American Academy of Political and Social Science*, Vol. 318, 1958.

shchev received a delegation representing an Indian organization known as "The Peace Fund Named after Gandhi." Khrushchev reportedly assured his Indian visitors that Soviet proposals for general disarmament under strict international control envisaged the prohibition and complete liquidation of nuclear weapons and also such measures of disarmament as would assure, in the first stage, the practical abolition of the threat of nuclear war. Further, Khrushchev asserted that all necessary conditions for the solution of the problem of a nuclear test ban existed. Reliable control over the fulfillment by the states of their obligations in the cessation of all tests of nuclear weapons could be assured, under present conditions of science, by means of national forces, without international inspection. Khrushchev went on to explain that if the western powers were not prepared at present to agree on the prohibition of all nuclear weapons tests, then the Soviet Union was prepared to sign an agreement on the prohibition of nuclear tests in the atmosphere, in outer space, and under water, while at the same time continuing negotiations regarding the cessation also of underground nuclear tests.

In reply to a question put by the delegation as to whether or not the Soviet Union was prepared to unilaterally make a declaration regarding the cessation of nuclear tests if no agreement could be reached, Khrushchev declared that while, in 1958, the Soviet Union had unilaterally ceased tests of all forms of atomic and hydrogen weapons and had called upon the western governments to do likewise, the United States and England had answered the "noble appeal" of the Soviet Union by conducting a new series of hydrogen bomb tests, on the largest scale yet. It was understandable, according to Khrushchev, that in view of this behavior on the part of the western powers the Soviet Union had been forced to take measures to strengthen its own security and to safeguard peace in the whole world.

Such statements by Khrushchev may indicate not merely confidence in the gullibility of non-communists, but also anxiety regarding the impact of Soviet nuclear tests on world public opinion. This would be particularly in countries such as India where the Soviet Union had considerable propaganda impact by being able to charge, over a period of several years, that it was not engaging in nuclear testing while the western powers, in spite of Soviet appeals for an end to testing by all countries, had continued to aggravate international tensions and to pollute the atmosphere by conducting nuclear tests.

The monster nuclear tests conducted by the Soviet Union in 1961 followed its unilateral disruption of the Geneva nuclear test negotiations. After these tests concern had been expressed in western diplomatic circles because the head of the Indian United Nations delegation apparently found it difficult to take anything but a neutral position regarding Soviet and American policies in this area. This may perhaps have been partly a reflection of the success with which Soviet propagandists pursued the initial propaganda advantage they had gained in 1955-1958.

It has often been precisely during periods when disarmament negotiations have been at a standstill that the Kremlin has launched its most energetic disarmament propaganda. The purpose may be to distract world attention from the infinitely complex technical and political problems of disarmament and to weaken the position of the anti-communist powers both with respect to disarmament negotiations and with respect to the defense measures necessitated by the refusal of the communist countries to seriously consider effective disarmament.

Khrushchev's 1959 and 1960 performances in the UN General Assembly support the above generalization. Following Khrushchev's 1959 speech and a Soviet resolution calling for universal and complete disarmament in four years—very similar to the proposals advocated by Litvinov at Geneva in 1927 and again in 1932-1934—the world-wide communist propaganda machine launched perhaps the most powerful disarmament propaganda in history. One of the principal printed media of this campaign was the magazine, *Problemy mira i sotsializma,* printed in most of the major languages of the world. Typical of the line taken in this publication was the thesis of its lead editorial in the November 1959 issue which maintained that following Khrushchev's UN proposals of that year disarmament was no longer a utopia.

According to the *New York Times* for September 27, 1960, Khrushchev declared at a luncheon at the Biltmore Hotel in New York arranged by Cyrus Eaton, that if the world powers would agree to disarm and disband their armies, he would be ready to accept "any measure of control anyone proposes." Unfortunately, this assurance was not backed up by concrete measures. Khrushchev apparently thought that he could make propaganda capital out of disarmament, for he engaged in an extensive correspondence with individuals and groups throughout the world designed to reinforce his desired image of a Soviet Union sincerely wishing disarmament. Under date of February 8, 1961, Khrushchev wrote to Norman Cousins and Clarence Pickett of the National Committee for a Sane Nuclear Policy, in reply to a letter sent by them. In his letter, Khrushchev reiterated the Soviet thesis that the "direct and certain path" to the prevention of atomic war and the ending of the arms race was universal and complete disarmament, for which the Soviet Union was patiently striving. He declared also that in spite of "serious concessions" made by the Soviet Union to the United States and Great Britain, these powers were pursuing a "negative position."

The U-2 episode of May 1960, which was employed by Khrushchev as a pretext for disrupting the conference of heads of state planned for that month in Paris, was seized upon by Moscow to enhance the plausibility of its disarmament and peace propaganda. The United States inaugurated the U-2 flights in 1956 because of concern over what was considered to be the danger of a surprise nuclear attack. When the plane piloted by Francis Gary Powers fell into Soviet hands on May 1, 1960, and when, unfortunately, the United States government assumed a confused and contradictory public posture, Khrushchev apparently felt that he had a golden opportunity to blacken the image of the United States as a "warmongering" nation. Soviet propaganda regarding the U-2 affair was utilized to build up the image of a peace-loving Soviet Union, to reinforce the Soviet image of a predatory United States, and at the same time, to terrorize small and weak nations. Soviet propaganda took no account, naturally, of the fact that the United States was constrained to employ unconventional means to gather information about Soviet military preparations because of a stubborn Soviet refusal to seriously consider a mutual exchange of information regarding defenses and weapons.[41]

To carry its peace, disarmament, and related propaganda to the peoples of the world, the Kremlin has from the very first days of its power in Russia employed mass propaganda campaigns, conducted both by communist parties and by a wide variety of "front" organizations, whose names, leadership, and slogans have often changed. These organizations have published newspapers, magazines, and books and in recent years have employed other mass media. Among their most effective methods for attracting attention have been the holding of conferences and congresses and the conducting of mass campaigns for the signing of petitions.

---

[41] Neal, *op.cit.*, defends Khrushchev's position on the ground that the U-2 flights could be construed by the Soviets as having aggressive intentions. Donald Dunham, in his study, *Kremlin Target: U.S.A.*, (New York, 1961) expressed the opinion that the hesitation of the United States in pressing its case before world opinion enabled Khrushchev to turn the U-2 episode to the advantage of the Soviet Union, despite the fact that it revealed glaring weaknesses in the Soviet military posture. See pp. 77-86.

One of the first important propaganda actions of the Soviet government was to promulgate the decree on peace, referred to at the beginning of this chapter, setting forth a demand for an immediate peace without annexations or indemnities. Even in the United States this early manifestation of the effort of the Soviet communists to associate themselves with the peace symbol led in December 1917 to the formation of the Friends of the Russian Revolution, an organization whose purpose was to support the Soviets' peace proposals. As Draper notes, "the Soviets demand for an immediate peace . . . was capable of soliciting broad support and led thence to President Wilson's Fourteen Points the following month."[42]

The horrors of World War I and the subsequent revulsion against war furnished a fertile soil for Soviet mass peace propaganda. This was to bear its most abundant fruit when, after the rise of Hitler, the communists succeeded in linking peace propaganda to the struggle against Fascism. The groundwork for the peace campaigns of the 1920's and 1930's was laid largely by Willie Muenzenberg, whom Neal Wood has called "the comintern's genius of propaganda."[43] Muenzenberg founded such communist-controlled organizations as the International Workers Order which carried on various kinds of communist propaganda, including Soviet peace propaganda. He also built up a vast publishing empire, and organized the distribution abroad of Soviet films.

In addition to his organizational abilities, Muenzenberg had great skill in attracting prominent intellectuals to the support of communist causes. His efforts were directed primarily toward concealing the Soviet and comintern control of the various propaganda spectacles which he staged. He was able to win to the support of Soviet peace drives such celebrities as the French

[42] Theodore Draper, *The Roots of American Communism* (New York, 1957), pp. 106-107.

[43] Neal Wood, *Communism and British Intellectuals* (London, 1959), p. 55.

115

author Henri Barbusse, who spoke at the opening of the Amsterdam Congress against imperialist war in 1932, British public figures such as Lord Marley and Allen Wilkinson, the American Negro leader James W. Ford and many others, including even, on certain occasions Albert Einstein.[44] Muenzenberg's influence reached its height during the Spanish Civil War, which was so energetically exploited by Moscow for its own propaganda purposes. Wood cites Arthur Koestler to the effect that the policy-making body of the Commission of Inquiry into Alleged Breaches of the Non-Intervention Agreement in Spain was a "communist caucus" consisting of two communist secretaries and others, under the direction of Muenzenberg.[45] Muenzenberg lost favor with Stalin in 1936-1937, and died under suspicious circumstances in 1940 in France, but he left behind him a tradition of effective manipulation of communist-dominated organizations, whose principal propaganda weapon was probably the symbol of peace.

The greatest impact of the mass peace drives of the 1930's was in western Europe. There, as Armstrong has pointed out, "the vociferous Soviet support of the League of Nations and collective security, the feverish communist efforts to mobilize organizations and opinion in the democratic countries against Fascist tendencies, and the real sacrifices of the communists in Spain, combined to create a new group of Soviet sympathizers, especially among the intellectuals. The process was most pronounced in France. . . ."[46]

Even in the United States communist propaganda achieved a certain effect. The efforts made by a congeries of communist-controlled organizations in the United States in the 1930's and even, for a time, following World War II, facilitated Soviet political exploitation of the strategic situation created by Red

[44] Guenther Nollau, *Die Internationale* (Cologne, 1959), pp. 148-150.
[45] Wood, *op.cit.*, p. 55.
[46] Armstrong, *op.cit.*, p. 46.

Army victories in Eastern Europe.[47] Ironically enough, however, Earl Browder who, as leader of the American communist movement, had done so much to propagate the "soft line," with its slogan "Communism is Twentieth Century Americanism," was himself to be denounced. In an article published by Jacques Duclos, one of Stalin's principal agents in the international movement, Browder was castigated for allegedly advocating "peaceful coexistence and collaboration in the framework of one and the same world," between capitalism and socialism.[48]

It is probably true, as Leonard Schapiro has observed, that by 1952 the "peace fronts" which had been set up in an attempt to camouflage communist organizations, had begun to be less successful than hitherto.[49] This was more true in western Europe and North America than in other parts of the world. For example, an expert on Japan wrote in 1957 that communist-sponsored choral and folk song groups which popularized such themes as "We Will Not Permit Atomic Bombings," were very successful in that country.[50]

The principal coordinating agency for the Soviet-dominated world peace movement following World War II has been and still is the WPC. It was organized at a "World Congress of Intellectuals for Peace," held at Wroclaw, Poland in August 1948, at which an "International Liaison Committee of Intellectuals" was elected. This body in turn summoned a "World Peace Congress" in Paris in April 1949. Because of the refusal of the French government to grant visas to known communist

[47] For a somewhat sensational but fact-crammed account of these efforts, see Eugene Lyons, *The Red Decade* (Indianapolis & New York, 1941).

[48] Robert V. Daniels, *A Documentary History of Communism*, Book II, p. 139.

[49] Leonard Schapiro, *The Communist Party of the Soviet Union* (New York, 1959), p. 542.

[50] Paul F. Langer, "Communism in Independent Japan," *Japan Between East and West* (New York, 1957), pp. 46-107; quotation on p. 67.

117

leaders, the congress was held simultaneously in Paris and in Prague. The Prague Congress set up a permanent organization which was called, at the beginning, the "World Committee of Partisans of Peace." The vast majority of the 138 members of this committee were known communists or communist sympathizers. This committee later changed its name to the WPC, a name which has been retained ever since.

The WPC became extremely active during the Korean War, when at times it acted as if it intended to set up an international organization to attempt to replace the United Nations. These threats reflected the Kremlin's irritation with United Nations action against communist aggression in Korea. In 1951 and 1952 the WPC established a number of regional organizations in western Europe, Asia, and the Pacific countries. It also established specialized groupings designed to appeal to businessmen, physicians, and other professional and occupational strata. It cooperated closely with other communist front organizations, such as the World Federation of Democratic Youth and the International Union of Students in bringing the peace theme into various youth and sports festivals. The main meetings, however, of the WPC have been its various World Peace Congresses held annually or semi-annually. These congresses have been used as sounding boards to launch major international communist propaganda campaigns. For example, shortly before the launching of the "Geneva spirit" at the meeting of heads of government in 1955, a World Peace Assembly was held in Helsinki, Finland. It, in effect, issued the necessary directives for actions throughout the world in support of the propaganda line taken by Bulganin and Khrushchev at Geneva.

In 1950, the campaign to collect signatures in support of the Stockholm Peace Appeal was inaugurated. Five hundred million signatures were claimed, but the overwhelming majority of these were obtained in the USSR and other communist countries. For the Warsaw Peace Appeal, conducted in

1950 and 1951, six hundred million signatures were claimed. Among relatively recent activities organized or supported by the WPC, mention should be made of the Fifth Conference Against Atomic and Nuclear Bombs, which was held in Hiroshima, Japan from August 5 to 7, 1961 to coincide with the national day of mourning for the victims of the Hiroshima bomb in 1945. Also prominent was the Latin American Conference for "National Sovereignty, Economic Emancipation, and Peace," held in Mexico City, from March 5 to 8, 1961. Khrushchev and other high-ranking communist leaders sent warm greetings to the latter meeting, urging the participants to "shake off foreign economic control and defend world peace."

Through the WPC, and in other ways, the Kremlin seeks to capture the minds of men. Both the WPC and the government of the Soviet Union itself award peace prizes. Five Americans, Cyrus Eaton, Paul Robeson, William Howard Melish, Howard Fast, and W. E. B. Dubois, have been awarded Soviet or WPC peace prizes. Perhaps the best known British recipient of a WPC peace prize is the actor Charles Chaplin. Other WPC activities have included the campaign in 1949-1954 for a five-power peace pact, active participation in the "germ warfare" campaign during and following the Korean War, and the "ban the bomb" campaign, which still exerts a certain influence on non-communist opinion, particularly in Great Britain. In an analysis of one of the current forms of anti-nuclear weapons agitation in Britain, Colin Welch, in articles in the London *Daily Telegraph*—reprinted in the September 1962 issue of *Atlas*—saw the Campaign for Nuclear Disarmament as, in part at least, a vehicle by which the communists hoped to recoup the losses they had suffered in British opinion following Russian suppression of the Hungarian revolution. Welch alleged that between a third and a half of the "active party workers" of the British Labor Party were C.N.D. "supporters." If his analysis is correct, the C.N.D. and other manifestations of nuclear pacifism serve Soviet purposes both by cloaking violent, destructive, subversive impulses in outwardly legitimate activity—which dupes many decent but gullible people, and also by creating a degree of confusion harmful to the functioning of the constitutional political order. Doubtless similar observations would be appropriate to Soviet "disarmament" agitation in other countries although its impact seems to be less in the United States, for example, than in Britain, some other commonwealth countries, and some of the underdeveloped countries, such as India.

In connection with the foregoing it is significant that a recent book by Soviet professors S. I. Tyulpanov and V. G. Onushkin, entitled, *The Crisis of World Capitalism*, stated that communists were the "soul" of peace campaigns such as C.N.D. and others. The Soviet scholars pointed out that by means of participation in such activities, the "masses" could be brought into "the struggle for the most basic social changes, into the anti-monopoly stage of the revolution."[51]

The activities of the WPC are closely coordinated with the Soviet effort since the death of Stalin to utilize cultural exchanges for propaganda purposes. Top leaders of the Soviet section of the WPC, such as Ilya Ehrenburg, Aleksandr Korneichuk, Wanda Wassilewska, and others are sent abroad as members of Soviet cultural exchange delegations, or act as hosts to such delegations in their home country. High-ranking Americans, such as former Senator William Benton, who have discussed problems of peace and coexistence with their Soviet counterparts, have testified to the extreme difficulties of communication involved in such meetings. An amusing but characteristic dispute went on for several years between Soviet scientists, and British and American scientists as to whether or not all of the numerous gatherings, of quite varied composition, at which problems of peace and disarmament, and

[51] S. I. Tyulpanov and V. G. Onushkin, *Krizis mirovogo kapitalizma* (Leningrad, 1962), pp. 206-207.

of the role of science in world affairs, have been discussed, should be called, as the Soviet representatives desired, "pugwash" conferences, after a series of meetings originated on the initiative of Cyrus Eaton at his estate in Pugwash, Nova Scotia, in the early postwar years. Trivial though it may seem, this semantic tiff illustrates the tendency of communists to seek to turn every aspect of peace discussions to the ends of communist policy. It is also interesting that a Soviet handbook on international organizations, published in 1962, devoted seven pages to the "Pugwash Continuing Committee," headed by Bertrand Russell.[52]

Moscow's effort to create the impression that it alone sincerely desires peace has normally been accompanied by systematic efforts to exclude from the internal Soviet communications network evidence that non-communists also conduct their own—from the Kremlin's point of view, hypocritical or naive—kinds of peace propaganda. A striking illustration was the order issued by Soviet authorities, in late October 1962, barring those aboard the "peace ship" Everyman III from disembarking at Leningrad. However, members of Everyman's crew were permitted to talk to an official Soviet delegation. This modestly hopeful omen was perhaps symptomatic of a turn toward a slightly more receptive Soviet attitude toward at least some kinds of non-Soviet peace efforts.

[52] *Mezhdunarodnye obshchestvennye organizatsii, spravochnik* (Moscow, 1962), pp. 428-435.

CHAPTER V

THE USES OF NATIONALISM

NO ASPECT of Soviet propaganda is more complex, indeed more tortuous, than its often successful effort to utilize the symbols of patriotism and even of the most traditional forms of nationalism for anti-patriotic, anti-nationalist ends. As professed Marxists, the Soviet communists claim to be internationalists. Communist "internationalism," to be sure, has found its typical expression in a ceaseless effort at subversion of "bourgeois" national governments—though not when this seemed detrimental to the interests of the Soviet state, as during the period of the Anglo-Soviet-American coalition in 1941-1945. It has also been associated with vigorous denial of the right of any non-communist international movement or ideology to propagate itself in a communist-controlled state, and by suppression of any such effort as a manifestation of "imperialist" influence.

Since 1917, the Russian communists, as rulers of a "multinational," but highly centralized, state, have displayed an impressive understanding of both the divisive and the cohesive potentials of national sentiments. Since the 1930's, they have made effective use of the doctrine of "Soviet patriotism," which performs somewhat the same integrating function in Soviet society as do nationalism and patriotism in non-communist states. In the non-communist world, however, communists seek to use nationalism as a political weapon against their "bourgeois" opponents. They strive to conceal their subversive intentions in familiar and, indeed, inspiring language.[1]

[1] On the development of Lenin's views on the national problem in Russia, see Richard Pipes, *The Formation of the Soviet Union* (Cambridge, Mass., 1954); on Soviet patriotism and related concepts, see Frederick C. Barghoorn, *Soviet Russian Nationalism* (New York, 1956);

The salient feature of the Soviet approach to nationality problems is the encouragement, exploitation, and whenever possible capture of anti-imperialist, national liberation movements in colonial countries. Propaganda and agitation directed to this end will be one of the central subjects of this chapter. Another significant theme revolves around the Soviet effort to prove to the peoples of the world, especially those of multi-national societies, that the USSR has achieved a model solution of the problems faced by such polities. With respect to this aspect of the "Soviet model," Selig Harrison has written that "the Marxist-Leninist scriptures on the national question seem to be addressed unmistakably to the special difficulties of economically less developed multi-lingual states."[2] Harrison calls attention to the close link in Soviet propaganda between problems of nationality and ethnic relations and those of economic development. While calculated encouragement of national liberation, and attractive advertisement of the Soviet success in the solution of nationality problems constitute perhaps the two main uses of nationalism in Kremlin world policy, they by no means exhaust its repertory in this field. Almost any national grievance or aspiration, whether of the least developed or of the most developed people may at times receive the attention of Soviet propaganda. Especially since the beginning of the cold war, with its division of the world into more or less clearly defined ideological blocs, communist propaganda has worked incessantly to set not only the less developed countries but also Britain, France, Germany, Japan, and other advanced industrial countries against the United States, by

---

also, Barghoorn, "Nationality Doctrine in Soviet Political Strategy," *The Review of Politics*, Vol. xvi, No. 3, pp. 283-304; on the persistent tendency of Soviet doctrine to envisage an ultimate "world state of no state," see Elliot R. Goodman, *The Soviet Design for a World State* (New York, 1960), and his article, "The Cry of National Liberation: Recent Soviet Attitudes Toward National Self-determination," *International Organization*, Vol. xiv, No. 1 (1960), pp. 92-106.

[2] Selig S. Harrison, *India: The Most Dangerous Decades* (Princeton, 1960), p. 309.

playing upon all national tensions and frictions which appeared to be susceptible of exploitation.

The Soviet approach to nationality problems began to take shape before World War I. The major works of Lenin and Stalin in which it is rooted are readily available in English and other western languages. Perhaps the most important of the Marxist-Leninist "classics" devoted to this problem was Lenin's 1914 study, "On the Right of Nations to Self-determination." Lenin argued that the Great Russians, who constituted slightly less than half of the population of the Russian Empire, were an oppressor nation. In order to gain the confidence of the non-Russian workers and peasants, the Great Russian proletariat would have to make it clear that it had no desire to oppress the non-Russians. One of the most effective means to this end would be espousal of the right to self-determination for the non-Russian peoples. Recognition of the right of self-determination was, according to this argument, a central element of the strategy of the class struggle which should be conducted, in the closest unity, by the proletariat of all nations. Lenin's emphasis, it is important to remember, was not primarily on self-determination itself, but on the proclamation of the "right" thereto.[3]

It is interesting to compare the position taken by Lenin in the above article with the statements about "oppressed" and "oppressor" nations contained in the program of the CPSU adopted by its Twenty-second Congress in 1961. Section VI of the program, which is entitled "The National-Liberation Movement," contains the following significant paragraph: "In many countries, the liberation movement of the peoples that have awakened proceeds under the flag of nationalism. Marxists-Leninists draw a distinction between the nationalism of the oppressed nations and that of the oppressor nations. The nationalism of an oppressed nation contains a general demo-

---

[3] Lenin, *Izbrannye proizvedeniya*, Vol. i, pp. 619-662.

cratic element directed against oppression, and communists support it because they consider it historically justified at a given stage. That element finds expression in the striving of the oppressed peoples to free themselves from imperialist oppression, to gain national independence and bring about a national renascence. But the nationalism of an oppressed nation has yet another aspect, one expressing the ideology and interests of the reactionary exploiting top stratum."[4]

Of course, many a zig and many a zag of the party line separates Lenin's seminal study from current directives on nationality policy. Lenin, in works written during World War I and after the bolshevik seizure of power, and Stalin, supplementing Lenin's work, added to the growing assortment of tactical devices disposed of by communist manipulators of national sentiments. As early as October 1916, Lenin, in an article entitled, "The Results of the Discussion on Self-determination," accused his Marxist opponents, in whose ranks were included such formidable figures as the leading left-wing German Socialist, of Polish origin, Rosa Luxembourg, of being indifferent to political realities in their opposition to his seemingly unorthodox—from a Marxist point of view—insistence on the right of nations to self-determination and even to secession.[5]

Lenin—and his chief collaborator Trotski—during the Brest-Litovsk peace negotiations with Germany and Austria in December 1917-March 1918 devoted part of their energetic propaganda effort to denunciation of the "annexationist" demands of the Central Powers. Soviet international propaganda

[4] *Program of the Communist Party of the Soviet Union*, published by Crosscurrents Press, Inc., New York, 1961, p. 46. Crosscurrents Press is an official Soviet agency. The Program is also available in other English translations, including one entitled "Khrushchev's 'Mein Kampf,'" published by Belmont Books, with an introduction by Harrison E. Salisbury.

[5] V. I. Lenin, *Polnoe sobranie sochinenii*, 2nd ed., Vol. xix, p. 245. A number of Lenin's important publications on the nationality question are contained in the English-language volume, V. I. Lenin, *Collected Works*, Vol. xix (New York, 1942).

thus early linked with its demands for peace and social justice an appealing—though deceptive—appearance of receptivity to the aspirations of the peoples of the world for national self-determination and sovereignty. At the same time, Soviet domestic propaganda early began to be couched in terms of an amalgam of Marxism and patriotism.

Lenin's realistic recognition that nationalism would long remain a force with which communists should learn to cope—and to turn to their advantage—found perhaps its fullest theoretical expression in his work, "Left Wing Communism, An Infantile Disorder." Lenin insisted in this major tract that even after the victory of socialism, it would not be possible to immediately eliminate the state and the nation. Lenin laid the foundation for the tough-minded power calculations with which Stalin and his successors were to approach problems of nationality and nationalism. Stalin was later frequently to express the view that "survivals of capitalism"—that synonym for all forms of evil in the Soviet political vocabulary—were more tenacious in the sphere of national sentiments than in any other field. Lenin, Stalin, and Khrushchev all realistically recognized that even when and if communism were to be established on a world scale, the struggle for the elimination of all forms of national consciousness and the ultimate "fusion" of nations would be long and hard, and would require stubborn effort on the part of the communist "vanguard" of the working class. Nevertheless, Lenin and his followers were committed to the long-range goals of elimination of independent sovereign states and to the amalgamation of nations, "in a single communist family." These goals were reiterated by Khrushchev in an important speech in Leipzig, Germany, on March 7, 1959.[6] However, in spite of numerous authoritative statements to that effect by Lenin, Stalin, and Khrushchev, the 1961 CPSU Party Program blandly asserted that "democratic forces establish the idea of national sovereignty in the

[6] Goodman, *op.cit.*, p. 49.

name of equality for the peoples, of their mutual trust, friendship and assistance and of closer relations between them, in the name of social progress."[7] It is clear that here, as elsewhere communists were using words in a communist sense, while hoping that their propaganda targets would understand the chosen words wishfully, in the very different connotations attached to them in non-communist political language.

The foregoing references to a few important documents in the Lenin-Stalin literature on nationalism and the nationality problem, particularly on national self-determination, indicate the conceptual framework which governs Soviet propaganda exploitation of nationalism. Communists seek to cause nationalists, liberals, and democrats to serve communist purposes. For this reason, while reassuring communists of faithfulness to Leninist anti-nationalism, Soviet propaganda often associates its messages with the language of traditional nationalism in its appeals to conservative and liberal nationalists.

Before turning to analysis of Soviet propaganda manipulation of the symbols of nationalism, particularly in the post-Stalin period, it will be useful to review briefly some pertinent aspects of Lenin's doctrine regarding the relations among major social classes. In early works, such as *What Is To Be Done?* and *Two Tactics of Social Democracy in the Democratic Revolution*, Lenin developed his theory that the "professional revolutionaries" whose chosen calling and destiny was leadership of the "proletariat" must gain the support of the majority of the peasantry, and of at least a part of the middle classes, including of course the "progressive" strata of the bourgeois intellectuals. These classes, particularly the poor and "middle" peasants, were later to be described by Stalin as "reserves" of the revolution. The peasants and a portion of the lower bourgeoisie, and even under certain conditions, of the middle or upper bourgeoisie, especially in "colonial" countries, were regarded as potential allies. Among these allies, some were to

[7] *Program of the Communist Party of the Soviet Union*, p. 48.

be treated as junior partners of the proletariat in overthrowing capitalism, establishing the dictatorship of the proletariat, and building a socialist society under the tutelage of the communists. Others belonged to the category of merely temporary allies, who must ultimately be denounced and suppressed as class enemies.

The bolsheviks, if they were to uphold their right to be considered Marxists, were logically compelled to categorize national sentiments as products of capitalism. They usually held that nationalism was a major constituent of bourgeois ideology and at the same time one of the most powerful of the instruments by which the bourgeoisie held the masses of workers and peasants in ideological bondage. Leninists considered that bolsheviks must wage a struggle to fan the flames of nationalism, at least when it could be expected to set various segments of the bourgeoisie against one another. At the same time they must wage an educational campaign designed to destroy the appeals of nationalism to workers and peasants, whose "consciousness" they sought, first to cleanse of prejudices and superstitions such as nationalism and religion, and then to stimulate into revolutionary action. This is a complex, somewhat contradictory and not always successful operation. To the non-communist it may seem like pure deception. To the communist, however, this exploitation of nationalism to dupe the political adversary, concurrent with a campaign to enlighten the workers and peasants as to the perniciousness of this sentiment, is but one of the duties of the revolutionary.

Implicit in Lenin's elitist and conspiratorial interpretation of Marxism, then, was a manipulative approach to the nationalist attitudes of the masses. Leninists have always denounced nationalism as a reactionary sentiment, as one aspect, in fact, of reactionary bourgeois ideology. The heirs of Lenin are still struggling to eradicate nationalism, or at least those aspects of it which they regard as harmful, from the thinking of the Soviet people. On the other hand, Lenin with his shrewd sense of political reality, realized early that some concessions had to be made to nationalist feeling, at any rate to the nationalist feeling of the workers and peasants. In a number of articles written between 1905 and 1914 Lenin arrived at a position which was later to be developed into a Soviet doctrine that while "bourgeois nationalism" is reactionary and evil, "Soviet patriotism" or "socialist patriotism," is progressive and positive. Borrowing the image of the "two nations" used by Benjamin Disraeli in his mid-nineteenth century novel *Sybil*, Lenin asserted that in every nation there were two nations, that of the landlords, clerics, and bourgeoisie, and that of the simple, virtuous workers and peasants. "In every modern nation," wrote Lenin in 1913, "there are two nations. In every national culture there are two national cultures. There is a Great Russian culture of such people as Purishkevich, Guchkov, and Struve, but there is also a Great Russian culture marked by the names of Chernyshevski and Plekhanov. The same twofold cultures exist among the Ukrainians, in Germany, England, among the Jews, etc."[8]

In 1914, Lenin published his article entitled "The National Pride of the Great Russians," perhaps the single work of Lenin on the nationality problem which is most frequently reprinted in the USSR. Lenin here asserted that the bolsheviks were not unpatriotic, that in fact they loved their language and their Russian motherland very deeply. Moreover, in such statements as his resolution, "The Tasks of Revolutionary Social-Democracy in the European War," written shortly after the outbreak of World War I, Lenin called for a "merciless struggle" against what he denounced as the efforts of the "bourgeoisie" to preach "chauvinism" under the cloak of "patriotism."

A doctrinal and propaganda position derived, in part, from Lenin's division of nationalism, in effect, into "good" and "bad" components is utilized by Soviet propagandists in our own

[8] V. I. Lenin, *Sochineniya*, 3rd ed., Vol. xvii, p. 143.

era to justify their claim to the leadership of the healthy patriotic forces of all nations. Stalin was making use of this device when in his farewell speech to the Nineteenth Congress of the CPSU in October 1952 he claimed that the bourgeoisie had sold out the rights of nations, and their independence, "for dollars," and that the "banner of national independence and national sovereignty" had thus been cast overboard. "There is no doubt," said Stalin, "that it is up to you, the representatives of the communist and democratic parties, to lift this banner and carry it forward if you wish to be patriots of your country, if you wish to become the leading force of the nation."[9]

Stalin's act of semantic expropriation climaxed years of increasingly audacious communist encroachment on the language of democracy, liberalism, and nationalism. While there is in this Soviet doctrine a measure of terminological continuity with Lenin's pre-World War I position, it is of course interpreted so loosely and arbitrarily by the Kremlin as to rob it of most of the measure of consistency and precision it once possessed. Even at best, Lenin's original "two nations" concept was not based on empirical evidence. Later, terms such as "nation" and "people"—like "working class" or "proletariat"—came to have whatever meaning the CPSU leadership decided they should have in a given historical phase, or in a particular political situation. This does not mean that unscrupulous juggling of the symbols of nationalism necessarily destroyed the effectiveness with which the communists exploited what to the targets of their manipulations were very real sentiments. The contrary, indeed, seems, in some instances, to have been the case.

Let us now examine in some detail the uses of nationalism in Soviet propaganda as exemplified mainly in the themes, first, of national liberation and self-determination, and, second, that of the Soviet model for the solution of the prob-

[9] *Current Soviet Policies*, Leo Gruliow, ed. (New York, 1953), p. 235.

lems of multi-national societies. Both of these themes, particularly the latter, acquired major significance only after the establishment of the Soviet state. Their exploitation in Soviet propaganda and agitation has played an especially significant role in two periods. These were, respectively, the period of the revolution and civil war, covering roughly the years 1918-1921, and then the years following 1945, when a once weak Soviet Union emerged from World War II with the immense prestige of victory.

Even after World War II, it took the Soviet Union roughly four or five years of consolidation of the gains resulting therefrom to place itself in a position to exploit with maximum effectiveness the claim that the USSR was at once the champion of the rights of all peoples to self-determination, and the mentor of all honest patriots desirous of realizing the full potential of their national heritage. Indeed, it remained for the propaganda conscious Khrushchev to exploit the potential of nationalism to the full, although as the above quotation from Stalin indicates, the Leninist effort was revived during the last few years of Stalin's lifetime. It must also be remembered that the nationalism of the emerging nations grew steadily in intensity during the late Stalin years and has flowered since his death, with the result that increasing opportunities became available to the communist bloc to turn nationalist forces against the west.

Since the bolshevik seizure of power, Moscow has consistently maintained that all of the legitimate political rights of the peoples under Soviet rule, including those in the sphere of nationality relations, either have been realized or are on the way to realization. The rationale of this position, including the claim that the Soviet Union and all other communist-ruled polities are "off limits" to doctrines competitive with communism, was suggested in a speech delivered by Stalin in Helsingfors, Finland on November 14, 1917.

Addressing the congress of the Finnish Social Democratic Workers Party, Stalin defended Lenin's slogan of the right of nations to self-determination but interpreted it in a novel fashion. Stalin declared that the Council of People's Commissars of the Soviet Republic must help the revolution in Finland, for the time had come to implement the slogan, "Workers of the World, Unite!" Thus Stalin was asserting that the "proletarian" regime had the right to extend its sway over other peoples by force. A few weeks later Stalin, writing in connection with the crisis in the Ukraine, asserted that the Soviet government could not permit national self-determination to serve as a cloak for counter-revolution. It became Soviet doctrine to limit the principle of self-determination to the "toilers," while refusing it to the bourgeoisie.[10]

Since the Eighth Party Congress in 1919, the communists have operated under a formula which, as Pipes puts it, "gave them a free hand to agitate for national independence and to attract the sympathies of the nationalists in those areas where the communists were trying to come into power, without hampering their efforts to overcome nationalist opposition where they were already in control."[11] Typical of the foreign policy application of this formula was an article published in the *Communist International*, No. 11, June 14, 1920. Lenin, in this article, defined the international situation as a struggle between Soviet Russia and the world bourgeoisie. Around Soviet Russia rallied, he said, "the Soviet movements of advanced workers of all countries on the one hand, and, on the other hand, all the national-liberation movements of the colonies and oppressed nationalities," who were convinced that there was no salvation for them except in a victory of the Soviet power over world imperialism. Similarly, the theses adopted in 1920 by the Second Congress of the Communist International stipulated that "the Communist International

[10] Barghoorn, "Nationality Doctrine," p. 296; Pipes, *op.cit.*, p. 109.
[11] Pipes, *op.cit.*, pp. 110-111.

must establish temporary relations and even unions with the revolutionary movement in the colonies and backward countries, without however amalgamating with them, but preserving the independent character of the proletarian movement, even though it be still in its embryonic state."[12] Thus the propaganda which sought to link up the communist movement with radical anti-colonial nationalism was carried on within the context of a "two camp" or bi-polar image of world politics. This image was included in the preamble of the first constitution of the Soviet Union, which took effect in January 1924.

Perhaps the most important forum for discussion of the significance of national-liberation movements for world communism was the Second Comintern Congress held in Moscow in July and August, 1920.[13] The general line taken at the Second Congress and during the period prior to the establishment of diplomatic relations between Soviet Russia and the great European powers, which ushered in some years of uneasy stability, was a very radical one. Soviet Russia was to assist, both directly and through local communist parties, the efforts of workers and peasants in colonial and economically backward countries to undertake radical nationalist and socialist revolutions. It was envisaged that these revolutions would probably, in most cases, not lead immediately to the establishment of socialist systems. However, the possibility, in certain favorable circumstances and special cases, of skipping the capitalist stage of development and proceeding directly to socialism in a number of backward countries was regarded as real. The preponderance of emphasis in the debates at the Second Congress was on limiting cooperation with bourgeois

[12] Quoted from *Blueprint for World Conquest* (Washington & Chicago, 1946), pp. 124-125.
[13] The debates, resolutions, etc., of the Second Congress are contained in *Vtoroi kongress kominterna* (Moscow, 1934). See especially pp. 98-161 and 490-499. See also V. I. Lenin, *Kommunisticheski internatsional*, Vol. II.

nationalist parties and movements only to cases in which it appeared that these movements had a clearly revolutionary potential.

This early, radical Leninist attitude toward national-liberation movements, which combined encouragement of and assistance, at least in the form of propaganda, to anti-colonial movements in their struggles for self-determination and national independence, was gradually abandoned after 1920. It was replaced by Stalin's policy of a temporary alliance between communism and the national bourgeoisie, as exemplified in China from 1924 through 1927. With the adoption in 1928 at the Sixth Congress of the Comintern of a new, radical line, there was a reversion to a position rather similar to that taken at the Second Comintern Congress in 1920. The theses on national and colonial questions adopted by the Sixth Congress urged a strategy of attempting to put the leadership of the revolutionary movement in the colonies in the hands of "a communist vanguard." They recognized that it might be difficult in many Oriental countries to attempt to proceed directly to socialism. The theses noted that "In its first stages, the revolution in the colonies must be carried on with a program which will include many petty bourgeois reform clauses, such as division of land, etc. But from this it does not follow at all that the leadership of the revolution will have to be surrendered to the bourgeois democrats."[14] The theses concluded with the expression of confidence that peasant and worker Soviets could be organized in colonial countries and that these Soviets would work in cooperation with "the Soviet republics in the advanced capitalist countries for the ultimate overthrow of the capitalist order throughout the world."

The rather futile radicalism of 1928-1934 was succeeded, as we have pointed out previously, by the popular front policy inaugurated in the latter year and elaborated at the seventh and last Comintern Congress in 1935. As far as nationality

[14] *Blueprint for World Conquest, op.cit.*, p. 130.

questions were concerned, the popular front policy encouraged attempts to form alliances not merely between communists, and socialists, and other left-wing parties, but also between communists and at least some bourgeois parties. For example, in Cuba before and during most of World War II the communist Juan Marinello held the post of minister without portfolio in the cabinet of Fulgencio Batista. Cooperation between the Soviet Union and local communist parties with bourgeois parties and even with non-communist governments became outstanding features of the post-World War II continuation of the complex strategy of collaboration, rivalry, and penetration inaugurated during the popular front years.

The full development of this policy did not take place until after the death of Stalin. Certainly there was no clear, simple line of demarcation. From time to time emphasis shifted from relatively flexible cooperation between the Soviet Union, local communists, and various groupings of non-communist leftist, liberal, and even sometimes conservative forces (provided the latter were anti-Nazi in the period 1935-1945 or anti-American after World War II) to relatively exclusivist policies such as that pursued by the Soviet Union in 1947-1949. And sometimes there was a shift to the policy of limited cooperation with bourgeois nationalist forces proclaimed at the 1960 Moscow meeting of the world communist movement.

On the whole, from the period of the Bandung Conference in 1955 to the present the Soviet policy toward national-liberation movements and also toward the emerging nations appears to have been one that was defined in an article by E. Zhukov, a leading Soviet Orientalist, in the Soviet monthly *International Affairs* for April 1956. In this article, entitled "The Eastern Peoples and the World's Destiny," Zhukov argued that new sovereign states in underdeveloped countries need not necessarily take the form of "people's democracies." In cases where the leadership of the national-liberation movement belonged not to the working class but to a bloc of anti-imperialist forces, or to the national bourgeoisie and elements close to it, the victory of the national-liberation struggle might lead to the establishment of an independent sovereign state in the form of a bourgeois parliamentary republic.

This somewhat flexible formula, within the pattern set by Khrushchev's proclamation in February 1956 at the Twentieth CPSU Congress to the effect that a vast "zone of peace," to which such countries as India or Indonesia belonged, had come into being, furnished a rationalization for more or less long-term collaboration between the Soviet Union and bourgeois nationalist movements, parties, and regimes. Needless to say, Soviet political writings contained many indications that this modern version of class collaboration was not regarded as permanent, and that Moscow continued to look to the day when countries such as India would be governed by communist dictatorships.[15]

We are now in a position to analyze some of the main themes of contemporary Soviet propaganda directed to national-liberation movements and to the governments established by them. This propaganda assumes many forms and is rather difficult to break down into distinct categories. Its most general feature is a pervasive attempt to inflame the hostility of the under-industrialized peoples against the west. Since we have already dealt with the negative aspects of Soviet propaganda on national-liberation themes, it will not be necessary to treat them here. The more positive themes of Soviet propaganda on this topic include expressions of solidarity and sympathy for peoples who are striving for political and cultural independence, expressions of respect for the culture and traditions of colonial and emerging nations, steady agitation in the United Nations for self-determination of de-

[15] For astute analysis of elements of continuity, change, and inconsistency in Soviet analysis of the situation of the emerging societies, see Walter Z. Laqueur, "Soviet Doctrine and the New Countries," *Survey*, No. 37, July-September, 1961, pp. 3-11.

pendent peoples, assurances of economic, educational, and other kinds of assistance to emerging countries, and, perhaps most important of all, emphasis on the role of the Soviet bloc in making it possible for underdeveloped countries to achieve and to retain political independence. As Indians with whom the writer has discussed problems of their country have emphasized, the peoples of formerly colonial countries tend to feel that colonial rule would not have ended without Soviet pressure.

At the end of November 1955, Khrushchev made a statement in Calcutta, India, which set the stage for much subsequent Soviet propaganda. He stated: "A great historic victory has been achieved by the peoples of Great China, our mutual friends and brothers. Great India has achieved political independence. Other peoples of Asia are freeing themselves from hateful colonial oppression. They are choosing the path of development and non-interference in the internal affairs of other states. We welcome the peoples of these countries in this great cause."[16] Khrushchev's statement indicated Soviet willingness, expressed with increasing force after Bandung, especially in statements addressed to non-communists, to describe such countries as India, Indonesia, Egypt, and others as independent states and not merely, as had earlier been Soviet practice, as semi-colonies of the west. This recognition was a necessary first step toward the cultivation of good relations with the governments of these countries. That, in turn, was required to gain access to and win the confidence of the middle classes and other non-communist propaganda targets in these areas.

While in 1955-1957 Soviet attention was directed primarily to Asia, the growth of nationalist and anti-imperialist sentiment in Africa and Latin America, especially from 1958 on, brought with it a widening Soviet interest in the political and

[16] Quoted in *Conquest Without War*, p. 113, from *Pravda* for December 1, 1955.

137

strategic potential of national-liberation movements on those continents. In February 1958, Khrushchev gave an interview to Manuel Mejido, a correspondent of the Mexican newspaper *Excelsior*, in which he stated, among other things, that "We, Soviet people, wholeheartedly sympathize with the yearning of the colonial peoples to throw off the shackles of slavery and the yoke of the imperialist powers." Khrushchev assured Mr. Mejido that the Soviet Union sympathized with "all the nations striving to win and uphold their right to independence." He warned the Mexican people that economic aid from "imperialist states" would lead to the loss of the freedom and independence of small countries. Finally, and typically, Khrushchev declared that the Soviet people had a sympathetic attitude to the "courageous people of Mexico and are deeply interested in their unique and ancient culture."[17]

By 1959, at the Twenty-first Extraordinary Congress of the CPSU, N. A. Mukhitdinov, a high-ranking CPSU leader of Uzbek origin, felt free to say that because colonialism had suffered a crushing defeat in Asia, imperialism was hanging on all the more stubbornly to Africa, which he characterized as "the last remaining colonial citadel." Mukhitdinov referred to various problems and crises both in tropical Africa and in such countries as Tunisia, Morocco, Algeria, and the Congo. While attacking western policy in the underdeveloped world, Mukhitdinov praised such leaders as Nehru for advocating democracy, and social and economic progress.[18]

As we have already pointed out, Castro's victory in Cuba greatly stimulated Soviet interest in Latin America. It probably also played a major role in the formulation of the concept of the "national democratic front" as a strategy by which Moscow hopes to transform "bourgeois" democracies into "peoples democracies." It should, however, be noted that B.

[17] Quoted in *For Victory in Peaceful Competition with Capitalism*, *op.cit.*, pp. 106-110, from *International Affairs*, No. 4, 1958.
[18] *XXI sezd kommunisticheskoi partii sovetskogo soyuza*, Vol. I, pp. 395-399.

Ponomarev, a leading Soviet theoretician—and CPSU central committee member—suggested in an article in *Kommunist*, No. 8, 1961, that while Cuba was already a full-fledged "national democracy," Indonesia, Ghana, Guinea, and Mali were moving in the same direction.[19]

Earlier, *Kommunist*, No. 6, 1961, in its lead editorial, had described a "national democracy" as "a state of a broad national front, which in its essence is, in the first place, anti-imperialist and in the second place unites all national patriotic forces and, thirdly, assures the active participation of the popular masses in the administration of their country." It asserted that Castro, "the outstanding leader of the brave Cuban people," had pointed out, correctly, that "imperialism" and "reaction" attempted to frighten the peoples by pinning the label of communism on agrarian reform, the nationalization of monopolies, the development of education, etc. If that is communism, Castro was reported as having said, "Then we agree with communism."

There occurred in Cuba a "convergence of communism and nationalism," to use John Kautsky's term. The communists, as soon as they became convinced that Castro was going to win, increasingly adopted Castro's radical nationalist slogans and many of his policies. Castro, in turn, increasingly subordinated his loosely organized "Twenty-Sixth of July Movement" to the disciplined, Soviet-controlled, Popular Socialist Party (Cuban Communist Party). Cuban "national democracy" thus moved toward "people's democracy," setting a pattern Moscow hopes may be repeated in other countries where widespread anti-Americanism, the weakness of non-communist political parties, and the absence of other pre-requisites for democratic political stability facilitate the growth of communist influence. From the point of view of the student of propaganda, a conspicuous feature of "national democracy" is the energetic use

[19] This was pointed out by Herbert Ritvo, in *The New Soviet Society* (New York, 1962), p. 90, note 110.

by communists of patriotic, democratic, and reformist slogans, under cover of which the communists expand and dispose their cadres in preparation for the establishment of a full-scale communist dictatorship. Also, an important role in this process of deception is played by the claim that opposition to and suspicion of the communists constitute treason to the nationalist revolution. This line was proclaimed by the Cuban communists from almost the first days of the Castro regime.

The ability of the Cuban communists to penetrate and exploit Castro's nationalist movement was probably greatly facilitated by years of Soviet cultural relations and other propaganda activity in Cuba. In 1944, the Soviet Embassy in Cuba organized a Cuban-Soviet Cultural Exchange Institute. A number of its officials became top executives of the Castro regime's educational and cultural agencies. Although during the second Batista administration, beginning in 1952, the Institute's activities were curtailed, it had laid a foundation for an image of the Soviet Union as a country which, unlike the United States, respected the cultural values and aspirations of Cubans and Latin Americans generally. Also, Soviet cultural activity, in cooperation with the Cuban communists, helped train communications specialists useful in the later capture and exploitation of the Castro movement. It is noteworthy that after Castro's victory a number of persons prominent in the Cuban-Soviet society became high officials of the Castro regime.

After Castro was in power, Moscow undertook a series of major moves designed both to bolster him, and to exert pressure on him, beginning with the opening in February 1960 of a trade and cultural exhibition in Havana by First Vice Chairman of the USSR Council of Ministers Anastas I. Mikoyan. Cuban mass organizations established close links with counterpart Soviet organizations, and an extensive exchange of persons began. The June 1962 issue of the communist magazine *Cuba Socialista* reported that 2,500 young Cubans were studying in the USSR. Of these, 1,000 were peasants studying agricultural techniques. In December 1961 Castro, after several premonitory but still cryptic utterances, openly proclaimed that he was and long had been a "Marxist-Leninist." Castroism, while it was in some ways embarrassing to Moscow—perhaps not to China—because its extremism tended to frighten some anti-American but still anti-communist Latin Americans, added a new string to the bow of Soviet propaganda regarding self-determination and national-liberation.

The period of Castro's rise to power and adherence to the Soviet bloc roughly paralleled less dramatic, but nevertheless highly significant trends in Indonesia. At the time of writing, in 1963, Sukarno has not permitted the Indonesian communists to gain nearly the degree of penetration of the Indonesian party-state machinery which Castro encouraged in Cuba. Nevertheless, there is in Indonesia a similar pattern of anti-western nationalism—political, cultural, and economic—and an organized communist movement. In the face of a high level of disorganization and incompetence in the non-communist political groupings and in the state machine, this situation may well lead Moscow to regard Indonesia as the country most likely to become the next "national democracy." Like Castro, Sukarno is impelled to seek a scapegoat for internal failures to gain mass support, and, as in Cuba, Moscow stands ready to pose as defender of the national revolution against western—in this case not so much American as Dutch—imperialism.

Against a background of such developments Khrushchev introduced in the 1960 UN General Assembly his resolution demanding the immediate granting of independence to the few remaining colonial countries and peoples. However, it should be noted that the resolution on this subject actually adopted on December 14, 1960 was not the one introduced by Khrushchev but the much milder one sponsored by the "Afro-Asian" group. Ironically enough, both the USSR and the United States abstained from voting on this resolution. The CPSU program, adopted at its Twenty-second Congress in October 1961, stated with evident satisfaction that: "The national states become ever more active as an independent force on the world scene; objectively this force is in the main a progressive, revolutionary and anti-imperialist force. The countries and peoples that are now free from colonial oppression are to play a prominent part in the prevention of a new world war—the focal problem of today. The time is past when imperialism could freely use the manpower and material resources of those countries in its predatory wars. The time has come when the peoples of those countries, breaking the resistance of the reactionary circles and those connected with the colonialists and overcoming the vacillation of the national bourgeoisie, can put their resources at the service of universal security and become a new bulwark of peace."[20]

The above quotation reflects confidence in the ability of world communism to reap further gains by association with, and eventual capture of, national-liberation movements. It further indicates clearly that Soviet interest in nationalism and anti-colonialism reflects not merely a desire to extend communist influence but also a desire to weaken the west in its struggle against further expansion of the Soviet bloc. Khrushchev's 1960 anti-colonial resolution was perhaps only the most spectacular of many Soviet attempts to manipulate the western idea of self-determination in the assembly halls of the UN. As Elliot Goodman has pointed out in telling detail, Soviet bloc representatives, beginning at the San Francisco Conference in 1945, and later in debates regarding such matters as the Universal Declaration of Human Rights and its implementation, from 1948 through 1958, sought, with considerable success in terms of winning votes, to pose as the only sincere advocates of equal rights and self-determination of peoples. However, this vehement advocacy was limited to

[20] *Program of the Communist Party of the Soviet Union,* pp. 48-49.

cases in which "such claims were raised within the confines of the non-Soviet world." All attempts to utilize the United Nations machinery to determine whether or not the right of self-determination, or any other human rights were effectively implemented in the Soviet Union were indignantly rejected by Soviet spokesmen as "incitement to, and encouragement of, the anti-patriotic activities of people who have broken with their own people and homeland."[21]

As we have already pointed out, a prominent feature of Soviet propaganda on the national-liberation theme is concerned with assurances of aid, comfort, and support to colonial peoples after they have achieved political independence. Soviet assurances of aid are accompanied by warnings that the independence of underdeveloped countries is still threatened by the great western powers. Such warnings meet with some sympathetic response on the part of peoples who have long memories of the humiliation associated with their former colonial status. They take on added significance when linked with assertions, on the whole perfectly correct, that the full meaning of national independence requires not only political sovereignty, but also economic and cultural development.

In his public speech to the Twentieth Congress in 1956, Khrushchev set the tone of the subsequent Soviet line on some of these matters. Noting the "growing friendship" between "eastern peoples who have thrown off the colonial yoke and the peoples of the socialist countries," he declared that, " . . . these countries, although they do not belong to the world socialist system, can draw on its achievements in building an independent national economy and in raising the standards of living of their peoples. Today they need not go begging to their former oppressors for modern equipment. They can get it in the socialist countries free from any political or military obligations."[22]

---

[21] Goodman, "The Cry of National-Liberation," p. 98.
[22] Quoted from *Current Soviet Policies* ii (New York, 1957), p. 34.

An important aspect of Soviet propaganda assuring support to the emerging nations is the expressions of respect and admiration for the "talent" and other good qualities of these peoples which this propaganda contains. For example, the *Pravda* editorial for October 2, 1960, hailed the collapse of colonialism and also declared that "The myth of the alleged inability of the colonial peoples to administer, to create, to build, has been shattered. The peoples of Asia, Africa, and Latin America have demonstrated their capacity to carry out internal reforms and at the same time to make an outstanding contribution to the development of international relations."

Expressions of solidarity with national-liberation movements in Soviet propaganda are reinforced, amplified, and significantly supplemented by the image which Soviet propaganda conveys of the USSR as a model multi-national state. This theme is complex, variable, and in some of its implications, subtle. Its ultimate significance is that real national liberation and the flourishing of national cultures can only be achieved in a communist society. Thus, the Soviet model of nationality relations is an instrument for the furthering of revolutionary movements and the building of communist parties. At the same time, the claim that the nationality problem has been "solved" in the USSR has, over the years, been one of the most successful of all Soviet propaganda claims in attracting the sympathy of many non-communist liberal and socialist intellectuals. While this seems to be particularly true in Asia, Africa, and Latin America, an appealing image of Soviet nationality policy has certainly had considerable impact on public opinion in western Europe and the United States. In a world in which ethnic, cultural, and national discrimination, and rivalry and tension bulk so large, it is not surprising that a state and a movement claiming to have the answers to these problems should attract attention to itself. It is possible that the facts regarding Soviet repression and destruction of national cultures so patiently unearthed by

Robert Conquest in his study, *The Soviet Deportation of Nationalities*, may in time diminish the impact on public opinion in the emerging nations of beguiling images of flourishing "socialist nations" in the USSR.[23]

During periods when the Kremlin is pursuing a "leftist," or "hard" policy, and when it subordinates alliances with non-communist social forces to the consolidation of the communist movement, emphasis in presenting the image of the multi-national Soviet society is placed upon the close association of Soviet nationality policy with proletarian revolution and dictatorship. When, however, as has normally been the case since the death of Stalin, the USSR is seeking to broaden its base of support in world public opinion and to infiltrate non-communist political parties and governments, the subversive implications of Soviet nationality policy are toned down, although they never become imperceptible to the attentive observer. In terms of ideological implications, there is not much difference between the "hard" and the "soft" line in projecting Soviet nationality policy to foreign audiences. The significant difference probably is in terms of presentation. Propaganda addressed mainly to communist and fellow traveler audiences contains explicit associations between nationality doctrine and the other main features of Soviet ideology. It may be interesting to recall, in this connection, an article by Khrushchev in *Pravda* on the occasion of Stalin's birthday, December 21, 1949. In this article, entitled "Stalinist Friendship of Peoples, Guarantee of Our Motherland's Invincibility," Khrushchev asserted that Lenin and Stalin "stood at the cradle of each Soviet republic" and nurtured each to its present state. He also declared that "All the peoples of the world see the fraternal friendship of the peoples of the USSR . . . as a great example for them. They are becoming convinced that the Soviet, the Stalin way, of solving the national question

[23] Conquest's book was published in 1960. See also Kolarz, *Russia and Her Colonies* (London, 1952).

is the only correct way."[24] A similar "hard" line was taken in the statements on nationality problems at the Nineteenth Party Congress in October 1952. L. P. Beria devoted more attention to this problem than did any of his colleagues in what was then still the Politburo. Despite Beria's subsequent execution as an alleged enemy of the people, his speech remains one of the best and most systematic presentations of the Soviet image of the model multi-national state and its international significance.

The speech emphasized particularly the gains achieved, according to Beria, by the non-Russian republics of the USSR, which were described by him as "states" or "nations." This attribution of statehood to the various constituent units of the USSR was in keeping with the doctrine propounded by Stalin in 1929, and first published in 1949, according to which "socialist nations" had developed in the USSR "on the basis of old, bourgeois nations as the result of the liquidation of capitalism." These nations, according to the doctrine, differed radically from "bourgeois" nations. The overthrow of capitalism in Russia and of "national oppression," had led to the efflorescence of national culture and to the "consolidation of friendly international relations among the peoples of our country."[25] This is, incidentally, one of the many basic Stalin doctrines that have not been abandoned in the years since the death of the now reviled dictator.

Beria devoted much of the above-cited speech to a comparison between the economic, political and cultural achievements of the ethnic groups organized in the Soviet republics, and the situation of the peoples of a number of non-Soviet countries. To emphasize the superiority of "socialism," the Soviet Central Asian republics were favorably contrasted in respect to various indices of "progress," with Egypt, Turkey and Iran, the Ukraine with France and Italy, the Baltic states

[24] *Current Soviet Policies* II, p. 9.
[25] J. V. Stalin, *Sochineniya*, Vol. XI, pp. 338-339, 353.

with the Scandinavian countries, etc. Beria concluded his speech by asserting that the successes achieved in the development of "the socialist nations within a single multi-national state are of tremendous international importance." The working class in capitalist countries saw in the Soviet state, affirmed Beria, the path "from the denial of rights to freedom and independence, from discord and enmity among nations to fraternal friendship among peoples, from hunger and poverty to a prosperous life, from illiteracy and cultural backwardness to the flowering of culture, science and the arts."[26] A major feature of Beria's speech, as of most late Stalin pronouncements on the nationality question was its emphasis on the "leading role" of the Russian people in making possible the achievements of the non-Russian peoples of the Soviet Union. Like other features of the Stalinist image of the ideal multi-national society which might be objectionable to bourgeois nationalists in the underdeveloped countries, this theme was muted after the death of Stalin.

The harsh, strident presentation of the model multi-national state, virtually undiluted by concessions to non-Russian, non-socialist, or "bourgeois" attitudes, was softened after the death of Stalin. The new position attempted to establish a kind of partnership with emerging "bourgeois" national movements in Asia and Africa.[27] In at least one Asian country—Indo-China—the communists almost immediately after World War II had been highly successful in mobilizing anti-colonialist, nationalist forces in a movement which they controlled but which, for propaganda purposes, spoke a political language more nationalist than communist. The situation in Indo-China was particularly favorable for the purposes of communist penetration, since the French colonial rulers had not permitted the

[26] *Pravda*, October 9, 1952. An English translation of Beria's speech is contained in *Current Soviet Policies* (New York, 1953), pp. 161-166. Quotations on pp. 162-164.

[27] I am indebted for some of the interpretations and data in the immediately preceding and following paragraphs to Mr. George J. Vojta.

nationalist intellectuals and middle class elements to organize political parties that might have effectively competed for power in a post-colonial situation.

The post-Stalin line emphasized similarities between the situations and experience of the underdeveloped countries and that of the Soviet Union at an earlier stage of its history. Since the Soviet Union claimed both "experience" and "success" in solving nationality problems and in promoting economic development, its "example" was worthy of serious study by underdeveloped countries in Asia, Africa, and Latin America. In the new presentation of the multi-national model, liberal and democratic phraseology was freely employed. For example, in an address to the Indian Parliament Khrushchev spoke of the equal rights of Soviet citizens, "regardless of nationality or race"; infringement of these rights was, he said, "punished by law" if committed on the "grounds of race or nationality." He also took pains to assert that "freedom of religion is recognized for all citizens," and is guaranteed by the state. He proudly proclaimed that "among Soviet citizens are Christians, Moslems, Buddhists, Baptists, and followers of other faiths." These facts, he said, were cited "not because I want to impose the Soviet path of development on you, but to give you a more complete idea of the difficulties our people met on their own path." In addition, Khrushchev assured his parliamentary audience that the Soviets "do not export revolution" and, finally, he declared that "we have acquired great experience in these years, and if you wish to use to any extent the experience we have gained . . . we shall willingly, in a friendly and unselfish way, share our experience with you and give you all possible assistance."[28]

Although nationality policy did not bulk as large at the Twentieth Party Congress in 1956 as it had at the Nineteenth Congress, considerable attention was paid to it in the speeches

[28] Quoted from the *Current Digest of the Soviet Press*, Vol. vii, No. 47, January 4, 1956, pp. 1-10.

by Khrushchev and others. The statements regarding this topic followed the relatively tactful line taken by Khrushchev and Bulganin on their journey to Southeast Asia. Thus, in his report to the Central Committee, Khrushchev emphasized that socialism led to the all-round development and flourishing of the economy and cultures of all nations and peoples, rather than to the erasing of national differences. In addition, he introduced the appealing thesis that the forms of transition to socialism would become more and more varied. This, together with the doctrine of the "parliamentary path" to socialism, and the assurances of Soviet desire to assist in the development of the national economies of the emerging nations, was presumably calculated to calm the fears of non-Marxist nationalists that the Soviet Union was still bent on subverting the political and social order of their countries.

A partial reversion to a more orthodox, "Stalinist" presentation of the multi-national model after 1956 was reflected in Mukhitdinov's 1959 speech at the Extraordinary Twenty-first Congress, parts of which have already been quoted in other connections. Mukhitdinov paid special attention to the international significance of "the successful solution of the nationality question in our country." However, he also mentioned favorably the fact that the "Balkar, Kalmyk, Chechen, Ingush, and Karachai peoples have been restored to statehood." This implicit denunciation of the treatment meted out to these "deported" peoples by Stalin indicated an intention to avoid reverting all the way back to the extremes of Stalinist nationality policy and propaganda. It may also, as Conquest was perhaps the first to stress, reflect Moscow's concern over the adverse effects—on Moslem opinion in particular—of increasing awareness of the fate of the Soviet "deported peoples."

Khrushchev, during his March 1960 visit to India, Indonesia, Burma, and Afghanistan followed the same general line as he did on his Southeast Asia jaunt in 1955. However, he was less tactful than before in his treatment of the national susceptibilities of the peoples visited. For example, he engaged in very frank criticism of Indian economic planning methods in an interview with Indian officials at the Bhilai steel plant.[29] Perhaps the prestige acquired by the Soviet Union in the interim as a result of its achievements in outer space impelled Khrushchev to strike a more confident, didactic note. Still, he continued to assure his listeners that the Soviet Union was willing to "learn" from other peoples, as well as to share its experience with them. In Indonesia, Khrushchev invited students "to come to the Soviet Union and see . . . how our country lives and develops." He stressed heavily the multinational character of Soviet society, where "more than one hundred nationalities and peoples live as one family."[30] It was also in Indonesia, on this trip, that Khrushchev announced the intention of the Soviet Union to launch one of its boldest experiments in both the practice and the propaganda of intercultural relations. In a speech in the Indonesian National University, Khrushchev stated that the Soviet Union "desiring to extend assistance to the countries of Asia, Africa, and Latin America in the training of their national cadres of engineers, agricultural specialists, physicians, teachers, economists, and specialists in other fields of knowledge," had decided to establish in Moscow the University of the Friendship of the Peoples.[31] The new university was jointly organized by the Soviet Committee for Solidarity of the Countries of Asia and Africa, the Union of Soviet Societies for Friendship and Cultural Relations with Foreign Countries, and the All-Union Central Council of Trade Unions. After the death of the Soviet-oriented Congolese leader Lumumba in February 1961, the name of this institution was changed to Patrice Lumumba University of the Friendship of the Peoples.[32] The Decree of the Council of Ministers of the USSR which announced the

[29] *Ibid.*, Vol. xii, No. 7, pp. 4-8.
[30] *Ibid.*, Vol. xii, No. 8, pp. 3-4.
[31] *Pravda*, front page, February 24, 1960.
[32] *Pravda*, February 25, 1961.

change of name referred to Lumumba as "an outstanding leader of the national-liberation movement of Africa, the hero of the Congolese people." Almost the whole of the front pages of *Pravda, Izvestiya,* and other Soviet newspapers for February 15 and 16, 1961 was devoted to eulogies and photographs of Lumumba and to accounts of organized demonstrations of protest against the Belgian and American "colonizers."

The exploitation of Lumumba's name may have been a clever stroke of semantics. According to Henry Tanner in the *New York Times Magazine* for January 14, 1962, the important African leader Kwame Nkrumah was embittered against the west because of Lumumba's death. Lumumba, according to Tanner, had promised to join Nkrumah's Ghana-Guinea Union, which might have made Nkrumah the most powerful man on the African continent. It is worth noting in this connection that in April 1962 it was announced in Moscow that one of five persons to receive the Lenin Peace Prize for 1961 was Mr. Nkrumah. Presumably this award represented a move to enhance Soviet influence among pro-Nkrumah Africans and was an indication of confidence that a significant impact had been achieved by Soviet propaganda alleging that the USSR is the most sincere and effective champion of African freedom and welfare. However, it should be remembered that Sekou Touré, the president of Guinea, received the same prize a year before Nkrumah, and that his relations with Moscow cooled considerably in late 1961 and early 1962.

It will probably be several years before it will be possible to appraise the success of Lumumba University. The opinion has been expressed that the establishment of this separate institution for students from underdeveloped countries was in effect a confession of failure as far as Soviet propaganda for the communist solution to nationality problems was concerned. According to this interpretation, the Soviet authorities were forced to segregate African and other students from Soviet students, with whom they had formerly studied together in such institutions as Moscow State University. This was necessary because the Afro-Asians learned too much about Soviet reality by rubbing elbows with regular Soviet university students and because this experience had a demoralizing influence on Soviet students as well.[33] There was, however, a possibility that the new institution—dubbed by some unfriendly critics "Apartheid University"—might serve Soviet purposes by educating an intelligentsia of a new type which might remain faithful to Soviet doctrine at least for one generation. This view was based upon the fact that students for this very special institution were to be drawn from the ranks of young people who "cannot get education either in their own native land or in western countries." This presumably meant that they would be persons who, because they had compromised themselves politically, or, in some cases, because they could not qualify for regular higher-educational institutions, would be especially grateful to the Soviet Union for making it possible for them to continue their studies.[34]

Whatever the pros and cons might be from an educational point of view, or with respect to the possible export of Soviet influence through Moscow-trained cadres, it seems likely that establishment of this institution will, at least for some time, serve dramatically to call attention to Soviet claims of leadership in solving the problems of multi-national societies. It should, of course, be remembered that Lumumba Friendship University is only one of many Soviet and Soviet bloc international educational efforts designed, in part, to exemplify and reinforce propaganda regarding nationality policy.

Foreign travel by well-briefed Soviet delegations, particularly those including skillful propagandists such as Khrushchev, has probably been the most effective instrument for projecting and dramatizing all of the propaganda uses of nationalism

[33] See, for example, David Burg, in *Problems of Communism*, Vol. x, No. 6, November-December, 1961, pp. 50-54.
[34] *Ibid.*, p. 53.

described in this chapter. An interesting example of some Soviet techniques designed to render plausible the official image of Soviet nationality policy is furnished by Khrushchev's speech in Soerabaja, Indonesia, on February 23, 1960. Khrushchev began by striking a note calculated to endear him to a nationalistic Indonesian audience by referring to Soerabaja as a city well-known for its revolutionary traditions, since it was there on November 10, 1945 that an armed uprising against "the colonizers" had begun.

Ironically, in view of the results of de-Stalinization following the Twenty-second CPSU Congress in 1961, Khrushchev compared Soerabaja to "the hero-city Stalingrad." Khrushchev in this speech mingled themes designed to appeal to Indonesian national pride and anti-colonialism with anti-Americanism, peace propaganda, and emphasis upon the growing capacity of the Soviet Union to render economic assistance to Indonesia. With particular respect to Soviet nationality policy, Khrushchev resorted to a favorite gambit of Soviet policy in exchanges of persons, especially with the peoples of Asia and Africa. Declaring that if his Indonesian hosts should come as guests to the Soviet Union they would find that it was a country consisting of fifteen republics with equal rights, Khrushchev then proceeded to illustrate the multi-national composition of the USSR by reference to the membership of the delegation headed by himself. He noted that the then Minister of Culture, Mikhailov, and the Chairman of the Committee for Foreign Economic Relations, Skachkov, were Russians, while Gromyko, also a member of this high-ranking delegation, was a Byelorussian. Going down the list of prominent members of the delegation, Khrushchev ticked off the following nationalities: Ukrainian, Azerbaidzhanian, Tadzhik, Georgian, Armenian, "and others." Careful selection of members for such delegations, together with solid training and good briefing are of course likely to enhance the effectiveness of Soviet propaganda regarding nationality themes, and, for that matter, in all fields.

The methods exemplified by this instance in Indonesia are of course employed in projecting the desired image of the Soviet multi-national society to the other countries of the world.

Khrushchev's reference to the USSR's political structure in the above-cited speech reminds us that a prominent feature of Soviet propaganda regarding the multi-national society consists of statements about the structure of Soviet government, especially as proclaimed in the Soviet constitution. In drafting constitutions Soviet leaders have always indicated concern about their public relations aspects. For example, at the Twelfth Congress of the Russian Communist Party in 1923—still perhaps the richest single source of information on Soviet nationality theory—Stalin argued in favor of a relatively large legislative representation for the small Eastern peoples under communist rule. He said "if we make a small mistake in the Ukraine this will not be felt in the west but if we make a small mistake in Adzharistan, with its 120,000 people, this will be reflected in Turkey and in the whole East, for Turkey is most closely connected with the East. If we make a small mistake with respect to the small region of the Kalmyks who are linked with Tibet and China, this will affect us much more than a mistake in the Ukraine."[35]

Similarly, Stalin in his speech of November 25, 1936 on the draft of the constitution of the USSR which went into effect in December of that year stated that "the international significance of the new constitution of the USSR can scarcely be exaggerated."[36] In the same speech Stalin claimed that the USSR was homogeneous in class structure but that with respect to its national structure it was "a fully formed multinational socialist state, which has stood all tests and whose capabilities might well be envied by any national state."[37] A

[35] *Dvenadtsaty sezd rossiiskoi kommunisticheskoi partii* (Moscow, 1923), pp. 605-606.

[36] J. Stalin, *On the Draft Constitution of the USSR* (English translation, Moscow, 1950), p. 65.

[37] *Ibid.*, p. 25.

number of important features of the 1936 constitution (which, with some amendments, is still in force), were determined in part by foreign propaganda considerations. Among them might be mentioned the right of the constituent republics to "secede," and retention of a bicameral legislature.

Among other developments which facilitated the propaganda of Soviet multi-national political structure and federalism—elements with obvious relevance to countries such as India—mention should be made of the constitutional amendment of February 1, 1944, granting to the constituent republics of the USSR the right to establish ministries of defense and of foreign affairs. A number of these ministries were established, in such republics as the Ukraine, Uzbekistan, Byelorussia, Georgia, Armenia, etc., and they have played a role in impressing upon the peoples of the world, particularly those of Asia and Africa, the desired image of a society in which cherished values, both social and national have been realized.[38]

Systematic analysis, country by country or continent by continent, of the themes and symbols identified thus far would require book-length treatment. It might, however, be appropriate to conclude this chapter with a brief survey of Soviet nationality propaganda concerned with certain key areas.

As befits its importance, India continues to receive much attention from Soviet propagandists. The Soviet Embassy in New Delhi issues a weekly mimeographed bulletin entitled *News and Views of the Soviet Union* which devotes a special section in each issue to the achievements of the Soviet Central Asian republics.[39] Multi-national India, with no single core nationality corresponding to Great Russia in the USSR, is perhaps particularly vulnerable, at least potentially, to the impact of the propaganda of the Soviet model of multi-nationality. In the opinion of Selig Harrison, Soviet and

[38] Vernon V. Aspaturian, *The Union Republics in Soviet Diplomacy* (Geneva & Paris, 1960).
[39] Harrison, *op.cit.*, p. 143.

Chinese claims of national equality in the home countries are significant primarily as a backdrop for the separatist political programs of local communist parties. However, following the period 1946-1953 when a disruptive policy in the nationality question was followed by the Indian communists, there came a period of "sweetly reasonable dedication to national unity when Stalin's death signaled a softened Soviet approach to Southeast Asia."[40] The Indian communists suddenly acclaimed Indian unity and encouraged the study of Hindi. Nevertheless, as Harrison warns, the Indian communists have not completely dropped from their political arsenal the doctrine that each "distinct nationality" in India could justly claim the right to secede from the Indian Union.[41]

It is probable that in the short run Soviet exploitation of Indian nationalism has been most successful when the Soviet leaders have associated themselves with such territorial-political grievances as those connected with Kashmir, Goa, and the like. During their trip to India in 1955 Khrushchev and Bulganin made a conspicuous effort to play upon the sensitive feelings of the Indian public in connection with these issues. According to an Indian political scientist interviewed by this writer, Indians wept when Khrushchev told one audience that Russia was ready to assist India to achieve its aspirations in Kashmir. The Indian situation is, of course, only one of many where Moscow can exploit the hurt pride and inflated egotism of emergent nations having scores still to settle with a once complacent and arrogant west.

In the Middle East Moscow has sought not only to turn the peoples of such countries as Iran and Iraq—and other Arab states—against Britain and America, but has also striven to apply pressure against these states by catering to the cultural and political aspirations of such widely dispersed minority

[40] *Ibid.*, p. 149.
[41] *Ibid.*, pp. 173-177. See also Chap. xx of Gene D. Overstreet and Marshall Windmiller, *Communism in India* (Berkeley & Los Angeles, 1959).

nationalities as the Armenians and Kurds. If it was true, as some reports indicated, that the overthrow of the Kassim regime in Iraq constituted a major defeat for Soviet policy, it may have reflected the limitations of Soviet exploitation of conflicting nationalisms.

In Africa, Russian efforts to exploit national-liberation and related aspirations began on a large scale in 1957 and 1958. Considerable increases occurred in exchanges of persons between Africa and the Soviet bloc, particularly in respect to Morocco, Tunisia, Ethiopia, and French West Africa. Immediately following the Afro-Asian Solidarity Conference in Cairo in December 1957, a great increase occurred in African student travel to the bloc, mainly via Cairo.[42] Of course, all kinds of Soviet propaganda in North Africa, as well as in the Middle East, benefited from the damage to western prestige which resulted from the Suez crisis of 1956, and from resentment engendered by years of French suppression of the Algerian national liberation movement.

As long ago as 1956 an African ethnographic symposium was published under the auspices of the Institute of Ethnography of the USSR Academy of Sciences. It was edited by the leading Soviet Africanist I. I. Potekhin. Like other works of Soviet ethnologists, this symposium cast its findings within the perspective of prospects for the development of the cultures analyzed toward "higher" social forms, leading, eventually to socialism on the Soviet model.[43] In February 1957, a comprehensive plan for research on Africa was drafted at a conference of representatives of the institutes of Ethnography, Oriental Studies, Geography, World Economics, and International Relations. In December 1959, a separate African Institute was organized within the Department of Historical

[42] *Communist Propaganda: A Fact Book* (Washington, D.C., 1959), pp. 69-70.
[43] "Russia Looks at Africa," issued by Central Asian Research Center (London, 1960), p. 9.

Sciences of the USSR Academy of Sciences. Potekhin was appointed director of this new institute.[44]

In the meantime, steps were taken to provide the Soviet public with information on African affairs. The major Soviet Journal of Oriental studies, *Sovetskoe Vostokovedenie*—superseded by *Problemy Vostokovedeniya* in 1959 and, subsequently, by a journal with the more popular title, *Narody Azii i Afriki (Peoples of Asia and Africa)*—began to include Africa in its field of interest. A Soviet delegation representing the Soviet Committee of Afro-Asian Solidarity—the Soviet affiliate of the similarly-entitled international organization, and headed by Potekhin—attended the First Conference of African Peoples, in Accra, in December 1958.[45] In April 1959, it was decided to establish in Moscow a Soviet Association of Friendship with African Peoples, under the chairmanship of Potekhin. It was stated that the association would "arrange meetings, social events, talks, and exhibitions devoted to the national holidays of the African peoples, to anniversaries of people outstanding in the cultural field in Africa, and to other important events in the life of the African nations."[46] The ubiquitous Potekhin visited Ghana in October 1957 at the invitation of the University College of Ghana and, among other subsequent activities, attended the Afro-Asian Solidarity Conference in Conakry, Guinea, in April 1960.

The major concerns of Soviet scholars and propagandists working on African subjects include the exacerbation of African anti-imperialist sentiments; one of their tasks is the strengthening of "African nationalist pride by emphasizing the civilized character of African societies before the coming of the Europeans."[47]

However, the Soviet appeal to African "nationalism" is carefully qualified and Soviet experts point to the dangers of uncritical support of nationalist ideologies, whether in the form

[44] *Ibid.*, pp. 10-11.   [45] *Ibid.*, pp. 11-13.
[46] *Ibid.*, p. 13.   [47] *Ibid.*, p. 15.

of nationalist movements of individual states, or in such forms as Pan-Africanism or "African socialism." Strong warnings to this effect were among the themes of an important article by Potekhin, in the first 1962 issue of *Narody azii i afriki*. The article, entitled "Some Problems of African Studies in the Light of the Twenty-second Congress," hailed the participation of delegations representing the ruling political parties of Ghana, Guinea, and Mali at the congress as symbolic of the "non-capitalist" and "positively neutral" policies of these states, and went on to emphasize an alleged community of interests between the "national liberation movement" of Africa, and the policies of the Soviet Union. In setting forth, rather systematically, directives for research by Soviet Africanists on social classes in African countries, Potekhin emphasized that in the majority of African countries, "objective conditions" existed for a "non-capitalist path of development"—because of the pre-capitalist, pre-industrial situation of African society. However, he pointed out, realization of this potentiality would depend upon the political strategy of the "working class" in Africa. Potekhin also stressed the role, in the African social transformation, of the "world socialist system," and especially of the USSR, as "guarantor of the political independence" of the African states, and as the source of "fraternal help" in the construction of a new and better life.

After African leaders, including heads of the most leftist-oriented states such as Mali and Guinea, had again, in 1962, reiterated their opposition to communism, articles appeared in the Soviet-controlled theoretical journal, *World Marxist Review*, for October 1962, indicating Moscow's impatience with this lack of receptivity. However, on the governmental and diplomatic level, Moscow continued to radiate friendliness for the "peoples of Africa" as evidenced in *Pravda's* cordial message, as well as in radio broadcasts in African languages, on "Africa Day," December 1, 1962. An impressive seven-member Soviet delegation, headed by Potekhin, attended the first International Congress of Africanists, at Accra, Ghana, from December 11 to 18, 1962. Also the USSR and other communist countries were quick to establish economic and cultural contacts with Tanganyika as that country achieved statehood. In August 1962, sixty Tanganyikan students reportedly left for Russia to spend up to five years there.

Khrushchev's message to the "Third Conference for the Solidarity of the Countries of Asia and Africa," held in February 1963, in Tanganyika, presented Soviet Cuban policy as evidence of Russian services to the cause of national sovereignty and independent political and cultural development for all underdeveloped peoples. Published prominently on the front page of *Pravda* for February 4, 1963—and broadcast throughout the world—the message asserted that "Soviet might" had saved Cuban freedom, as well as world peace, and that "life had shown" that the success of the Afro-Asian solidarity movement was dependent on the support of the "peoples of the socialist countries." In their further struggle against colonialism, concluded Khrushchev, the Afro-Asians could count on the firm friendship and support of the Soviet Union. Despite the intentions manifest in Khrushchev's message, however, the conference in Tanganyika apparently was a frustrating experience from the international communist point of view, since the gaucheries connected with intense Sino-Soviet rivalry proved to be a source of amusement, rather than of enlightenment to many Africans.

The same combination of politically directed scholarship, carefully planned exchanges of persons, and semantic enticements, including expressions of appreciation for cultural achievements and manipulation of the symbols of Soviet nationality policy as we have seen applied in Asia and Africa, has been employed in recent years to woo the peoples of Latin America. Robert J. Alexander dates the large-scale Soviet campaign in Latin America to 1959, following the advent of the Castro regime in Cuba, but he notes that this field was by no means neglected earlier, having been the recipient of constant attention since World War II.[48] An interesting fact that Alexander mentions is that thousands of influential Latin Americans travel annually to communist countries. Most of this political "tourism" is, according to Alexander, kept separate from communist party activity in the Latin American countries, with the result that many non-communist Latin American intellectuals and professionals become, perhaps without their knowledge, to some degree targets or instruments of communist propaganda.

The energy of Soviet propaganda in Latin America is reflected in some post-Castro Soviet propaganda activities in Mexico. Among Soviet propaganda efforts in Mexico, the industrial exhibition in Mexico City in November 1959, which was opened by Anastas Mikoyan, stands out. After opening the exhibition, Mikoyan toured a number of Mexican cities. In June 1960, the Georgian Republic Dance Ensemble arrived in Mexico City to open a tour. This is a good example of artistic embodiment of Soviet propaganda regarding the multi-national society. There has also been an energetic effort on the Soviet side to demonstrate a sympathetic interest in Mexican culture. Khrushchev, in a message addressed to Mexican President Lopez Mateos in connection with the one hundred and fiftieth anniversary of Mexican independence, stated that "the Soviet people have always displayed a deep interest in the highly original culture of your country."[49] As if to confirm the sincerity of these words, an exhibition on Mexican art was opened in Moscow in the fall of 1960. Later this exhibition moved to the Hermitage Museum in Leningrad, where it was still on display when this writer was in that city in late March and early April 1961. This was a very large and well-organized exhibition, placed near the opening of the huge Hermitage

[48] Robert J. Alexander, "Soviet and Communist Activities in Latin America," *Problems of Communism*, Vol. x, No. 1, January-February, 1961, pp. 8-13.
[49] *Pravda*, October 27, 1960.

Museum, where it could be seen by thousands of Soviet visitors, and of course could not fail to be seen by foreigners. When the exhibition was opened in Moscow, Mikoyan and other high Soviet officials were present.

A more negative kind of attention to Mexican national feeling was exemplified in an article published in *Sovetskaya etnografiya*, 1958, No. 6, by the anthropologist A. Zolotarevskaya. Entitled "The Mexicans of the United States of America," the article mingled historical, ethnographic, and political data and opinions regarding such matters as "the grievous position" of the majority of Mexicans in the United States. Among other things, it noted that the only state of the United States with a large Mexican population where Spanish is an official language is New Mexico, but that even there American "bureaucrats" did not know Spanish, and that they forced Mexicans out of official jobs.

The record we have analyzed reflects a determined and resourceful Soviet effort to exploit for the purposes of Soviet foreign policy the national sentiments of the peoples of the less-developed countries of the world. At least in the period since the death of Stalin, Soviet expressions of interest, sympathy, and solidarity have been couched more in non-communist than in communist terminology. The obvious purpose of this approach is to drive wedges between these peoples and the western industrial countries, while at the same time creating good will for the Soviet Union and other communist countries. From time to time, however, Khrushchev, echoed by Soviet scholars and journalists, makes remarks which reveal the temporary and tactical nature of the contemporary Soviet espousal of the cause of nationalism. For example, in July 1958, Khrushchev remarked, "The Arabs are not Marxists. They fight under another flag—under the flag of nationalism. We hail them. National liberation is the first step."[50]

Our attention in this chapter has been focused mainly on the

[50] Quoted in Goodman, *The Soviet Design for a World State*, p. 423.

underdeveloped countries, for they are the major contemporary arena of the world propaganda battle between communism and western democracy. However, it is perhaps appropriate to conclude this discussion by pointing out once again that Soviet exploitation of national sentiments is by no means limited to the cases of colonial and emerging nations.

Communist seizure of power in eastern Europe during and following World War II was of course facilitated by concealment of ultimate communist aims behind a facade of patriotic slogans. With regard to Germany, for example, Moscow had in 1943 created the Free Germany National Committee and the Union of German Officers, organizations which struck a strongly nationalistic note in their propaganda. After the establishment in 1946 of the Socialist Unity Party (SED) in East Germany, by merger of the communists and the socialists under Soviet auspices, the Soviets had a political instrument for systematic exploitation of such nationalistic sentiments as the desire, strong in varying degrees in all parts of Germany, for reunification. The Soviets and their German communist assistants almost from the end of the war have taken the position that reunification could be achieved were it not for the unpatriotic policies of the West German industrialists, stigmatized as the "chief allies" of the American "imperialists." At least in the early post-war years, the East German communists were under orders from Moscow to advocate a "parliamentary-democratic," rather than a Soviet-style path of political development for both East and West Germany, one in which, it was promised, the people would be granted all the normal democratic rights and freedoms.[51]

Later, the USSR and its West German communist supporters sought to undermine the "Adenauer regime" by depicting the Federal Republic as a puppet of American, British, and French "imperialism." The communists, seeking as they have so often

[51] See, for example, Carola Stern, *Porträt einer bolschevistischen Partei* (Cologne, 1957), pp. 18-20, 66-77, 98-104.

to exploit patriotism, attempted to convinĉe West Germans that, with Moscow's help, the German people could throw off the fetters of "foreign domination." Thus, once again, the communists tried to manipulate for their own purposes symbols of values profoundly alien to Soviet designs. The calculations underlying the Soviet attempt to turn German patriotism into an instrument for communist infiltration of the Federal Republic were spelled out in rich and convincing detail in legal proceedings against the West German communists held in 1955, at Karlsruhe.[52]

Soviet propagandists clearly regard fostering divisions among the NATO powers as an important activity, and employ for this purpose anti-Americanism, anti-German feeling, and other national sentiments and prejudices. Flora Lewis reported in the *New York Times Magazine* for January 7, 1962 that the Soviet ambassador in Washington had, privately, chided a group of US senators for being blind to the "German menace until they take over Florida." In the meantime, the Soviet ambassador in Paris was reportedly chiding Frenchmen for being blind to the "German menace until they take over Alsace-Lorraine." At the same time, Soviet propaganda was attempting to set West Germans against the United States by alleging that America was depriving Germany of huge markets in the Soviet bloc countries. Along the same general lines, the communist party of Great Britain in 1951 organized a campaign in defense of British "national independence" and of British culture! One feature of the campaign was a conference on "The American Threat to British Culture."[53]

As Pelling ironically observes, all the accumulated eighteenth and nineteenth century British criticisms of the United States, "based on aristocratic snobbery," were pressed into the service of international communism. The objective, no doubt,

[52] See the three volumes of *KPD Prozess* (Karlsruhe, Germany, 1956).
[53] Henry Pelling, *The British Communist Party* (London, 1958), p. 144.

was to turn to communist advantage the feeling of some British intellectuals that their country has become the victim of an "American invasion," especially in the industrial and cultural spheres.

An aspect of Khrushchev's handling of the crisis which arose in connection with President Kennedy's proclamation, on October 22, 1962, of a naval blockade to prevent supplying of offensive armament to the Castro regime in Cuba, was the effort to turn against the United States not only Latin American, Asian, and African national and anti-colonialist sentiments, but also western European nationalism. As Max Frankel pointed out in the *New York Times* for October 28, 1962, one of Khrushchev's objectives appeared to be "the engagement of the United States in a series of global bargains in which other nations would become pawns." Viewed in this perspective Khrushchev's suggestion, at one point, of a Cuba-Turkey bases deal was one more move in a long-standing Soviet diplomatic and propaganda effort to arouse suspicion against America by offering to "divide the world" between Moscow and Washington. From the point of view of analysis of Soviet propaganda strategy the immediate results of this gambit were less important than its illustration of the habitual effort of Moscow to play upon nationalist and other traditional sentiments in the populations to which it directs its messages.

CHAPTER VI

MODERNIZATION: THE SOVIET MODEL

THE communists of Russia, with a sensitivity reflecting Russia's long struggle to overcome its inferiority in many fields of technology, economy, and public services, have certain advantages in the current contest for the good will of the many peoples of the world aspiring to a higher standard of life than they presently enjoy. One of the most provocative themes of Soviet propaganda is that designed to exploit world-wide demands, articulated by politically active intellectuals in Asia, Africa, and Latin America, for full and equal participation in "modern" civilization. As industrialization engulfs new and larger masses of men, these demands are voiced with increasing insistency.

Soviet propaganda responds with the claim that Moscow has the knowledge and experience required to assure the rapid modernization of previously backward societies. To be sure, Soviet propagandists do not normally use such terms as "modernization"—they prefer to couch their assurances in terms of "progress" based upon the application of science, particularly the super "science" of Marxism-Leninism, for the solution of economic, social, and cultural problems. Thus, the present CPSU program declares that Soviet socialism can transform a backward country "into an industrial country within the lifetime of one generation and not in the course of centuries." Displaying awareness also of the emotional needs of people swept up in the torrent of social change, the program asserts that socialism is "the road to freedom and happiness for the peoples."

While such statements are drafted primarily with an eye on the non-western peoples, it would be a serious error to suppose that their authors do not assign universal applicability to the Soviet model. This claim of universality is indicated in the same party program when it states that "the CPSU sets the historically important task of achieving in the Soviet Union a living standard higher than that of any of the capitalist countries." Claims of economic, scientific, and technological success in the USSR and promises which may create the impression that communism can produce not merely rapid economic growth but also a superior form of the "welfare state" are calculated to appeal to world public opinion generally. They are not intended only for eager and impatient politicians and intellectuals in the underdeveloped countries.

The appeal of modernization, Soviet style, consists, Moscow believes, in creating good will toward the Soviet Union. However, the achievements of communism can inspire awe as well as admiration. This is particularly true, of course, in such fields as nuclear weapons, ballistic missiles, and space vehicles. The propaganda of Soviet achievements is an instrument not only of persuasion but also of intimidation. Whether or not even a decisive Soviet bloc "victory" in the battle of production would lead to political domination of the world by Moscow is debatable, but there is considerable evidence to indicate that the Soviet leaders believe that by outperforming the west in all of the major fields of human endeavor, economic, scientific and cultural, the communist countries can win world hegemony. It seems clear that a difference of emphasis regarding the capability of communism to persuade and overawe the non-communist world by force of example, and the pressures example can generate, is a significant source of differences between the international perspectives of the Soviet and the Chinese communist leaders. Moscow apparently believes that, at least for some time, the winning strategy for communism is to combine the building of a superior economic-scientific power base with economic pressures and skillful propaganda. If this estimate is correct, the direct application of military power would remain, at least for some years, a more subordinate element of communist world strategy than it was during the Stalin era.

Khrushchev at the Twenty-first Party Congress asserted that ultimate communist victory would be achieved "not through armed interference by the socialist countries in the internal affairs of the capitalist countries," but through conclusive demonstration that "the socialist mode of production possesses decisive advantages over the capitalist mode of production."[1] If and when such an objective is reached, Moscow may calculate that a new and decisive phase in the development of relations between "socialism" and "capitalism" will begin, characterized by: "the reactivation of the revolutionary potential in the west either through the inherent contradictions and crises of a capitalist society increasingly bereft of its colonial markets and sources of cheap labor and materials, through some sudden and spontaneous 'attraction' of the masses once the efficacy of the communist economic and social system has been adequately demonstrated, or through the active military intervention of the USSR if Soviet military preponderance makes such action feasible."[2]

Moscow presents its propaganda of the Soviet model of modernization within the framework of a professed belief that world politics is dominated by "the ever-increasing strength of the forces of socialism and peace and the simultaneous weakening of the forces of imperialism." The words are those of B. N. Ponomarev, one of the top CPSU central committee functionaries, with special responsibilities for Soviet relations with the international communist movement, in a significant article in *Pravda* for May 1, 1960. Ponomarev identified three main features of the contemporary world situation: the increasing struggle of the peoples of the world against the danger of war; the "gigantic upsurge" in the struggle of Asia,

[1] Quoted in Kovner, *op.cit.*, p. 107.
[2] *Ibid.*, pp. 107-108.

Africa, and Latin America for national liberation; and the intensification of the "labor and revolutionary movement in the capitalist countries." However, he regarded as more important than any of these, and indeed as the foremost factor in the world situation, "the powerful growth of the strength of the Soviet Union and of the entire world socialist system." The achievements of the socialist countries, and their ideas, he described as "a tremendous revolutionizing force, acting in the interests of all mankind.

Of a similar character was a long article in *Pravda* for September 14, 1962, by E. M. S. Namboodiripad, the new General Secretary of the Communist Party of India. Namboodiripad's article was entitled, "The Program of the CPSU and the Struggle of the Peoples of Asia and Africa for the Consolidation of Their Independence." It paid tribute to the inspirational effect of the Russian revolution, to which, according to the author, countries such as India, Indonesia, and Egypt owed their political independence. Namboodiripad also stressed the "practical" economic and military assistance of the USSR to underdeveloped countries. In particular, he emphasized that Soviet victory over the United States in economic competition would not only enable the Soviet Union to increase its aid to the "peoples of Asia and Africa" but would facilitate the social revolution on those continents. Namboodiripad called upon the Afro-Asians to support Moscow's struggle for peace, upon the results of which, he indicated, hinged the ability of the USSR to render economic and cultural assistance to the less-developed lands. Throughout his article, he put heavy emphasis upon the role of Soviet military power as a factor inhibiting plans of the "imperialists" (did he also have Communist China in mind?) to attack "independent countries," as they had attacked Egypt in 1956.

Perhaps the most forceful Soviet statement to date regarding the propaganda potential of Soviet-style modernization was contained in the declaration published in the January 7, 1963 issue of *Pravda*, already referred to in Chapter IV. According to *Pravda*: "In the countries of socialism the model for the future of all of mankind is being built. The peoples of our countries are obliged to exert all their effort to make that model as attractive as possible so that each working person, as he learns about the way of life of any socialist country, will say: 'that is my beautiful tomorrow, for which it is worthwhile to struggle, at all costs.' "

Contemporary Soviet efforts to associate Moscow with the universally appealing symbol of modernization must be viewed largely within the framework of power analysis. At the same time, we would underestimate the appeal of this most positive theme of Soviet propaganda if we overlooked its idealistic aspects. Skeptics may question the sincerity of practical politicians such as Khrushchev when they promise, sometime in the future, a world of peace, prosperity, and freedom for everybody, although many practical American businessmen and politicians, including former Vice-President Nixon, have expressed the view that Khrushchev sincerely believes in the slogans which he so ably articulates.

From the point of view of the propaganda analyst, the sincerity of Soviet statements is not as important as their impact. Western intellectuals, including even many Americans, tend today to be skeptical about the ideas of progress and the perfectibility of man. As Ulam observes, such catastrophes as the first world war "destroyed most of the appeal of liberalism as a proselytizing creed of modernization."[3] And yet, as another scholar has pointed out, "the vision of utopia, extinct in the west, continues to shine in the communist east, deriving its splendor from the artificial illumination of the propaganda engines of Agitprop." As this same scholar notes, Soviet philosophers at the Twelfth International Congress of Philosophers in Venice in 1958 portrayed "the future society to which the Soviet Union is allegedly advancing in terms worthy perhaps

[3] Adam Ulam, *The Unfinished Revolution* (New York, 1960), p. 243.

not so much of Marx as of his more imaginative predecessors—Condorcet, St. Simon and Fourier."[4] One of the distinctive features of Soviet propaganda, both domestic and foreign, since the death of Stalin, has been a partial return to the utopian visions contained in Marxist-Leninist doctrine. Certainly the new party program is replete with utopian phraseology. Once again the communists are holding out many of the values of the great world religions—the elimination of coercion, the achievement of equality, the possibility for mankind to realize the fullest development of the capacities of every individual. To be sure, careful analysis of communist texts reveals that what the communists promise envisages, in essence, a relatively conservative, regimented way of life. The CPSU program asserts that some twenty years will be required to build the "material-technical" foundations for communism. The prescriptions for continued direction and coordination of society by the party and its harsh warnings regarding the necessity for hard work are among indications that, as some western critics have pointed out, the only thing that will not be free in the "new" world of the future will be freedom itself.

Nevertheless, use of utopian phraseology, together with promises of such concrete benefits as free education for all, social security, full employment, and even, eventually, free bread, are certainly calculated to impress many people in all countries of the world. To put the matter in its broadest terms, Moscow seeks to associate Soviet socialism with all of the legitimate aspirations of mankind.

Most of this chapter will be devoted to such aspects of the image of Soviet-style modernization as industrialization, cultural development, social welfare, and, in the most recent years, spectacular Soviet achievements in science and technology, especially in the race, as Soviet sources put it "to master the cosmos." Before discussing these claims in detail,

[4] Erich Goldhagen, "The Glorious Future—Realities and Chimeras," *Problems of Communism*, Vol. IX, No. 6, November-December, 1960, pp. 10-18. Quoted material on p. 10.

we may usefully say something about the strategy employed by the Russians in presenting them. The manipulative-deceptive element, so unusually characteristic of Soviet propaganda, plays a less prominent role in connection with these matters than it does in other areas of Soviet foreign communications. To a considerable degree, Soviet propagandists can afford to tell the truth when they describe to the world the economic, technological, and educational achievements of their country and its social system. Certainly they can truthfully assert that in a remarkably short span of time the most backward of the great powers has become a formidable competitor of the most advanced industrial countries. Soviet leaders are shrewdly aware of the domestic and foreign propaganda implications of what is presented as an heroic struggle against backwardness. This is indicated, for example, by the fact that in his speech to the Twenty-second Party Congress entitled "Concerning the Program of the Communist Party of the Soviet Union," Khrushchev included, as had Lenin and Stalin before him on similar occasions, a famous quotation from the nineteenth century poet Nekrasov on the poverty and backwardness of old Russia. Khrushchev contrasted the Russia of today with the Russia of Nekrasov.

This is not the place to discuss the role of Russian revulsion against the shame of previous backwardness in spurring contemporary Russians to spectacular achievements. It seems likely that Russian experience in the struggle against backwardness imparts to Soviet propagandists a certain understanding of the mentality of other peoples engaged, or about to engage, in a similar struggle. Moreover, knowledge of the Soviet experience may generate, in underdeveloped countries, sympathy for the Russians. These are factors in Soviet Russian behavior of which we should be aware.[5] In this field, as in the

[5] A number of historians and social scientists have made important contributions to our knowledge of the role of economic and cultural backwardness, in the Russian revolutionary movement, and in the Rus-

understanding of the problems confronting multi-national states, Soviet propagandists have the advantage of a pattern of experience much richer than that of their western competitors. It should be noted here that while the propaganda of Soviet modernization has reached spectacular proportions since the death of Stalin, it is actually almost as old as the Soviet regime.[6] With the adoption of the first Five Year Plan in 1928 Soviet propaganda began increasingly to proclaim the superiority of Soviet planned industrialization over the "anarchic" American model. Molotov, in his address of March 14, 1939 to the Eighteenth Party Congress stated that the Soviet Union would within a relatively short time become "the most advanced country in the world in all respects."

The Soviet people have paid a high price in suffering, deprivations, and regimentation for communist industrial progress. Nevertheless, it would be idle and perhaps fatal for the west to fail to recognize the substantialness of Soviet industrial, technological, and cultural achievements. Soviet achievements in education, for example, may have been exaggerated by some western experts and journalists. Still, impressive evidence has been presented in a recent study to the effect that not only are Soviet elementary and secondary schools superior to American public schools in teaching mathematics and the natural sciences, but also that their curriculum and textbooks indicate substantial superiority in the teaching of such subjects as reading, literature, history, foreign languages, and geography.[7]

---

sian and Soviet attitude toward the west. Among them are Alexander Gerschenkron and Theodore H. Von Laue. See especially Von Laue's article, "Imperial Russia at the Turn of the Century: The Cultural Slope and the Revolution from Without," in *Comparative Studies in Society and History*, Vol. iii, No. 4, July, 1961, pp. 353-367.

[6] Kovner, *op.cit.*, presents evidence that Lenin, Bukharin and other bolshevik leaders envisaged the possibility that economic competition between socialist and non-socialist societies could supplement, or even be an alternative to military struggle.

[7] Arthur S. Trace, Jr., *What Ivan Knows That Johnny Doesn't* (New York, 1961), especially pp. 12, 18, 57, 112, 114, 122, 127, 158.

While we must, if we are to deal effectively with Soviet propaganda, recognize the elements of truth in Soviet claims, it is also necessary to be aware of what the American sociologist Alexander Vucinich describes as "the titanic and mostly unwitting publicity given to Soviet scientific and educational achievements in non-communist countries." Vucinich refers to this phenomenon as "the part of the total process which works in favor of the Soviet Union but is not sponsored by the Kremlin, and is not financed by the Soviet taxpayers."[8]

Not surprisingly, Soviet propaganda seeks to associate Soviet achievements with the ideology and practices of "socialism." As in the case of the exploitation of nationalism in Soviet propaganda during periods when the Soviet Union is pursuing a "hard" line in its international policy, Soviet-style modernization tends to be openly linked to social revolution and communist dictatorship. In the late 1920's and early 1930's the workers of the world were called upon to facilitate the progress of "socialist construction" in the USSR and of socialist revolution under the leadership of the Soviet Union.[9] In the May Day slogans of 1931, unemployment, famine, and the high death rate in capitalist countries were contrasted with "the flourishing life in the Soviet Union," and the international proletariat was urged to follow the path of the Soviet workers. Revolutionary propaganda was associated directly with the Soviet Five Year Plans. In those days, the association of "socialism" with economic and cultural modernization included explicit references to the necessity of violent revolution.

During the present era of coexistence propaganda, Soviet statements regarding the relevance of the experience of the USSR to the problems of non-communist underdeveloped countries create the impression that Moscow now admits that

[8] Vucinich's remarks were contained in a review of this writer's book, *The Soviet Cultural Offensive*, in the *American Sociological Review* for October, 1961. See p. 817.

[9] Lasswell and Leites, *Language of Politics*, p. 259.

substantial economic and social progress can be achieved, with Soviet help, without paying the high price of a Soviet-style social revolution. This would be especially true if the countries concerned proceed rapidly to eliminate western influence.

Frequently Khrushchev and other Soviet leaders assert that the USSR desires to help the countries of Asia, Africa, and Latin America solely because it wishes to contribute to their progress, strengthen their national independence and raise their standards of living.[10] Along the same lines, an article in a Soviet educational journal pointed out in the fall of 1960 that Friendship University would send students from underdeveloped countries home after five or six years of study "so that on the basis of the modern knowledge received by them they could contribute to the development of the economy and culture of their countries."[11] At least on the overt level, the pattern for Soviet participation in the modernization of underdeveloped countries is one of unselfish, disinterested helpfulness, with no ideological strings attached. What probably amounts to a directive for this kind of propaganda is contained in the important publication, issued as background for the 1961 CPSU program, to which we referred in another connection in the previous chapter.[12] A chapter in this volume by A. F. Yudenkov, entitled "The Program of the Party in the Sphere of Cultural Construction and Its Implementation," pointed out that one of the "general laws" of communism was the carrying out of a revolution in the field of ideology and culture, and the creation of an intelligentsia devoted to the working class and to the working people, as well as to the cause of socialism. Yudenkov described how this process had been carried out in the Soviet Union. He discussed the campaign against illiteracy, the establishment of educational and cultural institutions, the encouragement of scientific and ar-

[10] *Pravda* editorial, November 4, 1960.
[11] T. Samokhvalova in *Vestnik vysshei shkoly*, No. 9, 1960, p. 75.
[12] *O programme KPSS*, Part I.

tistic progress, etc. He contrasted Soviet cultural development with the results of Portuguese rule in Angola, noting, among other things, that only two per cent of the African population of that area was attending school. He also presented statistics to demonstrate the superiority of opportunities provided to Soviet citizens for higher education, in contrast to such leading western nations as France, Sweden, or the German Federal Republic. Against this background, Yudenkov made the following significant statement: "The Soviet Union and the other socialist countries, having achieved great success in the development of science, culture, popular education, etc., have the capability of rendering assistance to the poorly-developed countries of Asia, Africa, and Latin America, assisting them in overcoming their age-old backwardness, the product of colonialism. Cultural cooperation, the construction of institutes, of hospitals, of schools, of sports facilities, and so on, carried out by the USSR and other socialist countries in the nations of Asia and Africa demonstrates to the working people of these continents the achievements and the power of socialism, its internationalism and humanitarianism."[13]

Yudenkov also stated that "the new countries which sooner or later will embark on the path of socialist construction will be able to utilize the experience not only of the Soviet people but of other peoples, who are constructing or have already constructed socialism." Thus, although the Soviet message to underdeveloped countries emphasizes helpfulness and unselfishness, the desired political results of acquainting the peoples of the world with the Soviet model of modernization are by no means forgotten. Tact is, in the present period, normally exercised in presenting the Soviet model. Yet it is apparent that Soviet propagandists intend wherever it is expedient to offer selected aspects of the total model to create the impression that maximum progress toward achieving group and individual

[13] *Ibid.*, p. 537.

aspirations can only be made if the total pattern of Soviet experience is recapitulated.

At times, Soviet leaders, including Khrushchev, are candid indeed in associating Soviet achievements with communist ideology and institutions. Khrushchev, in replying to letters and telegrams reportedly received just before he made his visit to the United States in 1959, asked, "Why were the Soviet people the first in the world to successfully solve such a difficult and truly grandiose problem as sending a rocket to the moon—a problem with many unknowns?" His answer was that the Soviet people had "built a socialist society and are confidently building communism." This statement by Khrushchev was contained in a widely-distributed English-language publication entitled *Khrushchev in America*, published by the official Soviet Crosscurrents Press in New York in 1960. It will be recalled that the stage was set for Khrushchev's American journey by the sending of a Soviet rocket to the moon. Khrushchev took advantage of this spectacular scientific feat to enhance the world image of "the boundless possibilities for human progress offered by communism." However, in this statement and in his statements while in the United States, Khrushchev, while associating Soviet achievements with socialism and communism, carefully refrained from any propaganda for violent revolution inside the United States. On the contrary, he took the position that each country had the right to whatever kind of social system was desired by the "workers" of that country. However, he confidently expressed the opinion that the American people would eventually want to replace capitalism by socialism, because socialism was the superior system.

In addition to wholly or partially concealing communist insistence that violent revolution and dictatorship will ultimately be necessary for the completion of the revolutionary transformation of human society throughout the globe, the propaganda of Soviet-style modernization contains other elements of manipulation and distortion. One of the most obvious of these, but also one that can be most easily overlooked, is the habitual Soviet practice of associating with the magic symbol of "socialism" activities and practices which are, everywhere, concomitants of the universal, world-wide industrial progress of our era. Even the most commonplace functions of public authorities, such as planting trees on Moscow streets, are likely to be made the subject of self-congratulatory Soviet propaganda. Much more important, in terms of its impact on world public opinion, is the ability of the Soviet regime, while displaying selected aspects of Soviet reality—as in the case of guided tours offered to "progressive" intellectuals and politicians—to conceal the seamy side of Soviet life. This practice reinforces the favorable predispositions of those social and national groups impelled by the deprivations of the changes inherent in the world revolution of our era to want to believe what Soviet propaganda tells them. It helps Soviet communicators to strengthen their claim that the ideal society of the future is already under construction in the USSR. As Cantril notes, by portraying the "ideal society" as the communists see it, the Soviet leaders can continually raise expectations of what life should be, and can point to the gap between such expectations and the current state of affairs in underdeveloped countries "no matter how much the west gives to those people."[14]

The "technical modernization of society" has been described by one political scientist as the "universally accepted good" of our age.[15] Eagerness for speedy modernization is particularly strong among the radical nationalists of the emerging nations. A shared enthusiasm for rapid economic development undoubtedly constitutes one of the values common to the elites of such new nations as Ghana, Guinea, Indonesia, or

[14] Hadley Cantril, *Soviet Leaders and Mastery Over Man* (New Brunswick, N.J., 1960), p. 140.
[15] Zbigniew Brzezinski, "The Nature of the Soviet System," *Slavic Review.* Vol. xx, No. 3 (October, 1961), pp. 351-368. Quotation on p. 360.

India, and their counterparts in the USSR. For many years a conspicuous feature of Soviet propaganda, both domestic and foreign, has been the association of socialism with scientific and technical progress. A consistent feature of this propaganda has been the claim that only under the planned, socialist economy could assembly line production, automation, atomic energy, and other aspects of modern technology be systematically applied for the benefit of society. Claims of this sort have met with a certain response among western intellectuals, particularly among some natural scientists. In underdeveloped countries which aspire to the blessings, and know little about the defects of an industrialized society, they are likely to meet with a particularly sympathetic response. An anti-communist Indian author wrote in 1957 that, "passionately aspiring to rapid industrialization, Indian economists and intellectuals have turned to the Russian example."[16]

Soviet propaganda exploits its success as an example of rapid industrialization in a number of ways. Perhaps the most important is its claim that the USSR is uniquely capable and disposed to render unselfish assistance to underdeveloped countries aspiring to this indispensable basis of modernization. Moscow also stresses the special virtues of Soviet planned, state-directed economic development, exalts the value of trade with the USSR and the Soviet bloc generally, and backs up its claims with impressive statistics regarding the growth of the Soviet economy. It is interesting that in 1944 Jawaharlal Nehru wrote that "the inspiring record of the Soviet people in this war" was "due to a social and economic structure which has resulted in social advances on a wide front, in planned production and consumption, in the development of science and its functions."[17]

[16] R. Ramani, "Indo-Soviet Cultural Relations," *Quest* (Bombay), Vol. III, No. 2 (October-November, 1957), pp. 33-40. Quotation on p. 40.
[17] Jawaharlal Nehru, *The Discovery of India*, Anchor Books ed. (Garden City, N.Y., 1959), p. 392. This book contains other expres-

The image of the Soviet Union as the unselfish friend of the emerging, modernizing nations is fostered by world-publicized projects of economic aid and technical and medical assistance, of which perhaps the best known is Soviet assistance in the construction of the Aswan dam, in Egypt. According to the *National Observer* for January 14, 1963, President Nasser, at a ceremony marking the start of work on the main section of the dam, said "We hail the Soviet technicians and workers who have been working in a strange climate, who have endured the heat of our summer. We tell them the dam will ever remain a symbol of Egyptian-Soviet friendship." Thus, despite considerable Soviet-Egyptian friction, particularly over Nasser's repression of communist activity inside Egypt, Moscow continues to benefit by its participation in the modernization of the Egyptian economy.

Almost half of the space in *Pravda* for November 4, 1960 was devoted to describing Soviet foreign aid projects. The *Pravda* editorial for that date stated that the Soviet Union was furnishing economic assistance to fourteen countries of Asia and Africa, including India, the United Arab Republic, Indonesia, Afghanistan, Iraq, Guinea, Burma, Nepal, Ethiopia, and Ceylon. This assistance involved more than 300 industrial enterprises. The Soviet steel mill at Bhilai, in India, had at that time already produced 800,000 tons of pig iron and more than 300,000 tons of steel and it was supplying products to about 900 Indian enterprises.

Soviet propaganda, especially in the form of statements by Soviet representatives in UN agencies, heavily emphasizes the superiority of "socialist" to "capitalist" methods for the development of mineral, petroleum, and other natural resources. Soviet communications make frequent reference to the por-

---

sions of admiration, tempered by criticism, of Soviet achievements, and also indicates clearly Nehru's conviction that the economic regeneration of India required an economic policy based on a considerable measure of central planning.

tion of the Fifteenth UN General Assembly Declaration on Granting Independence to Colonial Countries and Peoples, which stated that "peoples can dispose of their natural wealth and resources to their own benefit." Soviet spokesmen allege that "foreign oil monopolies," and other foreign "cartels" violate this "right of the peoples." The Soviet delegation to the UN Symposium on Development of Petroleum Resources of Asia and the Far East, held at Teheran in September 1962 as one of a continuing series, presented a long, detailed paper portraying Soviet experience in the development of the oil and gas industry as a model for underdeveloped countries. On the other hand, the "international oil cartel" was accused of deliberately restricting the development both of crude oil production and petroleum refining in such countries as India, Ceylon, and Brazil. Also, in line with numerous other Soviet communications of recent years, the paper praised the governments of various countries, particularly Mexico and Brazil, for policies tending to reduce or eliminate the influence of American or other foreign oil companies on their national economies.

The Soviet paper also expanded on the aid and technical assistance in exploration and development of crude oil and natural gas resources, and in the creation of an oil producing and refining industry, which the Soviet Union was rendering to various countries of Asia, Africa, and Latin America, "on mutually favorable conditions and without any political terms." It argued that help rendered to India by Soviet engineers was responsible for the increase in Indian oil production since 1957. It also referred to similar Soviet activity in progress, or planned, in Afghanistan and Pakistan.

Moscow's attempt to play upon the hopes and fears of underdeveloped nations *via* UN channels confirms the correctness of Alexander Dallin's observation regarding the "dramatic change" in Soviet behavior within the UN specialized agencies, "from the near boycott of the Stalin era to the more recent awareness of 'public relations,' especially toward the non-Western world."[18] To the extent that the USSR can exploit and control UN economic aid and welfare activities, perhaps by placing Soviet personnel in key posts, its enthusiasm for this type of propaganda will probably increase in the future.

Experts on Soviet foreign economic policy have pointed to the apparent paradox of Soviet economic aid to non-communist countries. Why, they ask themselves, should the Soviet Union pursue policies which may strengthen the economy of "bourgeois" states? Apparently this question has been raised not only in the west but also by the Chinese communists. The answer appears to be twofold. In the short run, such assistance can gain the good will of radical nationalist governments and their supporters. It can also help the Soviet Union to influence the foreign policies of the emerging nations in an anti-western direction. In the long run, by fostering the development of an industrial proletariat and a radical intelligentsia, Soviet aid in the industrialization of underdeveloped countries can accelerate the movement of these countries toward the "inevitable" socialist revolution, as ordained by the sacred texts of Marxism-Leninism. Such aid may, of course, support many lesser, shorter-run political and propaganda objectives. Among these is the enhancement, by association with Soviet policy, of the prestige of local communist parties and pro-Soviet groups.[19] Despite the fact that the Soviet leaders must regard assistance in the industrialization of the less-developed countries, in the long run, as an instrument of social revolution, it may be viewed by the governments and political elites of some of these countries

[18] Alexander Dallin, *The Soviet Union at the United Nations* (New York, 1962), p. 68.
[19] On the motives and strategy of Soviet economic aid to underdeveloped countries see, for example, Joseph S. Berliner, *Soviet Economic Aid* (New York, 1958), pp. 8-29 and 137-143; see also Kovner, *op.cit.*, chaps. II, VII.

182

with greater sympathy and less suspicion than aid rendered by western governments and private firms. As Hans Heymann, in a perceptive article in *World Politics* (July 1960) pointed out, the Soviet Union possesses the advantage of lack of involvement in and responsibility for the existing system of institutions in underdeveloped countries and thus can avoid many of the delicate problems that confront the United States. Heymann expressed the view that in the short run Soviet economic aid was a potent factor in transforming political attitudes in Afro-Asia in favor of the Soviet Union.

Soviet propaganda regarding industrialization makes extensive use of statements by pro-Soviet and communist intellectuals and politicians. The Soviet-Cuban communiqué published in *Pravda* for December 20, 1960, following the signing of trade, technical assistance, and cultural exchange agreements, contained the following statement: "The Cuban mission became convinced that, thanks to its rapid tempo of development, the Soviet Union, with its socially just way of life and its scientifically planned economy will very soon catch up to the most developed capitalist country, the United States of America, and will quickly surpass it." The same newspaper for October 11, 1961 contained an article by Sanzo Nosaka, chairman of the Central Committee of the Communist Party of Japan, hailing the program adopted by the Twenty-second Congress of the CPSU. Nosaka expressed admiration for Soviet science, which had made possible the first flights of man into the cosmos. He quoted Khrushchev to the effect that the rapid development of the Soviet economy was the most powerful instrument for attracting millions of people in the capitalist countries to the ideas of communism. As in the case of propaganda regarding the Soviet solution of problems arising in the relations among the various nationalities of the USSR, Khrushchev often refers to the economic progress of the Soviet non-Russian republics as an example of successful modernization. *Pravda* for April 26, 1960 contained a statement reportedly made by Khrushchev in a speech in Baku on the fortieth anniversary of Soviet power in Azerbaidzhan: "There has been realized the dream of the great Lenin regarding the transformation of Azerbaidzhan and the other socialist republics of Transcaucasia and Central Asia into states which are models in every way for the peoples of the enormous multi-national East."

An appraisal of the propaganda impact of Soviet foreign aid must take into account not only such hopeful statements as those by communist leaders just cited, but the skeptical observations of non-Soviet economists such as Marshall I. Goldman. In an article reprinted in the *National Observer* for February 2, 1963, from an academic journal, Dr. Goldman indicated that economic aid to underdeveloped countries was bringing "diminishing returns" to Moscow for a variety of reasons. He discussed the damage to Soviet prestige resulting from mistakes in the administration of the aid and, above all, the fact that it had done more to promote the political independence of recipient countries than to facilitate Soviet policy aims.

Particular emphasis is, naturally enough, placed in Soviet propaganda on the virtues of economic planning. For example, an article published in *Kommunist* (March 1956) on the Indian government's second Five Year Plan "sought to create the impression that Soviet economists had had great influence on the formulation of the Indian plan."[20] The article noted that the Indian Statistical Institute in Calcutta, under the direction of Professor Mahalanobis had made use of the advice of Soviet consultants. In connection with Soviet comment upon and praise for Indian economic planning, Gene D. Overstreet has noted that the Soviet publication, while welcoming Prime Minister Nehru's brand of socialism, also pointed out that this version of socialism differed from the

[20] Gene D. Overstreet, "Soviet and Communist Policy in India," the *Journal of Politics*, Vol. xx, 1958, p. 193.

Soviet one. Insofar as the Soviet leaders regarded Nehru's emphasis upon expanding the state-owned sector in Indian industry as a "progressive" policy, they could consistently praise him. But if Nehru's successors should retreat from his program "the Indian communists might fall heir to the socialist tradition established by Nehru, and, by claiming this tradition as their own, gain a parliamentary majority." In this case, "the governmental apparatus, already geared to state planning and state ownership, could be taken over by the communists, to be used for their own more drastic purposes."[21]

As we have already indicated, it would be a mistake to assume that the Soviet leaders would be content with a situation in which the influence of Soviet economic and technical progress was limited to the underdeveloped countries. Certainly many authoritative Soviet sources indicate confidence that not only the "oppressed peoples" of Asia, Africa, and Latin America, but also the working people and "progressive" intellectuals of the west will respond to the appeals of Soviet-style modernization. For example, the important official history of the CPSU published in 1959 stated that "The successes of the Seven Year Plan in the USSR will exert a tremendous influence on the working masses of the capitalist countries, and will attract to the side of socialism millions of new supporters."[22] The party history argued that following the "defeat" of the United States in the sphere of economic competition, which would require some twelve years, a "decisive movement" in favor of socialism would take place in the world. This would be followed by the winning of a majority by communist parties in elections in a number of capitalist countries. The communists would wage a struggle both inside and outside of national legislative bodies and would turn them into an instrument "to create the necessary condi-

[21] *Ibid.*, p. 194.
[22] *Istoriya kommunisticheskoi partii sovetskogo soyuza* (Moscow, 1959), p. 706.

tions for the peaceful implementation of the socialist revolution." Along somewhat similar lines, Khrushchev in his highly
significant speech of January 6, 1961, delivered to the party
organizations of the Higher Party School, the Academy of
Social Sciences, and the Institute of Marxism-Leninism, expressed confidence that the time was not far off, "when Marxism-Leninism would dominate the minds of the majority of
the population of the earth." Khrushchev expressed the opinion
that millions of people would be attracted to socialism not
because they had read books and manifestoes, but because
they could see and "feel" the attractions of socialism "in life
and in practice." Doubtless—in this very pragmatic if boast-
ful statement—he had in mind the possible effects of such
forms of propaganda as Soviet participation in international
exhibitions, for example, and the impact of Soviet space spectaculars.

Post-Stalin Soviet propaganda revives the old Soviet view
that even the American and British peoples can be won over to
Soviet "socialism." The "dean" of Soviet economists, S. G.
Strumilin, on page 40 of his 1961 book, *Problems of Socialism
and Communism in the USSR*, indicates that the installation
of a "socialist" economy in the United States and England
would actually be easier than it was in Russia. Also, the "ideological servants of imperialism" were ridiculed at the Twenty-
second CPSU Congress for trying to "console" their "masters"
with the argument that communist ideas have no attraction
for western countries. Khrushchev, in his draft report on the
party program, asserted that communism was gaining strength
wherever working people were "humiliated by capitalism." He
cited a letter received by *Pravda* from an unemployed American, one Arthur Stone, who, he alleged, stated that the CPSU
program served as a source of strength to the workers in
capitalist countries.

Presidium member and Comintern veteran Otto Kuusinen in
an article in *Pravda* for April 23, 1960 made the following

statement: "We have an unlimited wealth of remarkable ideas—they would suffice also for America. For example, the brilliant idea of the complete elimination of both economic and political crises! The idea of the liquidation of unemployment! The idea of the shortening of the working day without reducing pay! The idea of eliminating the poverty of the popular masses! All of these ideas have been tried and proved in practice." Kuusinen went on to say that these ideas could not be applied by capitalist governments, which were controlled by the "monopolistic bourgeoisie." Consequently, the perspectives of contemporary capitalism were unenviable.

In their attempts to gain the good will of industrial workers, and also businessmen in advanced industrial countries, Soviet propagandists place heavy emphasis upon the alleged benefits of trade with the Soviet Union. The allure of trade is held out to industrial countries such as Germany, Austria, England, or Canada, while at the same time the United States is accused of attempting to control and restrict the foreign trade of these countries. This line of argument has been applied with particular assiduousness to West Germany ever since the death of Stalin. One of the first major post-Stalin efforts along this line was in a speech made by A. I. Mikoyan at the Fourth Congress of the Socialist Unity Party of Germany, in April 1954. Mikoyan set a pattern for Soviet post-Stalin propaganda. He accused the United States and the Bonn government of subjecting trade and cultural intercourse between East and West Germany to "unnatural" restrictions. The business and cultural circles of West Germany, according to Mikoyan, desired the re-establishment of commercial contacts between East and West Germany. Similarly, Khrushchev, in a speech delivered in Austria in 1960, argued that the Soviet Union offered the advantages of a stable market for Austrian goods that would be profitable for Austrian manufacturers and would furnish a guarantee to Austrian workers against unemployment. These and similar Soviet arguments regarding the value of trade with the USSR should be assessed within the framework of Khrushchev's admission that "we value trade least for economic reasons and most for political purposes."[23]

With the possible exception of Soviet space triumphs, industrial growth rates furnish the most telling evidence of the material success of Soviet socialism. Since this aspect of Soviet progress—and the propaganda connected with it—is well-known, we shall deal with it briefly. As Governor Nelson A. Rockefeller of New York pointed out at a conference on automation held at Cooperstown, N.Y., on June 1, 1960, "although the USSR's claims about the tempo of its economic progress are generally exaggerated, after all due allowance for overstatement is made the sober evidence emerges that her postwar growth trend has been at about six per cent annual rate as against four per cent for us." The Governor went on to say that the superior Soviet growth rate made it harder for the United States to combat Soviet propaganda in the underdeveloped countries and strengthened the Soviet claim that the Soviet system was the best for promoting the economic growth those nations sought. Naturally, rapid Soviet economic growth exerts its most profound effect on world public opinion during periods of recession in the United States. There is no doubt, as we have already indicated by reference to authoritative Soviet statements, that confidence in continued superiority of the growth rates of socialist economies over those of the capitalist countries constitutes the major basis for the Kremlin's belief that communism will achieve world hegemony.

Soviet propaganda, both domestic and foreign, includes a steady stream of statements, charts, diagrams, and statistics designed to drive home the point that the USSR is winning the battle of growth rates against the United States. A typical example was publication of statements on the front page of

[23] U.S., Department of State, *The Communist Economic Threat* (Washington: U.S. Government Printing Office, 1959), p. 4.

Pravda for November 18, 1961 asserting that by 1980 the USSR alone would produce one and one-half times as much electric power as present total world production. By 1980, according to the statement, the United States would be inferior to the USSR both in total output of electric power and in power output per capita. Similar statements were issued following the Twenty-second Congress concerning all of the other main indicators of national economic growth.

Appraisal of the validity of Soviet claims of superior economic growth is a highly technical problem with which we cannot concern ourselves here. Certain observations regarding the propaganda use made of growth rate claims are appropriate, however. The Soviet claims are generally highly selective, and tend to neglect fields in which Soviet performance lags far behind western countries, such as services, or certain new branches of technology. They also do far less than justice to the economic growth achieved since World War II by Japan, the German Federal Republic, Italy, France, Holland, and Belgium, which on the average have probably achieved even more rapid growth than the Soviet Union. They tend to ignore such matters as quality and variety of products. Above all, they tend to create the false impression that rapid Soviet industrial growth is automatically translatable into standards of living and of social welfare superior to those enjoyed in the western democracies.

We have already referred to Soviet expressions of confidence that the USSR will relatively soon enjoy the world's highest standard of living. The Soviet timetable, at least in terms of published statements, appears to be one of surpassing Europe "in the consumption of many of the most important articles" by 1965 and, as already indicated, getting ahead of the United States in per capita production by 1980. It should be noted, however, that statements made about surpassing American production levels do not specify articles of consumption. In fact, Soviet statements about specific items, such as shoes or articles of clothing, are vague and relatively modest. They are usually couched in terms of supplying "enough" of these articles. Such statements should be interpreted in the light of current Soviet doctrine that, while communism will create an economy of abundance, the tastes and requirements of communists should be "healthy" and "sensible"—presumably in terms of criteria established by the party.

If the USSR were to succeed in implanting in the minds of workers and farmers throughout the world an image of a "communist welfare state," this image might eventually become the most potent instrument of Soviet propaganda. Until recently, at least in advanced western countries, communism has been associated not only with police terror and intellectual regimentation but also with material poverty and drabness. As far as public health, education, and social insurance policies were concerned, the western appraisal of the Soviet record may have been excessively unfavorable even during Stalin's lifetime, when the foundations for the impressive progress of the last seven or eight years were being laid.[24] Summing up the Soviet record in social welfare, Alec Nove points out that even during the Stalin era "much attention was paid to the expansion and the improvement of health services and education, and fairly generous rules adopted in regard to such things as sickness benefits and paid vacations." However, in the late 1930's there was some retrogression in Soviet social services and "it was only after Stalin's death that moves got under way to restore the conditions which had prevailed until the mid-1930s." In recent years, "much more has been or is being done to improve old-age pensions and disability pay, to reduce working hours, to build more housing, and to pro-

[24] See, for example, Alec Nove, "Social Welfare in the USSR," *Problems of Communism*, No. 1, Vol. IX (January-February, 1960), pp. 1-10. This article, and the commentaries by Solomon M. Schwarz, Bertram D. Wolfe, Bertrand de Jouvenel, Peter Wiles, Richard Lowenthal, and Asoka Mehta present a well-balanced evaluation of the merits and defects of Soviet social welfare policies.

vide more consumer services, even though the Soviet citizen certainly still has—and probably will continue to have—much to complain about."[25] Mr. Nove's careful estimate should serve as a warning to the western democracies not to underestimate the material and organizational reality underlying the Soviet propaganda challenge, even in the field of social welfare.

However, in spite of recent improvements, which are continuing, there are still grave weaknesses on the Soviet side in terms of a comparison between Soviet and western European or American standards of living. In fact, some careful studies of official Soviet price and wage figures indicated that in 1959 the average Soviet worker had to put in about eight per cent more time than he did in 1928 in order to provide for his family the same average weekly supply of bread, potatoes, beef, butter, eggs, milk, and sugar. The work time required in 1959 for the purchase of clothing was estimated at from eight to sixteen times longer in Moscow than in New York City. As far as durable goods were concerned, a joint party-government decree published on October 16, 1959 envisaged considerable increases in production of refrigerators, television sets, washing machines, metal goods, electric irons, and kitchenware. Automobiles, the lowest priced of which cost about twenty-five thousand rubles and for which a Soviet citizen might expect to wait for many years, were not even mentioned in the above decree. Since prices of consumer goods have normally been kept high in the Soviet Union by a complicated system of sales taxes, often described as turnover taxes, Khrushchev's announcement in May 1960 of the intended abolition of personal income taxes by 1965 was relatively unimportant—especially in view of the partial suspension of this measure in 1962, and of the raising of prices of meat and dairy products in the same year.

Sharp inequality in wages and other forms of income has been a characteristic feature of the Soviet economy since the

[25] *Ibid.*, p. 8.

early 1930's. It is true that the post-Stalin regime, beginning in 1956, moved to raise the pay scales of the lowest paid workers. However, all relevant Soviet texts, including the recent CPSU program, make it clear that until the distant goal of full communism is achieved inequality of rewards will remain the basis of the Soviet system of distribution of goods and services.

Rents have always been very low in the USSR. Still, in terms of labor time required to pay for rent the Soviet worker may still be worse off than his American or western European counterpart. Despite considerable progress in recent years in solving the acute housing problem, the Soviet Union still is one of the most backward industrial countries in this crucial aspect of material and social welfare. This fact, generally recognized by all objective students of the Soviet economy, does not prevent such propaganda releases as the Soviet-Cuban communiqué referred to earlier from asserting that "in the USSR the problem of housing—one of the most difficult problems of humanity in the capitalist world—is being successfully solved." Timothy Sosnovy, probably the leading expert in the west on Soviet housing, wrote recently that "today, the predominant type of dwelling in Soviet cities is one room in an apartment shared with others, with a kitchen for common use."[26]

Article 120 of the USSR constitution provides that Soviet citizens have the right to "material security" in old age as well as in the event of sickness and loss of capacity to work. In this connection, the constitution refers to social insurance of workers and employees, medical aid, and the provision of health resorts at the expense of the state. The most comprehensive available American study of the organization of Soviet welfare services, published in 1961, stated that the basic social insurance system covered only about forty to forty-five per cent of the Soviet population. It applied primarily to wage earners

[26] Timothy Sosnovy, "Town Planning and Housing," *Survey*, No. 38, October, 1961, pp. 170-178. Quotation on p. 176.

and salaried office workers.[27] The Soviet pension system favors the "best" workers, trade-union members, and those in leading industries and unhealthy occupations. The pension system was greatly improved by the law of July 14, 1956, which increased the former minimum pension for old age by six times, and the former minimum for invalids and survivors by six to seven times.

The picture of considerable progress, accompanied by exaggerated claims, presented by Soviet social insurance is duplicated in the field of public health and medical services. It is true that medical services are free in the Soviet Union, although Soviet citizens of course indirectly pay for medical care in the form of taxes necessary to cover its cost. Citizens must usually pay for medicines and they may if they wish avail themselves of the services of relatively high-priced private physicians. As one would expect in such an elitist system, the highest-ranking party leaders and other executive personnel are treated in the best clinics and sanatoriums. The Soviet authorities claim that their country holds first place in the number of doctors relative to its population—a claim which makes a powerful impression in many parts of the world. At the same time, the Soviet press frequently voices criticism of defects in medical service, such as a shortage of medical equipment, the high cost of drugs, and the lack of first-aid facilities. Soviet sources also claim that the death rate in the USSR is the lowest in the world. They do not, however, furnish death rates for individual diseases. The death rate figures disseminated by the Soviet authorities reflect, according to non-Soviet experts, not only the commendable progress achieved by Soviet medicine, but also the very high percentage of young people in the Soviet population, resulting from such causes as very great losses among the older age groups inci-

[27] Bernice Madison, "The Organization of Welfare Services," in Cyril E. Black, ed. *The Transformation of Russian Society* (Cambridge, Mass., 1960), especially pp. 529-540.

dent to military operations, disease, and deprivations during World War II.

It is possible, as Mr. Nove suggests, that one of several motives for current Soviet improvements in welfare services is the realization on the part of the Soviet leaders that increased contacts with the non-Soviet world require such improvements if a favorable impression is to be made upon non-communist foreigners. When this writer commented favorably to a Soviet citizen of Jewish extraction, whom he met by chance in Kiev in 1956, upon some of the post-Stalin reforms, the latter immediately replied that these reforms were designed to impress foreigners. Whatever the motivation underlying them may be, however, the reforms are real and substantial, and their impact upon world opinion will probably increase in the future.

Soviet propaganda, in harmony with the official Marxist-Leninist ideology, emphasizes that Soviet socialism is a science both of mastery of the material world and also of the transformation of human nature. The "new man" created by the communist party and the Soviet state is, in this view, actuated by the principles of "communist morality." These are said to include socialist patriotism, internationalism, a conscientious attitude toward personal and social obligations, and "socialist humanism." All of these virtues are held to be the product of the "cultural revolution" which, according to such basic Soviet texts as the new CPSU program, has already been carried out in the USSR. The cultural revolution, according to the program, freed the working people of Russia from "spiritual slavery" and ignorance and gave them access to all of the cultural values accumulated by mankind. Even greater achievements lie ahead. The communist culture of the future "which will have absorbed and will develop all the best that has been created by world culture, will be a new, higher stage in the cultural progress of mankind."[28] As a skeptical American

[28] The fullest treatment of the "cultural revolution" available still appears to be G. G. Karpov, *O sovetskoi kulture i kulturnoi revolyutsii v sssr.*

political scientist puts it, the Soviet "cultural revolution" serves the purpose of educating the population for life in an industrial society and at the same time it also accomplishes the "political socialization of the entire population."[29] Isaac Deutscher notes that Adlai Stevenson, speaking from observation, has remarked that "education and the reading of serious literature are 'a universal pastime' in the Soviet Union." Mr. Deutscher then adds his own opinion that "they are a universal passion rather than a pastime." Literary classics, Russian and non-Russian are sold, Mr. Deutscher observes approvingly, in millions, even tens of millions, of copies, and he adds that the Soviet public is not exposed to the "gutter literature and gutter entertainment" rampant in the west.[30] The findings of Mr. Stevenson and Mr. Deutscher are significant in at least two respects. First, they are largely correct. In the second place, they indicate the powerful impression which Soviet cultural progress can make upon both non-socialist and socialist foreign intellectuals.

While the political partisanship and the utilitarianism dominant in the Soviet approach to education violate the traditions of western liberal education at its best, both the qualitative and quantitative achievements of Soviet education are most impressive. Soviet propaganda advertises these achievements energetically. A Soviet statistical handbook published in 1961 devoted one of its longest sections to attempting to prove that Soviet education was superior in every way to that of the United States. This publication claimed that there were more teachers, more students in higher educational institutions, and more engineers in Russia than in America.[31] Although such Soviet claims are false, insofar as they refer to numbers of students or percentages of the total population studying in the higher educational institutions, they are in large part correct

[29] Alfred G. Meyer in *Slavic Review*, Vol. xx, No. 3 (October, 1961), pp. 371-372.
[30] Isaac Deutscher, *The Great Contest* (New York & London, 1960), p. 27.
[31] *SSR-S Sha* (Moscow, 1961), pp. 113-126.

insofar as they refer to the training of qualified engineers and scientists.[32] The current achievements of Soviet education, especially on the university level, are based upon a solid foundation established under the leadership of Lenin and Stalin. According to a recent Soviet publication, by 1940 there were already 290,000 graduate engineers in the Soviet Union compared with 156,000 in the United States.[33] According to the 1959 Soviet census, 3,778,000 Soviet citizens had been graduated from higher educational institutions. From the Soviet equivalent of American secondary schools, 9,936,000 had been graduated. Including correspondence and night schools, which are highly developed in the USSR, about 50,000,000 persons were enrolled in educational institutions of all kinds in 1959. Some indication of the quantitative progress of Soviet education is given by the fact that, while at the time of the Bolshevik revolution there were about ninety institutions of higher learning in the Russian empire, Moscow alone has that many today.

To evaluate Soviet claims to world educational leadership involves as many technical problems as the appraisal of Soviet economic growth or the Soviet standard of living. Clearly, the Soviet educational achievement is a substantial one, and it makes a profound impression upon intellectuals, educators, and students from most countries of the world. Indeed, this fact itself is skillfully exploited by Soviet propagandists, who often broadcast expressions of admiration or even of alarm emanating from western educational sources. The encouragement of all kinds of education by the Soviet party and government leadership, and the obvious thirst for learning felt by all strata of the Soviet population are appealing.

Broad access to education in the USSR, and the fact that

[32] The *New York Times* for January 15, 1962 published an extensive summary of a study made by Nicholas DeWitt for the National Science Foundation indicating, among other things, that the dynamic growth of Soviet scientific manpower posed a serious threat to the western world.

[33] *O programme KPSS*, Part I, p. 510.

graduates of Soviet educational institutions are guaranteed employment, naturally meet with sympathetic responses, particularly in underdeveloped countries and also, to a somewhat lesser degree, in advanced industrial societies. The impact of these appeals would of course be greatly intensified if the western industrial nations were again to experience a major economic depression. In addition to these fairly obvious appeals of Soviet educational development, many foreigners are deeply impressed by the sense of moral purpose and dedication to social and cultural values professed by Soviet scholars, teachers, and students with whom they come in contact on what are often very carefully guided tours of the USSR.

Of course, the Soviet model of cultural modernization—perhaps not quite the correct term, for in so many ways Soviet culture strikes sophisticated westerners as Victorian—has, from the point of view of one who does not accept the ideological premises on which it rests, serious flaws. These include regimentation, censorship, secrecy, suppression, and other severe limitations on freedom of thought and expression. The 1961 central committee publication, *Problems of Ideological Work*, already referred to in this study, contained abundant evidence of the continued pervasiveness of these fundamental defects of Soviet cultural and intellectual life. For example, a Central Committee Decree dated July 31, 1959 and not previously published, sharply criticized the leading Soviet philosophical magazine because it was allegedly not sufficiently guided by Lenin's prescription that "without a solid philosophical foundation no natural science and no materialism can withstand the struggle against the pressure of bourgeois ideas and the restoration of the bourgeois world outlook."[34] Another decree published in this volume criticized the supposedly voluntary All-Union Society for the Dissemination of Political and Scientific Knowledge for permitting many of its workers and supporters to manifest "lack of principle" and

[34] *Voprosy ideologicheskoi raboty, op.cit.,* pp. 279-282.

197

even to present lectures of an "enlightenment" character. In communist terminology, this criticism constituted an attack on the "bourgeois" philosophy of the eighteenth century "enlightenment." It certainly indicates the continued intensity and thoroughness of the Soviet system for shaping public opinion.[35]

One product of Soviet efforts, and, according to Soviet sources, of the Russian social system, which reinforces the effects of all kinds of Soviet propaganda, is the success of Soviet activities in outer space. The launching by the Soviet Union on October 4, 1957 of the first artificial satellite attracted extraordinarily wide and keen attention. A distinguished social scientist has written that "the only other event in recent history that can match Sputnik in general public awareness was the explosion of the atom bomb in 1945."[36] The very widespread western use of the Russian word sputnik instead of the more cumbersome English term, artificial earth satellite, is, incidentally, a minor but significant indication of the propaganda impact of Soviet priority in many aspects of space technology. On the basis of the results of a number of public opinion polls, Almond found that, following the launching of the first Soviet earth satellite, "one of the most stable popular beliefs of the post-war era, the belief in the scientific and technological superiority of the United States," had been rudely shaken.[37] Moreover, public opinion polls showed that in a number of major western European countries, including West Germany, there was a considerable shift in estimates of the relative total military strength of the USSR and the United States in favor of the former. Another possible effect of the Soviet satellites was to produce shifts of opinion toward neutrality—although this

[35] *Ibid.*, pp. 137-143.
[36] Gabriel A. Almond, "Public Opinion and the Development of Space Technology," a contribution to unclassified RAND Corporation Report R-362-RC, "International Political Implications of Activities in Outer Space" (RAND Corporation, 1960), p. 112. Almond's article is on pp. 109-132.
[37] *Ibid.*, p. 115.

effect was not produced in Germany.[38] On the other hand, in Great Britain at least, the percentage polled who would side with the United States in the event of a Soviet-American war actually increased in the period from August 1955 to November 1957.[39] Almond concluded his article with a number of somber prognostications regarding the possible future impact upon NATO of a combination of Soviet superiority in space technology and concurrent reforms of Soviet internal policy. He expressed the opinion that "The current competition for economic growth and technological development may constitute a gradual and increasingly compelling demonstration of Soviet strength and moral and political tolerability," which might slowly turn NATO into a hollow shell and "put the European powers into a position in which they will have somehow to come to terms with the Soviet Union."[40]

The public opinion data on which Professor Almond's article was based were gathered in the United States and western Europe. It seems likely that the impact of Soviet space achievements was even greater in Asia, Africa, and Latin America. In Japan, according to a Japanese study supplied to us by official American sources, when the first earth satellite was successfully launched in the USSR on October 4, 1957, the Japanese became interested in Soviet science and technology at once, and newspapers and magazines printed articles on Soviet science and technology. Simultaneously, newspapers, magazines, and books imported from the USSR increased, and Nauka, the sales agent for Soviet publications, received orders for Soviet periodicals one and a half times as large as in the preceding year. Appropriate books were printed in second editions to meet the demand.

Soviet space science achieved a powerful impact even on Americans. Some American tourists in Russia were reported by

[38] *Ibid.*, pp. 115-118.
[39] *Ibid.*, p. 120.
[40] *Ibid.*, p. 131.

the *New York Times* for August 30, 1961 to be suffering from "Sputnikitis," consisting of "a deep feeling of inferiority relative to Russia, based upon the assumption that since Soviet rockets are better than ours then everything else Soviet must now be or will soon be better than what we have." This observation followed the earth-circling flights, in April and August, respectively, of Soviet "cosmonauts" Yuri Gagarin and Gherman Titov. As Almond's analysis indicated, the propaganda impact of Soviet space technology was somewhat mixed. In many ways it stiffened resistance to Soviet pressures by accentuating consciousness of the Soviet threat to the west. Certainly it served—to a degree impossible to estimate—as a stimulus to counter-measures, at least in the United States.

It is difficult to estimate the success achieved by Soviet propaganda in attempting to enhance the prestige of communist ideology and institutions by associating them with earth satellites, ICBMs, and cosmonauts. The propaganda effort has been enormous. *Pravda*, in an editorial for November 4, 1957 described Soviet earth satellites as "a vivid expression of the great advantages of the socialist over the capitalist system," and a direct result of the "wise leadership of the communist party." Similarly, immediately following Gagarin's flight, Khrushchev stated that the flight represented "a new triumph of the ideas of Lenin, a confirmation of the correctness of Marxist-Leninist teachings." Khrushchev also linked Gagarin's flight with "the movement of the peoples toward communism." As one can learn from an attractive brochure, "The First Man in Space"—with a smiling Gagarin on its front cover—the CPSU Central Committee and other leadership echelons of the USSR declared that the Soviet people placed its "victories" in space at the service of mankind, at the service of peace.[41]

The very name—Vostok—Russian for "East"—used for

[41] *Pravda*, April 14, 1961; "The First Man in Space," Crosscurrents Press (New York, 1961), pp. 56-58.

Soviet space ships, has obvious propaganda connotations. Soviet propaganda naturally made the most of the extraordinarily spectacular "group flight" of Andrian Nikolaev and Pavel Popovich, in August 1962 in the space ships Vostok III and Vostok IV. The Chuvash ancestry of Nikolaev, incidentally underscored Soviet claims regarding the advantages, for members of previously backward peoples, of Soviet nationality policy. Popovich was quoted in *Izvestiya* for August 13, 1962, as having said, just before his flight into space, "I go to cosmic flight with great pride for our great Soviet people, blazing a trail for all mankind to the communist future."

Khrushchev, according to the newspaper *Literaturnaya Gazeta* for August 19, 1962, referred—with the exploits of Nikolaev and Popovich fresh in the world's memory—to socialism and communism as the "reliable cosmodrome," from which mankind would storm the vastness of the universe. The achievements of the Soviet cosmonauts were brought to the attention of the world television audience and were for days top newspaper and radio news everywhere. It is a moot question to what extent their impact may have been offset by varied American achievements, earlier and later, in space science—both in manned flight and by Telstar, the Mariner II Venus probe, and other successes—and by the contrast between Soviet secrecy and relative American frankness and openness regarding the United States manned space program. The latter does appear to have been a significant factor as far as western European, and, of course, United States opinion were concerned—particularly highlighted, perhaps, at least for Americans, when Soviet cosmonaut Titov and American astronaut Glenn sparred in friendly verbal rivalry on joint television appearances during Titov's United States visit in April 1962.

As was noted in Chapter II, Soviet May Day slogans gave diminishing prominence to space achievements after 1958. This might be interpreted as indicating that the Kremlin regarded them as a wasting asset, as propaganda, on either the domestic or the international levels, or both. Such an estimate, if it was made, could of course change with the flux of international events.

A quantitative content analysis, by Donald Puchala, of Soviet radio broadcasts from August 11 through August 27, 1962, about the Nikolaev-Popovich exploits, yielded interesting results regarding the strategy by which Moscow links space achievements to modernization and other major propaganda themes. In 203 broadcasts thirty-four themes were identified. Technical and scientific themes were found to be most frequent, followed by political themes. In these the space achievements that had been emphasized by the scientific and technical themes were linked to the "socialist system" and to Soviet foreign policy or even to ultimate communist world revolution. A portion of the political propaganda consisted of allegations of dejection in American official circles because of the Soviet flights.

A great emphasis in the broadcasts to western Europe was placed on Soviet scientific prowess and superiority. Probably this emphasis was intended to foster the impression of overwhelming Soviet power. The broadcasts to Europe were mostly in English and were apparently directed toward an elite audience. However, those to Japan, in Japanese, to Indonesia, in Indonesian, and Latin America, in Spanish, were presumably intended for mass audiences. In contrast to detailed scientific reports to Europe, scientific reports to the non-western world were phrased in general terms of Soviet "progress," "welfare," etc. Also, the non-western world was warned of alleged United States plans to convert outer space to military uses. While seeking to undermine the confidence of the west, and to derogate America, the Nikolaev-Popovich propaganda—skillfully and systematically —sought to implant, especially in the under-developed countries, an image of Soviet and "socialist" scientific leadership.

The close concatenation of the Nikolaev-Popovich flight with that of American astronaut Walter Schirra offers an opportunity to obtain a rough comparative indication of Russian and American psychological impacts deriving from the space competition. For this purpose the reporting of these exploits in the leading French newspaper, *Le Monde,* was studied. *Le Monde* in seven issues in August 1962 and in two issues in October 1962, reported, respectively, on the Nikolaev-Popovich and the Schirra experiments. The Russian flights, besides being referred to in more than three times as many issues, were also reported much more prominently than was that of Schirra.

While most of *Le Monde's* reporting was informational rather than evaluative, the French opinion organ did say in its August 17 issue that "The Soviets have demonstrated that they have maintained their leadership in the space competition." Also, in commenting, on October 4, on Schirra's success, *Le Monde* stated that, "one can measure the distance that the Americans have still to cover in order to overtake the Soviets in this field."

Le Monde paid tribute to the magnificence of the Soviet scientific achievement, but at the same time—in an editorial published August 14—pointed out that admiration for the Soviet effort could not prevent "a certain apprehension concerning its possible use." It would be interesting to compare *Le Monde's* worried but generous response to the Soviet achievement—and its friendly reporting of the more modest American space victory—with those of representative Asian and African newspapers. One speculates that the results would demonstrate the complexity of the impact of the space race on world opinion, and especially the role of ideological predispositions in its evaluation.

We have dealt in this chapter with a few aspects of the propaganda of modernization, Soviet style. The basic theme of this propaganda is, as Armstrong puts it, that "the USSR must be emulated because it is—aside from 'historical accidents' like the United States—the most successful country on earth."[42] And, as the same author adds, the USSR insinuates that "its wishes must be followed and its controls accepted because it is the world's strongest country." Perhaps in conclusion it should be emphasized once again that while the emphasis in Soviet propaganda is upon success and strength, these terms are given a very broad application. Soviet propaganda seeks acceptance of the idea that Soviet socialism is already superior to western democracy in almost every field of human endeavor. As the editorial in *Kommunist*, No. 15, 1960, echoing Khrushchev's speeches, states, "The United States is losing its former exclusive economic position; the Soviet Union has already surpassed it in the development of a number of branches of science, and in the spheres of education, culture, and art." The editorial proceeded to state that it would not deal with the superiority of the Soviet political and social order, which it regarded as self-evident.

Soviet claims regarding artistic and cultural superiority, irritating though they may be to most Americans and western Europeans, should not be complacently dismissed. If Walter Z. Laqueur is right, "Soviet civilization is in some respects closer than the western culture to the feelings and aspirations of the intelligentsia in the backward countries, as Soviet economic planning is preferred to western capitalism—or a mixed economy."[43] Like other students of the socio-cultural scene in the underdeveloped countries, Laqueur sees in the pattern of poverty and anti-westernism much that predisposes the confused and struggling intellectuals of these lands to sympathy

[42] Armstrong, *op.cit.*, p. 346.
[43] Walter Z. Laqueur, *The Soviet Union and the Middle East* (New York, 1959), p. 292.

with Soviet "socialist realism." It may be that the very dog-matism and partisanship of Soviet culture which makes it repugnant to sensitive or sophisticated western intellectuals is appealing to peoples who have lost a sense of identity with their past and are looking for new and clear patterns.

Another aspect of the challenge of the Soviet model which should be mentioned is its appeal to the idealism, the altruism, and the craving for intellectual and emotional security of many artists and scientists in both East and West. Perhaps, as Ulam and others have suggested, the appeal of Marxism be-comes a wasting asset wherever industrial society strikes firm and stable roots. It is too early to be certain that Ulam's view is more correct than that of Lewis S. Feuer, who emphasizes that present-day America is "out of step" with most of the world, where "the magnetic power of Marxism, unparalleled in the history of mankind, has drawn into its ideological orbit peoples of different continents and races, from China to Burma to Ghana, Moscow to Belgrade and Djakarta."[44] As Feuer emphasizes, "the communist movement which invokes the name of Marx, has tarnished the ideal which inspired his work."

Whether or not one agrees with Feuer's general point of view, his remark points to a major ineptitude of much Ameri-can foreign propaganda, one which to some degree facilitates the effectiveness of the Soviet ideological offensive. This is the tendency of American spokesmen abroad to play down the elements of planning and of social reform in the American political and economic system and to over-emphasize "free enterprise" in countries where the magnitude of goals to be achieved rapidly under difficult conditions makes a heavy measure of government direction of economic development a necessity. In such countries, the predispositions of the political and intellectual elites are on the side of "socialism" and it is

[44] Lewis S. Feuer, ed. *Marx and Engels, Basic Writings on Politics and Philosophy* (New York, 1959), Introduction.

indeed folly for Americans to permit the representatives of what Alfred G. Meyer calls "USSR Incorporated" to claim a monopoly of public planning for community welfare. It would seem a wiser policy to emphasize the welfare aspects of American "people's capitalism" and the ruthless, repressive, and in many ways reactionary characteristics of what, for want of a better term, one might call the state-monopoly industrialism of the USSR.

CHAPTER VII

TECHNIQUES

IN the remainder of this study we shall examine what appear to be some of the most important methods developed by Soviet propagandists in their effort to shape world public opinion. This chapter focuses particularly upon Soviet techniques for securing access to the attention of foreign audiences and for bolstering the credibility of Kremlin messages. It is also concerned with methods employed by Soviet opinion moulders to cope with competing communications systems.[1] Soviet communications behavior reflects the elitist and conspiratorial nature of the Soviet political system. Kecskemeti correctly emphasizes the manipulative style of Soviet propaganda, appropriate to the political structure within which it operates, when he writes that Soviet communicators "conceive their role as consisting essentially in exercising control over the audience."[2] Lasswell, noting that the aim of Soviet propaganda is "to economize the material cost of world dominance," adds that it "acts upon pessimistic assumptions about the capabilities of mankind for enlightenment by peaceful persuasion."[3]

As we pointed out in Chapter I, the manipulative-coercive aspects of Soviet propaganda confer upon it both advantages and disadvantages. Soviet propagandists must, of course, take into account the resentment and fear aroused by the Soviet drive for world domination. The controllers of communications networks in all societies are normally on guard against

[1] On the more or less common tasks confronting all propagandists, see the contributions by Daniel Lerner, Herbert Blumer, Leonard Doob, and others in Schramm, *The Process and Effects of Mass Communication.*
[2] Kecskemeti, *op.cit.*, p. 303.
[3] Harold D. Lasswell, "The Strategy of Soviet Propaganda," p. 538.

penetration of these vital channels of influence by those who would subvert the established order. One way, indeed, of approaching Soviet international propaganda behavior would be to structure research in terms of the struggle conducted by Soviet communicators and their foreign assistants to deal with difficulties resulting from the exclusion of communist propagandists from non-communist communications channels. Soviet communicators, especially since the death of Stalin, have, to be sure, devoted much ingenuity to the task of overcoming the disadvantages inherent in Soviet ideology and subversive intentions.

Soviet communications specialists assigned to work in foreign countries are instructed to make full use of all available opportunities to obtain access to news sources and communications channels. In 1955, Nikolai Palgunov, then head of TASS, in his booklet, *Bases of Information in the Newspaper: Tass and Its Role* (in Russian), pointed out that "TASS demands" that its foreign correspondents avail themselves of all rights and privileges to attend court proceedings, witness political demonstrations to observe mass moods, receive official news hand-outs, be present at press conferences, etc. And, although very circumspectly, Palgunov also urged Soviet foreign correspondents to "extract information from the life" of the peoples among whom they worked, to understand the nature of social-political forces and groupings in the countries to which they were assigned, and so forth. *The Program in Journalism*, published in 1958 by the CPSU Higher Party School, contained in its last three sections implicit instructions to Soviet journalists working in "Latin America and the East" to establish cooperative relations with "the press of the national bourgeoisie, fighting for the liberation of the economic life of the countries of the East and Latin America from foreign influence."

The handicaps under which Soviet propagandists labor are balanced by immense advantages. Ours is an era of social and cultural revolution on an unprecedented scale. The "deprivational changes" inherent in this situation—to borrow a phrase from Lasswell—were compounded by the effects of two world wars. Moscow has labored hard to exploit both the discontents and the dreams generated by the world revolution of our time. Throughout this book we have been largely preoccupied with the persistent efforts of Soviet propaganda to link Kremlin objectives with the grievances and aspirations of the various world audiences. Consequently, we shall be less concerned in these concluding chapters with the content of Soviet propaganda than with its rhetoric, semantics, organization, and channels.

In their efforts to capture and hold the attention of those whom they hope to influence, Soviet propagandists have often displayed energy, resourcefulness, and a keen sense of drama, in addition to an almost instinctive political shrewdness. Since the death of Stalin these assets have, in the pragmatic atmosphere encouraged by Khrushchev, been more freely employed than before, and they have been supplemented by the increasingly vigorous efforts of Soviet scholars to assemble detailed information regarding the history and culture of all of the world's societies. Scholar-politicians such as the Africanist I. I. Potekhin or the Orientalist B. G. Gafurov roam the world in search of data which may be useful in furtherance of Soviet foreign policy objectives. The intensification of Moscow's political intelligence effort has led to an efflorescence of both scholarly and popular literature on foreign countries. It has, however, not resulted as yet in substantial modification of the dogmatic conceptual framework in terms of which Soviet policy-makers still appear to interpret world politics. Even substantial, well-documented studies published by the Academy of Sciences of the USSR amaze the non-Soviet reader by their extreme, archaic tendentiousness. For example, in 1958 the Academy published, in Russian, *The Economy and Politics of England since the Second World War*—a well-structured work which on its second page contains the conventional, Stalinist assertion that the "crisis of English imperialism" represents one manifestation of "the decay of capitalism in the epoch of imperialism." Typical of more popular literature on foreign lands is S. Datlin's 1960 booklet, *Africa Throws Off the Chains*, which begins with a florid contrast between the "hungry, unarmed" people of Africa and their enemies "who consider themselves the bearers of civilization." Nevertheless, by helping Soviet communicators to put some factual flesh on the bare bones of dogma, the literature to which we refer has probably increased the plausibility and hence the attractiveness of Soviet propaganda.

One aspect of the ceaseless Soviet effort to capture audience attention should be mentioned at the outset because it can so easily be overlooked. This is the inclusion of a propaganda component in major economic, military, or scientific policy decisions, or at any rate in their presentation to world opinion. It could be plausibly argued, for example, that Soviet space policy, particularly the decision in 1957 to use military rockets to boost heavy earth satellites into orbit, has been governed to a considerable extent by propaganda considerations. In contrast, the United States, especially in the early stages of what the American government at first refused to admit was a contest at all, pursued a policy which was in some ways idealistic, but which was unrealistic from the point of view of the international propaganda competition.

Propaganda considerations have clearly bulked large in both the policy and public relations aspects of the Soviet foreign economic aid program. This program is systematically meshed into over-all Soviet political, military, and cultural strategy. Soviet radio broadcasts, statements by Khrushchev, visits by Soviet statesmen, and coordinated agitation by local communist party members are organized to play up such attractions as low rates of interest on Soviet loans to Afro-Asian and Latin American countries, and the stability of markets allegedly available to businessmen or governments that trade with the communist bloc.

A kind of propaganda which the Kremlin is uniquely equipped to employ might be described as propaganda by implication. This consists, often, of "menacing reminders of its nuclear power and delivery capabilities."[4] Perhaps one might also classify under this rubric such techniques as the creation, or aggravation, of international crises, of which the Berlin crisis—that of 1948-1949, and the current one inaugurated by Khrushchev in November 1958, are conspicuous examples. The instigation and nurturing of crises, accompanied by promises of a relaxation of international tensions if only the western powers will display good will, and also by demands for "summit" conferences, appear to be devices designed not only to capture world attention but also to influence it in desired directions.

It is sometimes necessary to draw a distinction between Soviet techniques for gaining access to communications channels, on the one hand, and the messages which the Soviet leaders wish, or seem to wish to convey *via* these channels. Often Moscow may be less interested in conveying a particular message than in symbolizing its willingness to enter into some sort of relationship. In a word, gestures and tokens of willingness to communicate often, in Soviet policy, replace actual communication. Proclamation of willingness to communicate may serve to distract attention from Soviet obstruction of the kind of free and easy communication which western governments favor. The appearance of communicativeness, of course, is in itself an act of communication, sometimes intended to impress a much larger audience than the one that might be reached through a particular communications channel. These observations are prompted, in part, by the tendency of the

---

[4] For a brief list of instances in which such "blackmail" has been applied by the Soviet Union in international crises, see Hans Speier, *Divided Berlin* (New York, 1961), pp. 28-30.

Soviet government to publicly proclaim its enthusiasm about international "cultural relations" and other kinds of "contacts," while in fact usually restricting such relationships to a formal, tightly controlled pattern that severely restricts the creative and fruitful exchange of ideas which otherwise might take place.

One kind of Soviet propaganda ingenuity—which is not always successful in achieving its intended purpose—consists in the studied and implicit contrasting of a policy which has aroused resentment abroad with an allegedly "new" line, that may in fact have been forced upon the USSR by the actions of another power. When the new policy is a reluctant retreat, as in the October 1962 Cuba crisis, this fact is likely to be ignored in order to foster an impression of masterfulness and consistency. Indeed, for months following Cuba Moscow boasted that its action there had saved world peace.

Referring to Soviet-western economic rivalry, Henry G. Aubrey has pointed out that, "In foreign aid, too, the Soviet bloc has been able to attract a great deal of attention simply by doing what it has not done before."[5] One might add that the USSR sometimes attracts favorable attention by making an apparently conciliatory gesture immediately after it has alarmed the world by a particularly negative or menacing action. It thus gains, for a time, the gratitude sometimes accorded to one who withdraws a threat.

Perhaps relevant to this surmise is the behavior of Mr. Fedorenko, successor to the dour Valerian Zorin as head of the Soviet United Nations delegation. Interviewed on his arrival in New York in January 1963, Fedorenko apologized for not speaking English but then smilingly stated that Russian was a fine language for mutual understanding, frank conversation, friendship, peaceful coexistence, and progress. Thus he sought, perhaps, to alter the image of intransigence associated with

[5] Henry G. Aubrey, *Coexistence: Economic Challenge and Response* (Washington, D.C., 1961), p. 13.

Zorin's presentation of Soviet policy during the acute crisis over Cuba a few months before.

Moscow seems to enjoy, and often to achieve propaganda gains, by playing upon the hopes—and the lapses of memory—of "bourgeois" audiences. When the Soviet Union, in February 1962, released U-2 pilot Francis Gary Powers and permitted him to return to the United States, world attention was automatically attracted. There was a tendency for the American press to view this action as almost a benevolent one. Soviet propaganda hailed it as a step intended to relax international tensions. At the same time the Soviet communications media almost ignored the accompanying United States release of Soviet intelligence operative Colonel Rudolf Abel. Fidel Castro seems, incidentally, to have also used a Soviet-style threat-withdrawal technique in negotiations with the United States for release of prisoners taken in the abortive April 1961 Bay of Pigs invasion.

Closely associated with the persistent—and insistent—Soviet demand for attention is the predilection, probably stemming originally from the moral indignation so conspicuous in early Leninism, for "exposing" and "unmasking" non-Soviet politicians, diplomats, and national leaders. It will be recalled that Lenin, in *What Is To Be Done?* demanded that his followers be aware of—and react to—all forms of social injustice, and that they seek to merge all individual agitational and propaganda efforts into one formidable stream of pressure. Later, of course, this mobilization and focusing function was taken over by the leaders of the Soviet state. In the meantime, the use of such works as *What Is To Be Done?* in the training of Soviet propagandists has helped to preserve, in contemporary Soviet propaganda, Lenin's predilection for accusation, vilification, and "unmasking."

The continued influence exercised by this tradition is exemplified in such typical Soviet newspaper headlines as that of *Izvestiya* for June 29, 1960, reading, "The mask has been

213

torn off, the Pharisees are exposed." This headline, seeming somewhat out of place in the communist press because of its biblical connotation, related to Soviet "exposure" of the United States position at the ten-nation Geneva Disarmament Conference. The U-2 episode, a few weeks later, furnished a magnificent pretext for striking a lofty moral note. So too, did the death of Patrice Lumumba in 1961 and the subsequent tribulations of Lumumba's political associate, Antoine Gizenga. For weeks in late 1961 and early 1962, Soviet propaganda conducted a strident campaign for which the slogan was "The Life of Antoine Gizenga Is in Danger." And, according to *Barron's* Weekly for January 7, 1963, pro-Soviet elements in the Congo were forcing residents of Elizabethville to hang Lumumba's picture on their walls. Such vigorous agitation— Angola, Goa, and other trouble spots furnished additional opportunities—indicated the continued devotion of Soviet communicators to the Leninist tradition of simultaneously proclaiming Soviet virtue and righteous indignation, while contrasting this noble image with that of a malevolent but decaying "imperialism." Even such an episode as the sinking of the United States nuclear submarine Thresher in April 1963 was exploited by communist propaganda. The Soviet press echoed Leftist Japanese agitation which sought to turn the Thresher disaster into an instrument for weakening US-Japanese political-military arrangements, thus continuing an old effort to play upon Japanese anxieties and resentments dating back to the dropping of atomic bombs in 1945.

Soviet success in attracting attention is facilitated by the centralization of control of Soviet propaganda, and the very high degree of congruence between Soviet policy and propaganda. It also reflects Moscow's determination to exploit to the full its organizational advantages. The propaganda exploitation of diplomatic negotiations, and particularly of international conferences, is perhaps the oldest and most highly developed Soviet technique for attracting attention. An early manifestation of this aspect of Soviet international propaganda behavior was the organization, a few weeks after Soviet seizure of power, of an openly identified propaganda section in the Commissariat of Foreign Affairs, headed by Karl Radek. This agency published newspapers in German, Hungarian, Turkish, and other languages. After the signature of the Brest-Litovsk peace treaty, organizational direction of foreign propaganda activity was transferred to the central committee of the communist party, which in any case had already been making propaganda policy. This move, which set a pattern subsequently adhered to faithfully, was designed to partially blunt foreign criticism of Soviet subversive activity. It was also aimed to comply with provisions, in Soviet treaties with the central powers, pledging the Soviet government—but not the communist party—to refrain from conducting revolutionary propaganda against the governments of the other signatory states.[6]

One of the few published systematic case studies of Soviet propaganda exploitation of diplomatic negotiations is an article by Douglas Waples with the felicitous title "Publicity Versus Diplomacy: Notes on the Reporting of the 'Summit' Conferences."[7] As Waples observes, the Big-Three Wartime Conferences, as well as the Potsdam Conference of August 1945, "produced substantial results by means of compromise." The compromises resulted from private discussions and were reported only in official communiqués. In contrast, the highly publicized Summit Meeting of July 1955 and the Conference of Foreign Ministers of October 1955 did not produce any significant results. Waples' view that this difference in results was substantially affected by the "glare of publicity" which attended the 1955 conferences seems to this writer to be ex-

[6] Fischer, *Soviets in World Affairs*, 2nd ed., Vol. I, pp. 34, 45, 75-78; see also E. H. Carr, *The Bolshevik Revolution*, Vol. III (London and New York, 1953), pp. 18, 172-174.
[7] *Public Opinion Quarterly*, Vol. XX, Spring, 1956, No. 1, pp. 308-314.

aggerated. Nevertheless, his observations on Soviet exploitation of the propaganda possibilities inherent in the 1955 conferences are astute. Thus he points out that *Pravda*, before the Conference of Heads of State in July, "made big play of Bulganin's optimistic and conciliatory speech before leaving for Geneva and stressed the recent peace moves of the Soviet Union: the Helsinki and Leningrad Peace Assemblies, the World Mothers' Conference at Lausanne, Nehru's visits to Soviet capitals, happy Soviet relations with Tito, the Austrian Treaty, and others."

The Soviet propaganda machine, then, went all-out in drawing attention to happy prospects for improved international relations if only the other governments concerned supported the constructive proposals of the USSR. As Waples notes, *Pravda* purposely maintained a more hopeful attitude before, during, and after the Conference than did the western press. This official optimism was intended to facilitate the Soviet objective of creating the impression that a new era could dawn in international relations if only Soviet good will were shared by western governments.

In his comment on the October 1955 Conference, Waples emphasizes the use made by the Soviet delegation, and the Soviet press, of statements in western newspapers which could be cited to support the Soviet position. The Soviet Union, he believes, "profited from the 'discipline' of its press to the disadvantage of the Western powers." Waples also expresses the opinion that "Molotov's ability to work selectively on particular power audiences through his captive press is perhaps a sufficient reason for his insisting on an open conference despite the British preference for a closed conference." This statement is interesting, because it calls attention to one of the apparent paradoxes of Soviet international propaganda methods. Despite the extreme secrecy practiced by the Soviet rulers, they also make almost a fetish of publicity at international political conferences. While some western statesmen and scholars, such as George F. Kennan and Louis J. Halle, emphasize the importance of quiet and privacy if fruitful results are to flow from east-west negotiations, the Soviets persist in seeking to project their messages, over the heads of governments, direct to the "peoples."

Actually, of course, the Soviets are in a better position than is any western government to make political decisions in secret. For this very reason, they can afford to demand maximum publicity for the propaganda that they wish to disseminate at international conferences. These propaganda positions represent carefully designed and pre-arranged patterns and shed relatively little light on real Soviet intentions. Soviet insistence upon freedom of propaganda and agitation at international conferences and in the United Nations should be contrasted with Soviet aversion for freedom of information for foreign governments, and the foreign press, regarding conditions inside the Soviet Union or other communist countries. This aversion has been conspicuously displayed not only in connection with international disarmament negotiations but also in connection with Soviet and Soviet bloc behavior regarding, for example, the United Nations Security Council Commission to investigate Greek frontier incidents in the early post-World War II period, or in connection with the functioning, and the frustration, of such bodies as the Korean Armistice Commission, etc.

Soviet attention attracting capabilities were certainly greatly increased by Khrushchev's decision, in 1955, to make extensive use in Soviet foreign relations of exchanges of persons and of "personal diplomacy." Among Khrushchev's better-known ventures to date in the latter technique have been his trips to India, Burma, and Afghanistan in 1955, to India, Burma, Indonesia, and Malaya in 1960, to Great Britain in 1956, and to France in 1960 and, of course, his American journey of 1959. This latter trip included participation in the United Nations General Assembly, as did his 1960 experience

217

in the United States, which was confined to his agitation against "colonialism" and other propaganda exploits connected with the Fifteenth General Assembly Session. Commenting on Khrushchev's sojourn in New York in 1960, Harry Schwartz pointed out in the *New York Times* for October 9 that Khrushchev had met more key figures from Africa and Asia than in all the rest of his life, and that he had also "probably received more publicity for his ideas in the countries of those two continents than ever before." Mr. Schwartz added that "as the chief salesman for world communism, Premier Khrushchev may well believe that this personal and publicity impact upon the neutral world will richly repay him in the long run." In this connection it may be worth recording that a perceptive African diplomat assigned to the United Nations told this writer in the spring of 1962 that, while Khrushchev's table-pounding offended the sophisticated, his personal lobbying among Africans, and his dramatic visit to Harlem to hobnob with Fidel Castro, gained him great good will among many simple Africans and Latin Americans.

Among the extra propaganda dividends which have accrued to the Soviet Union as a result of Khrushchev's travels and his participation in international conferences, have been pretexts afforded by such activities for publication and distribution in foreign languages of pamphlets and books related to them. For example, Khrushchev's 1959 and 1960 trips to the United States resulted in publication by a Soviet agency in New York, Crosscurrents Press, of *Khrushchev in America*, dealing with the 1960 trip. This volume includes several glossy photographs showing Khrushchev, smiling broadly with Prime Minister Nehru, Fidel Castro and several political leaders of "neutral" countries.

Also, in connection with various travels, as well as in the general framework of post-Stalin "cultural diplomacy," Khrushchev and other Soviet leaders have been able to make a considerable number of appearances on American and other foreign television programs. One of the most successful of Khrushchev's television appearances was his performance on the "Open End" program in 1960. As one observer noted, Khrushchev probably succeeded on this occasion in conveying to many Americans an image of himself as "peace-loving as any grandfather."

Perhaps of more relevance to Soviet domestic than to foreign propaganda—but also important for the latter—is the use of travel or study by Soviet citizens in "capitalist" countries to train Soviet propagandists and to bolster the credibility of Soviet attacks on the policies of those states. As one of this author's colleagues remarked, a young Soviet diplomat who spent a year ostensibly doing historical research at an American university made use of the experience to prepare himself for service in the Soviet United Nations delegation as chief expert on "American cannibalism."

It seems probable that face-to-face communication has been more successful, both in attracting attention and in exercising persuasion, than any other Soviet propaganda instrument. Among other advantages, it permits greater flexibility in dealing with the problem of multiple audiences than do the mass media. It facilitates deception of "bourgeois" politicians—to whom soothing reassurances of Soviet peaceful intentions may be offered "in confidence." Certainly Khrushchev himself has shown keen awareness of his own value as a propaganda instrument. In this connection it is interesting that Otto Kuusinen, writing in *Pravda* for February 4, 1959, poked fun at the "ossified bureaucrats" of the "anti-party" group, who had, he charged, opposed Khrushchev's policy of making use of "personal contacts" in foreign policy.[8]

In many other ways, Soviet propagandists and their artistic, scholarly, and scientific collaborators have in recent years attracted the attention of various world audiences. Among

[8] Cited by Herbert Ritvo in *American Slavic and East European Review*, April, 1961, p. 215.

the devices are exhibitions, participation in international trade fairs, foreign performances by Soviet athletes, dancers and singers, and the export of books, periodicals, musical scores, and films. According to United States government sources, the Soviets claimed that 1,400,000 persons attended a Soviet exhibition in Colombo, Ceylon, in 1959, and that 1,000,000 attended the Soviet exhibition in the same year in Mexico City. During 1960, members of the Sino-Soviet bloc were represented in over 40 international trade fairs and, in addition, they staged over 30 unilateral trade or industrial exhibitions abroad. An unclassified American official report cited Soviet sources to the effect that between 1946 and September 1960 the Soviet Union took part in 155 exhibitions and fairs in 40 countries with a total attendance of 178,000,000 persons. We shall deal subsequently in somewhat greater detail with channels and media of Soviet foreign propaganda. The above details are presented to indicate the increasing versatility and energy displayed by Soviet propagandists, especially under Khrushchev, in obtaining access to foreign audiences.

While seeking systematically to bring Soviet messages to each and every appropriate world audience, the Soviet regime continues to deny to foreign communicators all but a very limited access to Soviet communications media and refuses to permit foreigners, including communists, to have unfettered face-to-face contact with Soviet citizens. This is true despite the fact that there is a considerably greater flow of persons and of information across Soviet frontiers than in Stalin's day. The general pattern of Soviet restrictions on international communication is well known, and we shall deal here only with a few outstanding recent developments.[9] In Chapter I mention was made of Khrushchev's angry rejection, after his 1959 visit to the United States, of American proposals for a mutual United States-Soviet relaxation on controls over exchanges of

[9] See, for example, Frederick C. Barghoorn, *The Soviet Cultural Offensive* (Princeton, N.J., 1960), pp. 99-124.

radio, television, and other kinds of communication between the two countries. It is true that, in the following years, modest progress was made in expanding communication, especially in the field of scholarly exchange. For example, in 1962 Professor Richard Pipes of Harvard University lectured at Leningrad University on "Liberal and Conservative Trends in Russian Social and Political Thought of the Nineteenth Century." However, despite the probability that the invitation to Pipes had been cleared with higher authority, Leningrad University was sharply attacked, in *Kommunist*, No. 8, May, 1962, for having allowed Pipes to dispense "bourgeois ideology" to Soviet students.

In September 1962 the important propaganda organ, *International Affairs*, published an attack on NATO, entitled "New NATO Weapon: Ideological Subversion." The article, by Yuri Zhukov, was devoted mainly to charges that the NATO countries were attempting to use cultural exchanges to carry the cold war into the territory of the socialist countries. Zhukov defended Soviet restrictions on the importation of western, "bourgeois" publications into Russia. He concluded by asserting that "revolutionary vigilance" remained an "unalterable principle" of Soviet life.

An attack in *Izvestiya* for January 20, 1963, on the distinguished Soviet poet and dramatist, Victor Nekrasov, was particularly revealing of Kremlin attitudes toward the politics of cultural relations. The unsigned article, entitled "Tourist with a Walking Stick," criticized Nekrasov's two articles, published in the November and December 1962 issues, respectively, of the literary magazine *Novy Mir*, for allegedly taking a "fifty-fifty" attitude toward the "bourgeois" culture he had observed while traveling in Italy and the United States (he had been in America with a high-level Soviet cultural delegation in November, 1960). Nekrasov was accused of such heresies as "bourgeois objectivity" and advocacy of "peaceful coexistence in the field of ideology."

The real reason for the castigation of Nekrasov, or at least for its severity, may have been the fact that in the second of his *Novy Mir* articles he was bold enough to sharply criticize the standard Soviet practice of attaching to Russian delegations on cultural exchange missions security agents whose presence, surveillance, and intimidation considerably inhibit freedom and spontaneity of contact and communication.

The wave of repression of experimental, nonconformist, and independent Soviet intellectuals which began in December 1962 brought with it various new restrictions on freedom of communication and of movement. For example, the trip planned by the well known Russian poet Evgeni Evtushenko to the United States for April 1963 was cancelled. Also—among other similar episodes—the Soviet authorities suddenly canceled a conference, scheduled for April 17 in Moscow, at which British politicians, journalists, and radio broadcasters had planned to discuss problems of mutual concern to them and their Soviet counterparts.

In negotiations for their 1961 exhibition in Moscow, French representatives were told that they could exhibit books, but only "under glass." A similar position was taken toward the book display of the American Exhibition in 1959, and toward a special British book exhibition, also held in Moscow in 1959. In addition, the efforts of all three of these governments to secure permission to open reading rooms for the display and use of books, magazines and newspapers published in their countries, under the management or with the participation of French, British, or American citizens, continue to be rebuffed by the Soviet authorities.

Although it has permitted more foreign visitors to enter the Soviet Union than had ever before been admitted, the Khrushchev regime has continued to maintain an elaborate system of closed areas where access is denied both to foreign officials and to tourists. No type of interpersonal contact is without its special pattern of controls and restrictions. Perhaps the

222

most important and fruitful of all areas of personal exchange between the Soviet Union and non-communist countries is the exchange of graduate students and young scholars. However, very few of the American graduate students and scholars who have studied in the Soviet Union since 1958 have been permitted access to archives, and when they have it has been for very brief periods. Severe travel restrictions, even with respect to areas of mainly historical interest, such as the cities of Rostov or Suzdal in central Russia, are imposed on the American students and scholars. Requests to visit such areas are denied on the ground that this would be "tourist," rather than academic travel. Moreover, none of the American graduate students, as of the end of 1962, had been permitted to engage in any sort of systematic interviewing of Soviet officials or other citizens in connection with their research projects.

Despite the continued maintenance of the "closed society" in the Soviet Union, with its attendant advantages and disadvantages in foreign propaganda, there is no doubt that Khrushchev has displayed a certain willingness to pay a price, in terms of relaxation of controls, for his policy of utilizing exchanges of persons and of cultural materials as an instrument of foreign propaganda. It is probably for this reason that the Soviet "conservatives" were appalled by his bold new policies. One could compile an interesting list of indices of reduction of Soviet secrecy since the death of Stalin. However, the question might be raised whether these actions resulted from a conscious intention to reduce secrecy, or were unintended consequences of major policy decisions designed to increase national efficiency or relax internal social tensions. These indices might include increased face-to-face contact, expansion of the geographic area of the Soviet Union open to foreigners, increasing choice of modes of travel (somewhat cut back early in 1962), access to previously closed types of institutions, contacts between members of occupational groups which formerly did not participate in any kind of international communication. Also might be included are increased access to foreign reading matter, both in the original languages and in translations, increased printing of American official statements in Soviet newspapers, substitution of selective for total radio jamming, and opportunity for Soviet citizens to participate in international meetings.[10]

It should be emphasized that the trends referred to above are of limited scope, and may be subject to reversal. Indeed, the period since 1961 has in some ways been one of retrogression in Soviet communications practices. The expulsion in 1962 of *Newsweek* correspondent Whitman Bassow and the forcing out in February 1963 of the Moscow bureau of the National Broadcasting Corporation were significant negative developments. Even more important was a drastic reduction in 1962 in tourist travel by Soviet citizens to western Europe and the United States. Thus, according to United States official sources, only 77 Soviet tourists came to this country in 1962, in contrast to 400 in 1961. Moreover, the trend toward restriction of this kind of interpersonal exchange, important because even in the Soviet pattern of shepherded travel it is somewhat more informal than travel by official delegations, continued into 1963. As of early June, only one party of Soviet tourists had visited the United States. In part, this reduction in Soviet tourist travel to America—and also to western Europe—may have been the result of a shortage of foreign exchange caused by such expensive Soviet commitments as Cuba, for example, entailed. In 1962, and up to the time of writing, in June 1963 Moscow was on the whole systematically fulfilling its schedules of exchanges of scientific, educational, artistic, and other personnel under the various treaties and agreements to which it was a party.

Following the trial for espionage of the Soviet official Oleg

[10] This last point was discussed by Peter Juviler in the *American Slavic and East European Review* for February, 1961, in an interesting article entitled "Interparliamentary Contacts in Soviet Foreign Policy."

Penkovski, in May 1963 the Soviet press once again began to sharply warn Soviet citizens of the possible risks involved in unauthorized association with foreigners, whether tourists or diplomats. However, as Seymour Topping pointed out in the *New York Times* for May 31, 1963 the warnings, unlike those issued in the Stalin era were sufficiently ambiguous to give rise perhaps to doubt as to whether or not the Kremlin was certain how far it wanted to go in discouraging East-West communication.

The partial erosion of the traditionally rigid pattern of Soviet secrecy is one of the potentially hopeful aspects of current developments in current Soviet-free world relationships. In the short run, however, it also has the beneficial effect, from the point of view of the Kremlin, of calling increased attention to every aspect of Soviet propaganda and, of course, of helping to break down established non-communist images of Soviet obscurantism and isolationism. The propaganda gain to the Soviet Union can be particularly great if the advantage of continued communications controls can be combined with the appearance of the relaxation of controls. Such a combination can permit continued tight control of domestic Soviet public opinion, and can achieve the advantage of secrecy in preserving the integrity of the myths about Soviet affairs projected by Soviet foreign propaganda, together with the added advantage of the favorable alteration, in the eyes of many foreigners, of their image of Soviet Russia.

Let us now examine the adaptive devices by which the Kremlin has sought to identify its policy objectives with the varied aspirations of target audiences. One might say that in aspects of this strategy the Soviet Union seeks "innocence by association." The term might be applied to the familiar Soviet device of quoting, often out of context, excerpts from the "bourgeois" press in support of the authenticity of Soviet statements. Related to this device is that of attempting to associate respectable non-communist political, business, or cultural leaders with Soviet or communist causes and movements. Deception, or even outright lying, are often involved in the employment of such methods. The degree to which the deception involved can be successful depends upon a number of factors, including strict Soviet control over access to information about conditions inside the Soviet Union, and the intellectual and political astuteness of the individuals to whom such tactics are applied. In connection with Soviet propaganda exploitation of the non-communist press, for example, it is worth noting that its effectiveness depends in considerable measure upon the degree to which those who read Soviet publications or listen to Soviet broadcasts check on the accuracy of quotations contained in Soviet propaganda messages.

Soviet propaganda, as we have emphasized, seeks to harness to Kremlin policy the grievances and aspirations of the most diverse social, national, and ethnic groups. Perhaps it would be useful here to note that Soviet propaganda is directed, at times, to the most conservative sentiments, such as religion. In fact, Soviet propaganda, in its effort to mobilize world opinion against the western democracies, seeks to present the USSR as, at one and the same time, the champion of traditional values, including the most ancient folk cultures, and also the driving force of anti-traditional, revolutionary modernization. Successful implementation of this formula involves, at times, the playing down of the class struggle and violence aspects of Marxist-Leninist doctrine and the display, for example, of evidence of respect for religion.

It is doubtful if Soviet exploitation of religious sentiments has been a very significant factor in the total Soviet propaganda effort. Nevertheless, there is something so intriguing about the attempt by an avowedly anti-religious regime to exploit religious sentiments that it may be valuable to linger for a few moments on this aspect of Soviet propaganda. In December 1917, Lenin and Stalin signed a proclamation ad-

226

dressed to the "Laboring Moslems of Russia and the East," which was, essentially, a revolutionary appeal addressed to a religious group, in which close attention was paid to nationalist sentiments. In September 1920, the Comintern organized, in Baku, a "Congress of the Peoples of the East." Among the slogans issued by this congress were those calling for a "holy war." During World War II, besides reestablishing the patriarchate of the Russian Orthodox Church, and subsequently making extensive use of religious connections to further Soviet foreign policy in the Balkans and the Near East, the Soviet regime also engaged in such religiously-tinged propaganda activities as the organization and activation of the anti-Fascist Jewish committee. This committee, in 1943, sent the famous Jewish Shakespearean actor Solomon Mikhoels and the poet Itzik Feffer to the United States on a speaking tour. Both Mikhoels and Feffer, incidentally, disappeared during the "anti-cosmopolitan" campaign of 1948 in the Soviet Union. Mikhoels had been one of the leading actors of the Jewish theatre in Moscow. When this writer asked the head of the Department of Culture of the city of Leningrad in 1956 why the Jewish theatre had been closed, the Soviet official answered that this step was taken because of the threat posed by the Germans to Moscow. This was an untrue answer since in fact the Jewish theatre had remained open until 1948.

Pravda for October 1, 1962, reported that Khrushchev, in a speech in the Central Asian republic of Turkmanistan, made the following statement: "I have occasion to meet and talk with representatives of foreign Moslems. They say that the life which they see in our eastern republics is what the peoples of their countries dream about."

Examples of Soviet determination to exploit connections between peoples under Soviet authority and religious groups throughout the world, could be multiplied. And yet, at the same time, all churches in the USSR, including the relatively favored Russian Orthodox Church, operate under severely restrictive laws. They also remain the object of increasingly intense anti-religious propaganda. Intensification of such pressure is indicated, for example, by sections of the new CPSU program, by speeches at the Twenty-second Party Congress, and by vitriolic editorials such as the attack on religion as a "survival of capitalism" in *Pravda* on September 26, 1962.

The Soviet combination of relentless single-mindedness in the pursuit of power with flexibility in the exploitation of shifting situations is reflected in an article by L. Ilichev, who as central committee secretary in direct charge of propaganda and agitation and head of the "ideological commission" established by the November 1962 party plenum, is perhaps the top Soviet policymaker of Soviet propaganda. Published in *Kommunist*, No. 14, September 1960, Ilichev's article was entitled "Toward a New Upsurge of Ideological Work."[11] Ilichev warned that it was necessary to "unswervingly defend the purity of communist ideology from distortions." It was also necessary, he emphasized, to be able to "perceive and most boldly generalize the newest processes in international life, and not to cling to the letter at the expense of the spirit of Leninism." In illustrating this vague but significant statement, Ilichev noted that the Soviet Union, on the basis of its increased power, was "creatively" interpreting current developments and breaking new paths in the solution of the problems of mankind. It was thus conducting a policy which was "driving the imperialists into a corner," and stimulating the revolutionary activity of the popular masses. Ilichev expressed satisfaction with the "Leninist peace-loving foreign policy" conducted by Khrushchev at the General Assembly of the United Nations. Khrushchev's activities, he stated, were at the center of attention of world public opinion. Khrushchev had posed "the most burning problems of the present era." Interestingly enough, in view of Soviet propaganda exploitation of national

[11] *K novomu podemu ideologicheskoi raboty, Kommunist*, No. 14, pp. 22-40.

and religious sentiments, Ilichev warned that it was necessary to be on guard against national and religious prejudices, and he called for further strengthening of the "atheistic education of the workers."[12]

Ilichev's article is worthy of note, because, among other things, it indicates continued Soviet adherence to the Lenin-Stalin propaganda style. As a study of communist propaganda made during the Stalin era noted, "In communist propaganda, as in war propaganda, there is a very high degree of self-enemy polarization. Whoever the devils and angels may be at any given moment, a sharp dichotomy is drawn."[13] In keeping with this high degree of "polarization," and consequent rigid patterning, Soviet propaganda seems to strive to achieve a kind of "magical" quality, with its frequent invocation of ritualistic phrases and symbols. As one scholar notes, "Soviet Marxism is built around a small number of constantly recurring and rigidly canonized statements to the effect that Soviet society is a socialist society without exploitation. . . ."[14] In a somewhat similar vein, Alfred G. Meyer has written that "Ideology is to hide the fact that the very goals of the revolution are being violated. It serves as a set of magic formulas for the purpose of creating a fictitious image of Soviet society as the best of all possible worlds." Its purpose is "to veil the reality of the Soviet social system."[15]

While these authors and others who have offered perceptive comments on various fundamental features of Soviet ideology and propaganda differ in many respects in their interpretations, their views tend to bring out certain general characteristics of Soviet propaganda. It is a very carefully "patterned" propaganda. It strikes a clearly self-righteous tone. It tends

[12] *Ibid.*, pp. 30-32.
[13] Nathan Leites and I. de Sola Pool, "Interaction: The Response of Communist Propaganda to Frustration," in Lasswell, *Language of Politics*, p. 345.
[14] Herbert Marcuse, *Soviet Marxism* (New York, 1958), p. 86.
[15] Meyer, "USSR, Incorporated," p. 375.

to command, rather than to persuade. It ignores evidence which is not consistent with its demands. It insists that it represents a cause which will inevitably be victorious. It persists in blackening the motives of opponents. To non-communists or others not predisposed to be influenced by it, it seems irrational and absurd. To the outside observer, Soviet propaganda, for the most part, seems like the output of tense, disturbed, and angry individuals—a fact which may help to explain its success in certain situations and with certain audiences, caught in the grip of crises and frustrations.

Even after the death of Stalin, as Kirkpatrick has noted, in commenting on the reaction of the Soviet regime to changed propaganda conditions within the Soviet bloc, "Attempts to adjust to the new situation were superficial and limited to some of the more 'technical' aspects of propaganda media operations."[16] Kirkpatrick goes on to point out that the remedies suggested for the situation, in view of admitted "failures of indoctrination," involved an intensified application of the orthodox principles of communist propaganda rather than a fundamental discussion of the relationship between propaganda and reality. On the whole, the student of post-Stalin propaganda is likely to agree with Kirkpatrick, even with regard to the period since 1956. Despite the element of flexibility in Soviet international propaganda, to which references have been made in this study, Soviet propaganda still operates to an overwhelming degree in terms of attitudes and categories which often seem to have little relation to the reality they purport to describe.[17] If this is true even with respect to underdeveloped countries, it is still more true with respect to the advanced industrial countries of the west. This lack of "fit" between Soviet propaganda charges, accusations, and exhortations, on the one hand, and the "reality world" of such a large

[16] Evron M. Kirkpatrick, *Year of Crisis* (New York, 1957), p. 59.
[17] See, for example, Walter Z. Laqueur, "Soviet Doctrine and the New Countries," *Survey*, No. 37, July-September, 1961, pp. 3-11.

part of the foreign audience, helps to explain the incredulity, amusement, or irritation often expressed by Americans listening to Soviet representatives at United Nations debates.

Before turning to some illustrations of the persistence of inflexibility and dogmatism in Soviet propaganda, even under Khrushchev, it should be noted that the handicaps of ideological and organizational rigidity are not as severe, in the case of Soviet propaganda, as they might appear to be if one confined one's study solely to propaganda disseminated by Soviet periodicals, the publications of communist parties outside the Soviet Union, or Soviet radio broadcasts.

Despite its lack of subtlety, Soviet propaganda is associated with Marxist ideology which still has great prestige with many world audiences. The degeneration of Soviet social theory has not completely destroyed the advantage to the Soviet Union of this association. Also, Soviet propaganda is associated with the power, the economic growth, and the scientific strength of the USSR. Finally, it is more flexible, especially in the area of "cultural diplomacy" than a mere study of printed texts would indicate. Besides, flexible or not, Soviet propaganda is energetic, vigorous, persistent, and ever-ready to take advantage of the mistakes and shortcomings of the "capitalists" and the "imperialists."

A study of Soviet propaganda regarding the Cyprus problem, between the spring of 1950 and the end of 1959, based on Soviet publications in Russian and in English, revealed that the various participants, as seen through Soviet eyes, were all "typecast." Throughout the period the British were characterized as "imperialists," as "colonialists," as "terrorists," etc. Their policies were always dictatorial, ruthless, deceitful, demagogic, savage, reactionary, medieval, etc. The Americans were characterized as "blackmailers, bosses, and imperialists," and their behavior was "brazen, curious, and covetous." The Turks, playing a minor role, were "agents of the British Secret Service, fellow plotters." Each and every British proposal to settle the problem of the future of Cyprus was attacked as hypocritical or disingenuous. Although throughout the period Soviet propaganda advocated "self-determination" for Cyprus, Soviet propagandists never clearly indicted or specified what they meant by "self-determination." Nor did they indicate what the possible consequences of self-determination might be. The objectives of Soviet propaganda regarding this thorny issue appear to have been: a) To prolong the crisis as long as possible by presenting every proposed remedy as being fraudulent and unacceptable; b) To persistently propose a simple and appealing solution, self-determination, which had the dual advantage that it was impossible to apply and, consequently, that its advocates would be in a position to demand the revision of whatever settlement was agreed upon, and to bid for the support of those whom that settlement dissatisfied; c) To weaken the authority of the Greek and Turkish governments by presenting them as regimes lacking any sort of autonomous will, and—at least in the case of the Greek government—as traitors to its own national interest; d) To present the United States and Great Britain in the worst possible light—in this case as the malicious oppressors of a small people fighting for their liberty.

It would appear that the first and the fourth of the above objectives were to a considerable extent realized although one cannot of course attribute this result entirely to Soviet propaganda. The Cyprus issue damaged British prestige considerably, especially in the Middle East. And, despite the poor showing of the Cypriot communists in the war of liberation on the island, the Soviet Union was able to effectively move into the troubled situation which developed on Cyprus following the London settlement of 1959.[18]

Soviet reporting of the Hungarian Revolution in 1956 and after furnishes a pertinent example of the application of tech-

[18] The above material on Cyprus was drawn from an unpublished study by Mr. M. O'D. Alexander.

niques of biased communication in the presentation of an event of world significance. Thirty-six hours after violence erupted in Hungary, *Pravda* published a report which set a pattern for interpretation of the events in that country. It must be admitted that although a careful reader, provided he has access to non-Soviet sources of information, can detect implicit inconsistencies and even glaring omissions in Soviet reporting of the Hungarian Revolution, this reporting was distinguished by considerable deftness. Certainly Soviet reporting achieved a high level of consistency in the language used to describe Hungarian developments. The outline of the situation in Hungary set forth in the first *Pravda* article referred to above was preserved nearly in its entirety throughout and after the revolution. The main points of the interpretation are as follows.

1. On the afternoon of Tuesday, October 23, 1956, the "honest," socialist, Hungarian working people staged a demonstration against the anti-party mistakes committed by the Rakosi and Gero governments.

2. Fascist, Hitlerite, reactionary, counter-revolutionary hooligans, financed, trained, and equipped by the imperialist, capitalist west, took advantage of the demonstration to begin a counter-revolution.

3. The honest Hungarian working people under Imre Nagy appealed to Soviet forces stationed in Hungary under the Warsaw Pact for assistance in restoring order.

4. The Nagy government proved to be weak, and it permitted counter-revolutionary influences to penetrate its ranks. It became helpless and fell apart. This is demonstrated by the fact that Nagy denounced the Warsaw Pact.

5. The Hungarian patriots under Janos Kadar broke with the Nagy government and formed the Hungarian revolutionary workers and peasants government. This genuinely popular government asked the Soviet command for help in suppressing the counter-revolution.

6. The Hungarian patriots, assisted by Soviet forces, smashed the counter-revolution.

Naturally, this version of the Hungarian events contrasts sharply with that set forth in the *New York Times* or other representative western non-communist newspapers. The most obvious contrast arises from the comparison between the variety and even confusion contained in western press reports with the unison with which all Soviet newspapers reported the events. Soviet reporting was, by western standards, unnaturally consistent. The language used in Soviet reports was, in keeping with this pattern, extremely repetitive. Reading Soviet press reports of the hectic Hungarian events one feels that an all-seeing, invisible being is reporting them. This impression is intensified by the complete lack of any effort in the Soviet press to support or document its descriptions of events. One finds in the Soviet reports no evidence of any attempt on the part of Soviet newspapermen to check the accuracy of statements issued by the "patriotic" Hungarian forces. There is no indication of the process by which it was decided that Nagy, for example, was first a "patriot" and then became a "traitor."

One is also struck by the prejudiced interpretation achieved by the subjective manner in which events were reported. The reader is not furnished information upon which to base his own conclusions. He is, rather, presented with conclusions together with facts selected to conform to these conclusions. In other words, he is given a carefully digested version of events which he is asked to accept. To be sure, some slight flavor of "objectivity" is perhaps achieved by funnelling the party line from Budapest through a satellite newspaper to a Soviet newspaper.

As noted earlier, certain evidences of suppression and distortion are available to the attentive reader even in this neatly tailored version of events. Thus, the first Soviet reporting of the anti-government demonstration in Budapest came twenty-four hours later than in the western press. The appeal made by Nagy to the United Nations was not reported at all. The fact that Nagy was arrested was also not reported. The Soviet press reported total calm in Budapest when, according to the western press, a revolutionary crisis was breaking out. Without offering any supporting analysis or assembled evidence which a critical western reader would demand, the Soviet press expected its readers to believe that the majority of the Hungarian people were opposed to the uprising from the very beginning.

Most puzzling of all is the fact that Imre Nagy, praised at first as a loyal member of the Hungarian Communist Party, suddenly became an anti-party defector. Doubtless it was because of such inconsistencies and silences as these that some critical Soviet readers, particularly university students in Moscow and Leningrad, did take a skeptical attitude toward Soviet reporting of the Hungarian uprising. On the other hand, the Soviet presentation was a plausible one and may well have been accepted by many people, not merely in communist-ruled countries, who would have been puzzled or confused by less carefully organized interpretation of a political explosion whose complexity will undoubtedly baffle historians for a long time to come.

Soviet propaganda tactics in regard to Cyprus, the Korean War, the Hungarian uprising, the Suez crisis, Cuba, Berlin, the Congo, and innumerable other situations, have been basically similar. Soviet propaganda substitutes vague symbols for specific referents. It relies on a limited number of incessantly repeated concepts. This technique readily lends itself to manipulation, since events and actors are identified only in vague terms and the Soviet press cannot easily be forced to make retractions in previous interpretations. Such symbols as "forces of reaction" can be easily shifted from one group to another, since the specific group representing the current "forces of reaction" is seldom clearly identified.

This kind of propaganda represents a system of clues, to which the reader is expected to make appropriate responses. It is obvious that Soviet foreign propaganda, like Soviet domestic propaganda, is completely indifferent to the distinction between "news" and "opinion," which is so important in the best western journalism. By the "scientific" and "objective" standards which permeate the thinking of many British or American government officials, journalists, and scholars, Soviet foreign propaganda appears to be steeped in demagogy.

Distortion is perhaps the most generally used single technique of Soviet propaganda. Its employment is inherent in the propaganda approach discussed in the preceding paragraphs. Deliberate suppression of aspects of Soviet or communist reality considered inappropriate in particular situations, is another important Soviet and foreign communist propaganda technique. For example, in the Indonesian general elections of January 1955, the communists, in their overt propaganda, explicitly disavowed revolutionary goals. They became, in effect, more nationalist than their nationalist opponents. They denied that the communist party desired a revolution and they stopped using such terms as "class struggle." In addition, they set up various affiliates in labor, peasant, and other groups which were ostensibly separate from the communist party of Indonesia, although communists sometimes ran as "non-party" candidates of these affiliates.[19] This tactic in Indonesia was part of a general strategy adopted by the Kremlin in 1955. It was fostered by the efforts of Khrushchev, beginning in that year, to achieve a measure of "respectability" for the Soviet Union and international communism by the practice of personal diplomacy, in association with the heads of "bourgeois" governments.

It is worth noting that the Soviet press, in describing the

[19] The foregoing material is taken from a doctoral dissertation on the Indonesian general elections submitted to the graduate faculty of Yale University by Stephen B. Hosmer.

results of Khrushchev's personal diplomacy, takes a militant line, and fits it into the generally offensive pattern of Soviet ideology. For example, Vadim Kozhevnikov in an article in *Pravda* for October 2, 1961, stated that the time had come when the "old world" had been "forced to attentively listen to the frank and open words of the head of the Soviet government, from the tribunal of the United Nations, and in the cities of America." Kozhevnikov also made the characteristic statement that "in the sacred struggle for peace, for communism, a worthy place is occupied by Soviet literature. Its most effective instrument is vigorous publicity."

Character assassination and other devices intended to arouse hatred of the "class enemy" have always bulked large in Soviet propaganda. Before and during the early, relatively frank period of Soviet propaganda activity, the use of lies as political instruments was openly advocated. For example, *Izvestiya* for January 1, 1919 quoted the Soviet diplomat Joffe as saying, "To deceive your class enemies, to violate, to destroy a treaty imposed by force, but never to sin against the revolutionary proletariat, never to violate the obligation taken on yourself before the revolution—those are the true revolutionary methods of the revolutionary struggle." Soviet foreign policy and propaganda today, despite the ever-widening gulf between Soviet ideology and the domestic and foreign reality which it purports to describe, justifies unlimited opportunism in the name of the struggle for the lofty goal of "communism."

This rationalization permits the communists to feel free to engage in a broad gamut of activities, ranging from trivialities to the most blatant political forgeries.

The most extensive and systematic treatment of Soviet use of forgery as a propaganda weapon now available is the 121-page study published in 1961, by the United States Government Printing Office. This document is based on a hearing held in June, 1961 before the Internal Security Subcommittee of the Senate Committee on the Judiciary. This study describes

Soviet techniques for circulating rumors charging that anti-De Gaulle French generals had enjoyed support from the Pentagon and the United States Central Intelligence Agency. Testifying before the Committee, Richard Helms, assistant director of the Central Intelligence Agency, noted that the Soviets used a variety of devices "to nurse a little plant into a big lie." According to Mr. Helms, "one is to print a local or planted rumor as a news article, using both bloc and free world papers as outlets. Another is to lend the tale a seeming authenticity by replaying through bloc media stories attributed to the western press. A third device is the allegation that the current Soviet charges are proven by secret western documents—documents that do not even exist as forgeries. The fourth trick is the tape-recorded telephone call." Mr. Helms testified that in four years no fewer than thirty-two forged documents designed to look as though they had been written by or to officials of the American government had been discovered. He expressed the opinion that the purposes of Soviet forgeries were to discredit the west in the non-western world, to sow suspicion among the western allies and, finally, to drive wedges between the peoples of non-bloc countries and their governments. The testimony of Mr. Helms offers impressive evidence regarding the hostile intentions and the expertise devoted by Soviet propaganda to the employment of fraud and forgery. While, in the long run, these methods may be self-defeating, since they arouse mistrust and anger, they can often achieve a significant short-term impact. Their effectiveness is, of course, determined in large part by the sophistication and vigilance of the publics and governments which they are designed to deceive.

Besides the primarily negative or accusatory Soviet propaganda techniques already discussed, many others might be mentioned. Operating behind its shield of domestic secrecy and equipped with extensive intelligence gathering facilities throughout the world, Soviet propaganda is in a particularly good position to make use of the already described technique of discrediting opposing communications systems by quoting foreign sources in criticism of their own governments.[20] A rather special but important aspect of Soviet propaganda, both foreign and domestic, consists of attacks on foreign radio broadcasts, such as those disseminated by the Voice of America, Radio Free Europe, Radio Liberty, and the BBC.[21] Of a somewhat different order is the use by Soviet propaganda of manipulation in the translation of official documents. As Peter Tang has noted, "the intent and effect of applying this linguistic weapon to a psychological offensive by an ideologically strongly armed communist movement against the comparatively loose ideology of the free world is to create a receptive atmosphere."[22] Other important devices include attacks on the western world in statements by, or attributed to, Soviet defectors who for one reason or another have returned to their homeland. Also employed are attacks on their native countries by defectors from the west, such as the Englishmen Burgess and McLean, or the Americans Mitchell and Martin.

Soviet propaganda also continues its efforts to discredit American scholarship on the USSR. A typical example of this form of negative Soviet foreign propaganda was an article published in *New Times*, No. 47, 1960, entitled "A World of Unrealities: America's Anti-Sovieteering Experts and Agencies." Very similar in spirit, but more factual in content, was a study, in the May-June 1962 number of the USSR Academy of

[20] The article by Waples already cited in this chapter contains interesting material indicating how the Soviet representatives at the 1955 Geneva Conferences "had large benefits from the undisciplined western press whose skilled analysts supplied *Pravda* with an abundance of anti-western arguments well-stated in the western idiom."

[21] See, for example, Alex Inkeles, "The Soviet Attack on the Voice of America: A Case Study in Propaganda Warfare," *American Slavic and East European Review*, Vol. XII, October, 1953, pp. 319-342.

[22] Peter S. H. Tang in *Introduction to Pamphlet Study* by Natalie Grant, entitled "Communist Psychological Offensive: Distortions in the Translation of Official Documents," published by The Research Institute on the Sino-Soviet Bloc (Washington, D.C., 1961).

Sciences' journal, *Istoriya* SSSR (*History of the USSR*). This study analyzed and vigorously criticized, as a "fiercely anti-Soviet" mouthpiece of the "ruling circles" of the United States, a leading American scholarly journal, *The American Slavic and East European Review*.[23]

Considerable emphasis has been placed in this chapter upon the hostile, negative, and destructive intentions and efforts of Soviet propaganda. This emphasis seemed justified in view of the essentially negative character of communist political communication and also in view of the effort made throughout this study to pay due attention to the positive themes in Soviet propaganda. It might be well to conclude this chapter with a reiteration of an earlier suggestion that anti-communists can make a serious political mistake by overlooking the positive, or seemingly positive, appeals of Soviet propaganda. In their efforts to woo some audiences, especially in the newly emerging lands, and in particular publication enterprises and cultural relations activities, Soviet communicators have often displayed tact and sensitivity to the attitudes and aspirations of target groups.[24] Aubrey has brought out very well some important positive aspects of Soviet propaganda: "Through numerous cultural exchanges in music, the dance, and the theatre, plentiful supplies of inexpensive literature in the vernacular, and scrupulous attention to anthropological details, the Russians have outdone the West in paying tribute to the deeply rooted predilections of many peoples in Asia and Africa. In this manner, they are able to enlist for their cause the thirst of the inhabitants of economically backward areas for the better things of life. Many of these lands can point to much more ancient cultural traditions than the United States. Moreover, a picture of American attachment to material things,

---

[23] See also the attack on the quarterlies, *Russian Review* and *American Slavic and East European Review*, in *Voprosy istorii*, No. 4, April, 1961, pp. 172-177.

[24] On this point, see, for example, Barghoorn, *The Soviet Cultural Offensive*, especially Chaps. vi, vii, viii and ix.

partly true and partly distorted, serves to suggest a greater affinity between the poor countries and Russia, a country priding itself not only on great material achievements in spite of a late start, but also on outstanding attainments in science and the arts."[25]

An example of Soviet propaganda tact and careful audience analysis in dealing with a western country is furnished by the magazine *USSR*, the official English-language monthly distributed in the United States in exchange for the American Russian-language publication *Amerika*. Unlike Soviet radio broadcasts in English to North America, the tone of which resembles that of *Pravda*, *USSR* emphasizes similarities between Soviet and American people and problems. Another area in which Soviet cultural exports are selected with an eye to the taste of foreign audiences is that of films. Such Soviet movies as "The Cranes Are Flying" and "Ballad of a Soldier," which have enjoyed widespread success abroad, particularly in the United States do not conform to the orthodox canons of Soviet cinema art, which is expected to embody such themes as the class struggle and "socialist construction." Despite the accolades which they have received in the west, these films were coldly handled by official Soviet motion picture criticism.[26] Along the same lines, Soviet dance groups abroad have often won the enthusiastic good will of audiences by performing traditional Indian folk dances in New Delhi or the Virginia Reel in New York. Despatching Soviet party leaders of non-Russian, particularly of Central Asian origin, to Africa and Asia, or bringing Indians, Indonesians, Ceylonese, and other Asians to Soviet Central Asia are among other evidences of Soviet cultural sensitivity.

Moreover, in recent years Soviet social scientists have been encouraged to renew their study, prohibited in the late Stalin

[25] Aubrey, *op.cit.*, p. 17.
[26] On this subject, see, for example, Reference Paper No. 23, 1960/1961, distributed by the Soviet Affairs Analysis Service of the American Committee for Liberation.

era, of western empirical social science techniques.[27] The benefits to Soviet foreign propaganda of renewed interest in the behavioral sciences appear so far to lie mainly in a substantial improvement of quality of presentation or in the achievement of mildly sensational effects such as the finding, reported by correspondent S. Vishnevski in *Pravda* for December 31, 1962, on the basis of a "public opinion poll" conducted in Union Station, in Washington, D.C., that the average American desires peace with Russia!

The Soviets have, however, begun in their now very substantial studies of the languages and cultures of foreign countries, to lay at least the foundation for sophisticated cross-cultural communication and these programs are growing in scope and maturity. It remains to be seen to what extent it will be possible under Soviet conditions, where scholars must execute the directives of politicians, to make effective use of social science concepts which, experience to date indicates, flourish best in a democratic, pluralistic society. Also, it is still not known to what degree rubles, energy and organization can offset, except where audience predispositions are very favorable the handicaps imposed upon Soviet propaganda by its association with an archaic ideology. The possibility that Moscow will achieve increasing success in its effort to utilize social science for power purposes cannot, however, be excluded and its progress or lack thereof in this field should be alertly followed. It is significant that M. V. Keldysh, the president of the Academy of Sciences of the USSR in an address to the Twenty-second Congress of the CPSU, reported in *Pravda* for October 22, 1961, asserted that upon the progress of Soviet social science research depended success in such tasks

[27] Evidence of familiarity with the content—but not the spirit, one might say—of contemporary European and American social science, literature is available, for example, in V. A. Yadov's book, *Ideologiya kak forma dukhovnoi deyatelnosti obshchestva* (Leningrad, 1961). See also the impressive review of the literature of western social psychology in A. L. Shnirman and A. G. Kovalev, *Kollektiv i razvitie lichnosti* (Leningrad, 1962).

as "the propaganda of the great superiority of the socialist system." Perhaps of even more fundamental importance was inclusion of a similar statement in the 1961 CPSU program. t is also highly significant that the Academy of Sciences has s up "scientific councils" to apply such techniques as "cybe netics"—very broadly defined in the USSR—to such areas as "the developmental laws of socialism" and "the economic competition of the two systems."

In recent years a measure of sophistication and of apparent accommodation has been introduced into Soviet propaganda activities in many countries, including the United States. For example, the Soviet agency, Crosscurrents Press, Inc., and the Soviet press agency, Novosti, for a time supplied some of the material distributed by a translation service known as *Current Soviet Documents*. Later the name of this translation service was changed to *Soviet Documents*, the title by which it is presently known. However, for a time it was believed by some American Sovietologists that the name *Current Soviet Documents* had been designed to compete with the *Current Digest of the Soviet Press*, established in 1949 by a number of scholars to supply accurate and representative translations of significant Soviet material. According to documents introduced in hearings before a Congressional committee in May 1962, the Soviet Government had paid Crosscurrents Press, Inc. a sum in excess of $240,000 for its publications since September 1959.

As of 1964 a check revealed that Crosscurrents Press had the same mailing address and occupied the same office space as the Four Continent Book Company, Bookfield House, and the International Arts and Sciences Press, a group of related agencies engaged in publishing in the United States a weekly magazine, three monthly journals, and seven quarterlies. Some of this output, for a time at least, was mistaken in the United States—and also in India, whither some of it was exploited— for that of other publishers.

✦✦✦ ➤ CHAPTER VIII

ORGANIZATION AND MEDIA

SOVIET propaganda circulates through a world-wide system of interlocking organizations and channels which may be divided into three main categories. The heart of the system is located in the central control mechanism of the CPSU, which, through its Department of Propaganda and Agitation, directs both domestic and foreign propaganda. Until recently the CPSU was able, as a rule, to make use of foreign communist parties for purposes of infiltration, propaganda, or insurrection as it saw fit. Even in the present era of relatively "polycentric" communism, most of the communist parties of the world, except those heavily influenced by Communist China, are still more or less pliant instruments of the CPSU. However, international communism has probably partly lost one traditional source of its power to impress, namely, that conferred upon it by the purposeful consistency of its propaganda "line" at any given time. We shall be only incidentally concerned in this chapter with the propaganda activities of foreign communist parties. Some aspects of international communist activity, such as the strategy of the united front are, however, so significant for the study of Soviet foreign propaganda generally that we must take them carefully into account.

The second major category of organizations consists of various "front" or peripheral organizations—sometimes also called "cover" organizations, such as the World Peace Council (WPC), the International Institute for Peace, the World Federation of Trade Unions (WFTU), the World Federation of Democratic Youth (WFDY), the International Union of Students (IUS), the Women's International Democratic Federation (WIDF), the International Association of Democratic

Lawyers (IADL), and others. In addition to these broad international organizations, set up either to exploit such universal sentiments as the desire for peace, or to represent particular social or occupational strata, there are regional groups that communists seek to control or influence. An important example is the Afro-Asian People's Solidarity Organization, which grew out of the Bandung Conference of 1955 in Indonesia, and has, since a conference held in December 1957 and January 1958, had its headquarters in Cairo. It has a Soviet affiliate in which prominent Soviet literary figures such as Anatoli Sofronov and Mirzo Turzun-Zade play leading roles. Of a somewhat similar character are the increasingly numerous, active, and growing Soviet "friendship" societies, which engage in nominally unofficial cultural activities, including the exchange of books, photographs, exhibitions, and many other kinds of materials, as well as exchanges of persons.

The Yearbook of the Great Soviet Encyclopedia for 1962 indicated that as of the end of 1961, the Union of Soviet Societies for Friendship and Cultural Relations with Foreign Countries included thirty-eight affiliated associations for friendship and cultural relations with various countries and groups of countries. Its Moscow House of Friendship in 1961 was visited by fifty thousand foreigners from 80 countries. The Union coordinated the work of fifteen sections, bringing together figures in various fields of science and culture. There are also fourteen affiliated societies for friendship and cultural relations with foreign countries with their headquarters in the various constituent republics of the USSR. The associations formed since 1959 include one for the countries of Latin America and one for the peoples of Africa, and also societies for relations with the Netherlands, Iraq, Iceland, Afghanistan, and Canada. In November 1961 a "USSR-Switzerland Society" was founded. The Latin American society already, in 1959, had relations with fourteen Latin American countries, while the African society had links with more than thirty African countries. The Union as a whole had cultural ties as of 1961 with one hundred and eighteen countries of the world.[1] It publishes in Russian and other languages the magazine *Culture and Life* and it also publishes in English, French, etc., the newspaper *Moscow News*.

Illustrative of the organization and scope of Soviet cultural propaganda efforts in Japan—to mention one important country—is the fact that in 1958 the Japan-Soviet Association had the following affiliated groups: the Japan-Soviet Library, Japan-Soviet Academy, Japan-Soviet Scientific Library Center, Japan-Soviet Translation and Publication Coterie, Soviet Students' Association, Japan-Soviet News Agency and the Friends of the Russian Language Association. The Japan-Soviet Association was, according to U.S. official sources, a bridgehead for Soviet cultural activity in Japan. The Association worked in close liaison with the Soviet State Committee for Cultural Relations, the Ukrainian Cultural Liaison Association, the Tass News Agency, the Lenin Library in Moscow, and the Friendship Associations in Czechoslovakia and Hungary. The Japan-Soviet Association is a good example of an active and powerful, but subordinate affiliate of the Soviet-oriented international cultural exchange network.

Since its founding in 1961, the Novosti (News) press agency, sponsored by the Union of Friendship Societies, as well as by the Union of Soviet Writers and the Union of Soviet Journalists, has actively disseminated Soviet propaganda abroad. In 1961 it supplied literature and photographs to Soviet publications in 38 countries, with a circulation of one million three hundred thousand copies, according to the above-mentioned *Yearbook*. Some of Novosti's material is reprinted in publications of International Arts and Sciences Press without indication of its source or of changes from the original Russian.

[1] *Ezhegodnik bolshoi sovetskoi entsiklopedii* (Moscow, 1960), p. 17; *Ezhegodnik bolshoi sovetskoi entsiklopedii* (Moscow, 1962), pp. 25-26.

For the purposes of this study the most important international propaganda channels are those directly controlled by the CPSU and the Soviet state. These include Intourist, the Soviet state monopoly for tourist affairs, as well as the agencies of party and government concerned with radio broadcasting, Soviet fairs and exhibitions abroad, the publication and export of printed matter, etc. Another major communications agency is TASS whose foreign correspondents act both as information-gatherers and as Soviet propagandists. A very important role is played, of course, by the State Committee for Cultural Relations. Also, as has already been indicated in previous chapters, Soviet diplomatic missions, as well as Soviet personnel representing the USSR in the United Nations or employed by the UN, perform propaganda functions. A startling example of Soviet exploitation of a supposedly non-political UN agency for propaganda purposes was reported in the *Wall Street Journal* for February 18, 1963. According to the *Journal*, the United Nations Educational, Scientific, and Cultural Organization, to which the United States is the largest single financial contributor, had just published a booklet by two Soviet citizens denouncing "colonialist oppression" by western nations, and attributing it to the "capitalist" system.

In addition to the foregoing, the following agencies and organizations, listed in *The Handbook of the Great Soviet Encyclopedia*, 1962 edition, contribute to the orchestrated pattern of Soviet world propaganda. The Committee of Youth Organizations was described as maintaining "constant communication" with more than one thousand youth and student organizations in one hundred and one countries of the world. In 1958, the Committee established a Bureau of International Youth Tourism. In 1959, it conducted a seminar on higher education in the USSR, as well as various sports and other international activities. In 1961 it sent abroad more than six hundred Soviet youth delegations. In the same year it organized the "World Youth Forum" in Moscow. The Committee operates, among other services, the Sputnik travel agency, a youth travel organization which furnishes low-cost accommodations for foreign young people traveling in the USSR under various exchange programs. Judging from conversations with a member of one such group from Britain, Sputnik not only provides economical services but can also generate a friendlier, more informal atmosphere than is usually produced by Intourist.

An article on the Sputnik agency in the July 1961 issue of *Molodoi Kommunist* (Young Communist), the magazine of the Young Communist League central committee, struck a note of the most cordial hospitality. Sputnik's president, N. Novokreshchenov, quoted from a letter received from an English youth group, who apparently were overwhelmed by the warmth of Russian hospitality, which so reassured them as to mankind's future that—according to the account—they left the USSR confident that "peace would be preserved." Novokreshchenov stated in the above article that by the summer of 1961 "several tens of thousands" of young people from 27 foreign countries had visited the Soviet Union under the auspices of Sputnik. Many had made use of the youth camps, hotels, and other facilities of the society, and all had benefited from such features of Sputnik's operations as the fifty per cent reduction in railroad fares which it offers to those using its services. According to Novokreshchenov, in 1960 alone 1,080 young people from France, about 500 from England, 340 from Austria, 270 from the German Federal Republic, and 200 from the United States availed themselves of these services. In turn, Sputnik, in 1960, sent groups of young Soviet tourists to 18 countries of Europe, Asia, and Africa, where, the article concluded, they helped many young people to "objectively evaluate" the life of the Soviet people, "engaged in building a communist society."

Sputnik is not the only Soviet agency which supplements Intourist's tourist services—the Soviet trade unions also do, mainly in connection with visits to the USSR of labor union tourist groups from "socialist" countries.

The Committee of Soviet Women, to mention another agency active in the exchange of persons field, in 1959 invited to the USSR 44 foreign women's delegations from 31 countries and its representatives participated in many gatherings in foreign countries. In 1961 the Women's Committee invited 41 foreign women's delegations from 23 countries. The Slavic Committee of the USSR holds various commemorative meetings jointly with representatives of Slavic countries. In 1961 the Slavic Committee organized a meeting against the "military attack by the USA on Cuba." The Union of Societies of the Red Cross and Red Crescent of the USSR, founded in 1925, participates in exchanges of delegations with various communist countries, as well as with organizations in Denmark, India, Finland, Libya, Iraq, etc. It also operates hospitals in Iran and Ethiopia and is represented by medical groups in India and Cambodia.

The Organization of Soviet War Veterans, founded in 1956, received delegations from the United States, Greece, and other countries and sent delegations to Italy, France, Austria, Norway, and Belgium. The Soviet Association for International Law, founded in 1957, is a member of the Association of International Law, with its headquarters in London. The Soviet Committee for Solidarity with the Countries of Asia and Africa, the Soviet affiliate of the Cairo-based Afro-Asian Solidarity Committee, founded in 1956, and headed by the above-mentioned Central Asian poet Mirzo Tursun-Zade, had three commissions: for relations with the countries of Asia and Africa, for problems of culture and cultural collaboration, and, finally, for Africa. In 1959, it significantly expanded its foreign connections. It engaged in a number of activities "in support of the national-liberation struggle of the Afro-Asian peoples, in defense of the victims of imperialistic repressions, for the strengthening of universal peace, for the prohibition of atomic weapons, and in support of proposals for general and complete disarmament."[2] In 1961, among other enterprises, it donated 20,000 American dollars to the "fund for Afro-Asian solidarity," and contributed to the "International Committee for Aid to the Congo and Algeria."

In a very special category is the nominally independent but state-influenced Russian Orthodox Church, which plays a considerable role in certain aspects of Soviet foreign propaganda, particularly in the Middle East, but also to some degree in relations with the United States and Great Britain. Its activities include maintenance of a permanent representative to the World Council of Churches in Geneva, Switzerland. The activities of these various agencies and groups, backed by the power and prestige of the Soviet state, are probably vastly more significant in their world impact than are either the foreign communist parties or the front organizations.

The Comintern, nominally federative in structure but actually so much dominated by Moscow that Stalin felt free to order the execution of many of its leaders, and the much less significant Cominform—in existence from September 1947 until its dissolution in May 1956—only partially masked Kremlin control over foreign communist parties. Since the dissolution of the Cominform, Moscow has felt that it must get along with a minimum of formal, overt machinery for coordinating the activities of foreign communist parties. Since September 1958, the *World Marxist Review*, published in Prague in many languages, has acted as a central theoretical clearing-house for international communism—it has been conspicuously Moscow-dominated, and has only infrequently offered its pages to the

[2] *Ibid.*, 1960 edition, pp. 18-20.

Chinese communists. While communist secrecy makes it difficult to obtain reliable information on the mechanisms by which propaganda and other directives are conveyed from Moscow to foreign communist parties, it seems clear that such organizations as the Comintern and Cominform never played more than a subordinate role in the process. The Report of the Royal Commission in Canada in 1946 brought out interesting material regarding the control exercised over espionage and propaganda activity in Canada by Gusarov, a Second Secretary of the Soviet Embassy in Ottawa, who acted as a direct representative of the Central Committee of the CPSU. It would, however, be a mistake to assume that the process of direction of foreign communist party propaganda activity has always been one of direct dictation from Moscow. Consultation and discussion, particularly in recent years, have played important roles in the process of interaction at the top levels of international communism. Moreover, communication of the "party line" does not take place exclusively, or perhaps not even primarily, through secret directives conveyed by such individuals as Gusarov or dispatched by couriers from Moscow. There is considerable evidence to indicate that Moscow normally exercises its leadership over foreign communist parties mainly by virtue of such media as short-wave radio broadcasts or by articles in *Pravda, Kommunist,* or other authoritative periodicals.[3] Such international communist congresses as the Moscow Meetings of November 1957 or November 1960, the congresses of the CPSU itself which are attended by delegates from foreign communist parties, and, as in the case of the Twenty-second Congress, attended by representatives of non-communist parties (the ruling parties of Ghana, Guinea,

[3] On the role of Soviet publications, particularly those of the Academy of Sciences of the USSR, in setting the "line" for foreign communist parties, see, for example, John H. Kautsky, *Moscow and the Communist Party of India* (Cambridge, Mass., 1956).

and Mali sent delegates) play a major role in coordinating propaganda activities of the international communist movement.

The international communist apparatus remains formidable, although in many countries outside the Sino-Soviet bloc, communist parties have diminished in numbers and ideological élan for several years. As long ago as 1954, according to a survey by the United States Information Agency, the strength of communist parties in western European countries had declined greatly since its peak in the early post-war years. As Anne O'Hare McCormick pointed out in the *New York Times* for April 12, 1954, the refusal of the Soviet leaders to permit free elections in any of the territories they had annexed indicated that they had no illusions that their system would be the "people's choice." Mrs. McCormick added, quite correctly, that the concern of the Soviet leaders was not—at least in the west—with the influence of communist parties but was directed toward "selling Soviet policy to the non-communist majorities in the free world."

At the end of December 1959, according to an official but unclassified report of the United States Department of State, the total communist party membership for the 86 countries where a count was possible was about 35,000,000, of which 85 per cent was accounted for by the Sino-Soviet bloc. The report noted that the position of the communists in Europe, as indicated by party membership figures and election results, continued to deteriorate in 1959. Since 1959, the decline in the strength and ideological vitality of communist parties in the advanced industrial countries has continued, with the disturbing exception of Italy, when, in the April 1963 parliamentary elections the communists received 4 per cent more votes than in 1958, when the last election was held. This rather surprising event casts some doubt on the fullness of distribution, or the impact, of Italian prosperity and it reminds us of the skill and determination with which Italy's communists, led by the master propagandist, Palmiro Togliatti, exploited the opportunities created by the collapse of fascism and the prestige of Russia. Total world communist party membership increased to about 40,000,000 by the end of 1961, owing to increases in CPSU and Chinese Communist Party ranks. A decline in communist party influence is indicated, however, by decreasing circulation of party newspapers and magazines.

An important aspect of the ebbing vitality of communism, which set in as Europe, especially, recovered economically from the effects of war, was its diminishing appeal to youth. For example, according to the State Department source cited above, "the party attracts fewer young people than formerly; only about ten per cent of its current members are under twenty-five years."[4]

However, in some of the underdeveloped countries, especially Indonesia, and, after the victory of Castro, in some Latin American countries, the communists have continued to grow in numbers and influence in recent years. As of mid-1963 communist penetration of the leadership elements of several countries, of which Indonesia, with its vast population, tremendous resources, and shaky economy was probably the most important, appeared to have reached dangerous proportions. On the other hand, the apparently glowing prospects opened up for communist penetration in the Middle East following the Suez crisis of 1956 have not materialized. Radical nationalism as represented by Gamal Abdel Nasser in Egypt, has thus far proved more attractive than communism even in the Arab countries, with their strong anti-western emotions, stimulated by the Arab-Israeli, the Algerian, and

[4] "World Strength of the Communist Party Organizations," Intelligence Report No. 4489, R-12, issued by Bureau of Intelligence and Research, Department of State, Washington, D.C., January, 1960, p. 9. See also Intelligence Report No. 4489, R-14, which is the 1962 version of the above series.

other problems. In Iraq, particularly, the overthrow of the Kassim regime was a severe blow to Soviet hopes in the vital, oil-rich Middle East. In evaluating the significance of international communism as a device for extending Soviet influence, it should of course be remembered that the influence of communist parties is often far greater than their numbers might indicate. The communist parties remain formidable because they represent a disciplined network of experts in subversion, propaganda, and agitation, prepared at any time to act energetically to exploit opportunities which may become available to them because of emerging social and political crises. As Gabriel A. Almond stressed with regard to the Italian and French parties in his earlier-cited study, *The Appeals of Communism*, communist parties can render enormous services to the Soviet Union even without seizing power.

The CPSU and other communist parties continue to display impressive energy and determination, and considerable skill in their efforts to exploit political movements resulting from the effects of rapid social change. For example, Moscow-directed communists have for some time been engaged in a systematic effort to convert Castroism from a somewhat unorthodox movement of the "Jacobin Left" into a reliable Soviet instrument.[5] As Robert J. Alexander pointed out in *Problems of Communism*, for January-February, 1961, "the advent of the Jacobins in Latin American politics makes it possible for the communists to develop a protective coloration which has been difficult for them to achieve hitherto. Behind the screen of an 'indigenous Latin American revolution' ostensibly led by the Jacobins, the communists are attempting to become an ally or even an integral part of a movement for fundamental change

[5] According to the *New York Times* for March 10, 1962, at least ten communists were included in the twenty-five member directorate set up in Cuba. Among them, reportedly, were two Comintern veterans. The expression "Jacobin Left" was coined, apparently by Robert J. Alexander.

in Latin American countries." Important services to Soviet subversive activities have been rendered by Cuban communications agencies, especially the official press agency, Prensa Latina, which both openly, and clandestinely, distributes inflammatory agitational material, particularly to Latin American students. According to a study made by an eight-nation group of the Organization of American States, reported in the *New York Times* for June 6, 1963, such activity greatly increased in 1962. The situation in Latin America, as well as in Indonesia, where Dipa N. Aidit, chairman of the communist party, is one of the four deputy chairmen of the People's Congress (a body attached to but not an integral part of the supreme political authority in the country) serves as a reminder that communist parties are still employing the traditional communist technique of the united front with impressive success.

The united front involves both semantic tactics and organizational strategy. Its principal ingredients are deception, corruption, or intimidation of non-communist politicians, and penetration of non-communist organizations with a view to influencing, controlling, and eventually incorporating them into the communist system of power. A detailed history of communist use of united front tactics would be extremely valuable. In the absence of such a history, and for the purposes of this study, it is sufficient to say that united front tactics are representative of numerous Soviet and communist devices for deception and manipulation and that their forms are adapted to changing circumstances as interpreted by communist leaders. Sometimes, as in Germany shortly before the accession of Hitler to power, or in Argentina today, the communists practice a kind of parallel action, supporting, for their own purposes, the Nazis and Peronistas whose ideologies are obviously irreconcilable with their own. It is probable that extreme rightist parties that engage in some sort of arms-length cooperation or parallel action with communists have a better chance of surviving and even gaining from the experience than do leftist or liberal parties. The latter, because of the apparent similarity of their values with those of the communists, are more susceptible to communist influence than are the fanatical and relatively highly disciplined rightist totalitarian movements.

Such a conclusion seems warranted by the experience of the socialist and democratic parties of eastern Europe during the early post-war years. Of course, the pressure of Soviet power was an important if not decisive element in the process whereby the coalitions of independent political parties set up in 1944 and 1945 in eastern Europe were reduced to a monolithic structure, completely controlled by the communists. However, the process was facilitated and to a considerable extent concealed from the outside world by communist tactics of deception and infiltration. Matyas Rakosi, who engineered the process in Hungary, pointed out in a lecture delivered on February 19, 1952, that in the early stages of the communization of Hungary the problem of revolution was not discussed openly at all. This was because even a theoretical discussion of the dictatorship of the proletariat would have caused great alarm among the communists' partners in coalition and would have hampered the communists' efforts to win over the majority of the small bourgeoisie and even of the working masses.[6] The adoption at the November 1960 Conference of Communist Parties of the formula of the "national democratic front" for underdeveloped countries indicates that the communists in those countries entertain some hope that the process carried out in eastern Europe under cover of the Soviet armed forces may perhaps be repeated today in non-contiguous areas by local communists, backed by Soviet economic aid and helped by the awe inspired by Soviet power.

[6] For a detailed description of the process of communist take-over in eastern Europe, including its propaganda aspects, see Zbigniew Brzezinski, *The Soviet Bloc* (Cambridge, Mass., 1960), Part I.

There is a certain division of labor between the CPSU and the national communist parties which support it. Commenting on one aspect of this CPSU-local communist party coordination, Selig Harrison notes that in India "Soviet and Chinese claims of national equality at home are significant primarily as a backdrop for the separatist political programs of local Communist parties." Local communist parties naturally focus their propaganda somewhat more narrowly than does the CPSU. For example, a comparison of statements on race relations in the United States, and other non-communist countries, during 1957, on Radio Moscow broadcasts in English to western Europe and also in the British *Daily Worker*, revealed that of thirteen references to this topic on the Soviet radio all, whether concerned with South Africa, America, or other countries, attributed the evils attacked to "American imperialism." The London *Daily Worker*, on the other hand, devoted much more attention to race relations—more than one hundred references were noted—but attacked the United States in only about half of the cases analyzed.[7] A systematic analysis of this pattern of coordination would be useful, but could only be undertaken on the basis of case studies not presently available. On the basis of knowledge now available, it appears that while local communist parties play a significant role in strengthening the impact of Soviet propaganda, they lack the flexibility and the sophistication which would be necessary to operate on a really high level of effectiveness.

The united front, the popular front, the national front, or the national liberation front all represent types of coalition which communists seek to utilize for their own purposes. The other main type of international communist organizational structure with national affiliates that requires discussion here is the Soviet-dominated international front organization. The role of the World Peace Council in Soviet international prop-

[7] Harrison, *op.cit.*, p. 146. The above comparative study of Soviet and British propaganda was made by Mr. David E. Price.

aganda has already been described in Chapter IV. Other international communist fronts backstop the peace propaganda of the WPC and at the same time disseminate demands and promises appropriate to particular groups. Following World War II, as Seton-Watson has pointed out, there was "a widespread feeling, not shared by experienced western union leaders, yet no less powerful for that, that the Soviet Union, one of the great allies, stood for the rights of the workers."[8] Capitalizing on this mood, the Soviet leadership brought about the foundation of the WFTU in 1945. Soviet efforts to utilize this and other international organizations primarily as instruments of Soviet propaganda soon led to a considerable degree of disillusionment in the west. In December 1949, non-communist trade unions decided to form the International Confederation of Free Trade Unions (ICFTU), and the WFTU has devoted a large part of its efforts ever since to attacking this organization, which is denounced for allegedly being under the domination of the western "monopolists." In recent years, the main themes of WFTU propaganda have been "peace" and "anti-colonialism." By far the largest part of the membership of the WFTU consists of the trade unions of the Soviet Union, communist China, and the eastern European countries. These unions are, of course, tightly controlled by the ruling communist parties of those countries. The most important foreign labor movements belonging to the WFTU are the French CGT, the Italian CGIL, and the Indonesian SOBSI. A major Indian labor union federation, the TUC, also belongs to the WFTU.

The Declaration issued by the November 1960 Communist Conference in Moscow included an appeal for the "restoration of unity in the trade union movement in countries where it is split." This objective has been pursued with a certain amount of flexibility. It does not necessarily imply an imme-

[8] Hugh Seton-Watson, *Neither War Nor Peace* (New York, 1960), p. 162.

diate attempt to bring all trade unions in non-communist countries into the WFTU. For example, Moscow supported the establishment in May 1961 of an All-African Trades Union Federation (AATUF), spearheaded by labor congresses in Ghana and Guinea. The AATUF resolved that its constituent national members divorce themselves from formal affiliation either with western or communist international labor groups. It appeared that the USSR was prepared to back this policy in order to capitalize on neutralist sentiment in Africa. In Latin America also, communist policy is to promote the formation of united trade union groups, not necessarily affiliated with the WFTU. Soviet policy toward the Latin American labor movement, however, has tended to involve an emphasis on "revolutionary struggle" inappropriate in Africa, where Moscow's policy, despite some aberrations, is still basically one of wooing national governments, such as those headed by Kwame Nkrumah in Ghana or Sekou Touré in Guinea. Rodney Arismende, First Secretary of the Uruguayan Communist Party, wrote in an article in *Kommunist*, No. 5, 1961, that the working class bore the principal responsibility for the outcome of the Latin American revolution, and that it worked primarily through the communist parties and the trade union movement. He particularly praised the unified labor federations of Chile, Cuba, and Uruguay. He also commented favorably on various political general strikes in Chile, Argentina, Uruguay, Cuba, and Venezuela.[9]

At the Fifth Congress of the WFTU held in Moscow from December 4 to 15, 1961, Louis Saillant, its Secretary-General, took the traditional line that any cooperation between the WFTU and the non-communist labor unions must be under communist leadership. Characteristically, Novella, the main spokesman of the Italian delegation, criticized as excessively inflexible Saillant's extreme subservience to Soviet policies.

[9] Some of the above material was drawn from a Radio Free Europe Research and Evaluation Bulletin, dated August 29, 1961.

Both in the WPC and in the WFTU, the Italians have in recent years favored a more flexible policy than that backed by the USSR or by the extremely rigid, "Stalinist" French Communist Party. On the other hand, the Chinese representatives in these organizations have since 1957 argued for revolutionary militancy against "American imperialism." They have also urged more vigorous struggles against western influence in the underdeveloped countries than has the USSR and have indicated impatience with the Soviet tendency to support, in the present era at least, "bourgeois nationalist" regimes in formerly colonial countries.

Two communist front international youth organizations, namely, the World Federation of Democratic Youth and the International Union of Students, have played a considerable role in contemporary international communist propaganda.[10] Both of these organizations are closely linked to the Komsomol, the official, monopoly internal Soviet youth organization. In 1956 there was also set up in the Soviet Union the already-mentioned Committee on Youth Organizations (CYO), which negotiates youth exchanges with youth organizations outside the Soviet Union. Like the WFTU and the WFDY, the IUS was launched on the wave of enthusiasm following World War II. Its constitutional convention took place in Prague, in August 1946. Following the communist coup in Czechoslovakia, in 1948, considerable disillusionment with the activities of the IUS developed in Western Europe. One reason for this disillusionment was the failure of the IUS to intervene on behalf of students of Charles University arrested in connection with the coup. According to Apeland, "from 1948 on, the IUS could not truly speak for any major portion of the world's students

[10] The most useful single source of information on these organizations is the study, *Communist Front Youth Organizations*, by Nils M. Apeland (Bombay, 1959). Current information on these organizations, and other aspects of Soviet international youth activities is contained in *Youth and Freedom*, published since 1957 by the Institute for International Youth Affairs, New York City.

other than the officially sponsored federations of those nations occupied by Russian army troops."[11] From 1948 until after the death of Stalin both the WFDY and the IUS acted as agencies for the dissemination of violently anti-western propaganda. Beginning in 1955-1956 the two organizations have emphasized "cooperation" with non-communist youth organizations and at the same time have echoed the general Soviet propaganda of anti-colonialism.

The most dramatic propaganda efforts sponsored by these two organizations are the World Youth Festivals. The sixth, probably the most successful in terms of its international impact, and certainly the most lavish and expensive, was held in Moscow in 1957. The seventh took place in Vienna in 1959, and the most recent one was in Helsinki in 1962. The Vienna Festival was the first of these mammoth spectacles to be held outside the Soviet orbit. Despite the opposition of Finnish youth organizations and of Finnish public opinion generally, the authorities responsible for Soviet international youth propaganda arranged the Eighth World Festival of Youth and Students in Helsinki in July and August 1962.

Estimates of the cost of the Moscow Festival in 1957 have gone as high as $200,000,000.[12] In this connection, it is interesting that the Soviet magazine *New Times*, No. 30, 1957, reported that for this Moscow Festival, 1,075 railway carriages, 7 ships, "many" aircraft, and 2,600 busses would be placed at the disposal of the visitors.[13] The results of the 1957 Moscow Festival apparently were not entirely satisfactory to the Soviet leadership, at least as far as internal effects were concerned. It was followed by official warnings, which continued through 1962, regarding the dangers to Soviet youth of unrestricted contacts with foreigners. Contacts between Soviet participants and foreign delegates at the 1959 Vienna Festival

[11] Apeland, *op.cit.*, p. 29.
[12] *Ibid.*, p. 53.
[13] *Ibid.*, p. 52.

were much more sharply restricted than had been the case in Moscow in 1957. In keeping with this trend toward tightening of controls on contacts between Soviet youth and the "bourgeois" world, the World Youth Forum, held in Moscow from July 25 through August 3, 1961, was a relatively secretive affair. In an apparent effort to conceal its sponsorship by the WFDY and the IUS, the organizers of the Forum presented it as a more or less spontaneous project of Soviet youth groups whose activities in organizing it were reported as if they were not under centralized political control.

The Forum was an interesting episode in the Soviet campaign for the political exploitation of youth. The following information is based upon bulletins issued by the press center set up to publicize its activities that were supplied to the author by a western student participant. The Forum was opened by Petr Reshetov, then Chairman of the Soviet Committee of Youth Organizations. Sergei Pavlov, Secretary of the Central Committee of the Komsomol, read a message of greetings from Premier Khrushchev that emphasized the representative character of the Forum, the opportunities it opened to youth in the struggle against colonialism, and its value for peace and social progress. Khrushchev also attacked "reactionary forces" in the west who allegedly wanted war. Khrushchev's message, together with other militant speeches, particularly those of the Algerian and Ghanaian representatives, reflected the intensely political character of this gathering. The Forum differed from the more open and carnival-like youth Festivals due to this heavily political emphasis. At the same time, however, the Forum press releases claimed that the assemblage represented most of the world's youth, as well as students' and children's organizations of the most diverse religious and political trends.

In support of this claim to representativeness, lists of organizations which had sent messages of greetings to the Forum were read. Greetings were reportedly sent by Radha Krishna,

Vice-President of India, Subandrio, Minister of Foreign Affairs of Indonesia, the American millionaire Cyrus Eaton, the World Peace Council, the Communist Party of France, the Trade Union Association of Colombia, and many others. While the representative and universal aspects of the Forum were stressed, many American and western European youth organizations were criticized for refusal to participate. The propaganda strategy underlying this gathering appeared to be one of linking up communist propaganda lines with non-communist aspirations.

Some of the promotional activities connected with the Forum included an international photography contest with cash prizes organized by the Soviet youth newspaper *Komsomolskaya Pravda*, and an international fund-raising drive. It was announced that funds had been collected in such countries as Argentina, Venezuela, Cuba, Brazil, Guinea, and Ghana. Participants in the Forum heard concerts presented by leading Soviet choirs, visited a variety of points of interest in the Moscow area, watched athletic events and motion pictures, and met with officials of the Union of Societies of Friendship with Foreign Countries, and with leaders of Soviet youth and sports organizations. They also had meetings with members of the editorial board of *Komsomolskaya Pravda*, and with members of the Economic Committee of the Soviet of Nationalities of the USSR Supreme Soviet.

Both the WFDY and the IUS carry on extensive publication programs. In East Berlin the WFDY publishes *World Youth* in English, French, Spanish, German, Chinese, Polish, Hungarian, Rumanian, Russian, Arabic, and Swedish editions. The WFDY also publishes six other periodicals and issues press releases, publicity and documentary materials, and special publications for World Youth Festivals. The principal magazine of the IUS is *World Student News*, published monthly in Prague, in Arabic, English, French, German, Italian, Norwegian, and Spanish. It also publishes a Russian version in Moscow.

In October 1960, the IUS held its Sixth Congress, in Baghdad. This Congress, the first major meeting that the IUS had held outside a communist country, appeared to be part of a larger effort to capture organized world youth for communism, to which purpose the Forum was later to contribute. According to information gathered by the Independent Research Service, a private American youth organization, the Baghdad Congress was a completely rigged affair, and the meetings and seminars were utilized to pass unanimous anti-western propaganda resolutions. Such resolutions are disseminated by communist propaganda media everywhere as representative of the opinions of the "progressive" youth of the world.[14]

The seventh IUS congress, which took place in Leningrad from August 18 to 29, 1962, was the scene of rather sensational verbal fireworks. Representatives of the extreme leftist, somewhat Trotskyite-oriented Japanese students' organization, Zengakuren, which has for years been the spearhead of anti-American agitation among the student youth of Japan, attacked Soviet nuclear testing and also denounced Khrushchev's peaceful coexistence policy. The latter, they asserted, prevented the mounting of a genuinely revolutionary struggle of the workers of the world against imperialism. Even before this, Zengakuren representatives had demonstrated in Red Square against Soviet testing and had been detained by the Soviet police. After the congress, the Japanese Communist Party began a campaign to eliminate the influence of what it described as anti-Soviet "gangsters" from the Japanese youth and students' movement.

While the Zengakuren revolt was embarrassing to the seasoned Soviet leaders who continue to control the IUS, the seventh congress apparently also scored some successes, par-

[14] See *Bulletin* of Independent Research Service, 333 West 81st St., New York City, February 1, 1961.

ticularly in its effort to exploit anti-Americanism among Latin Americans. One of the most fiery speeches was delivered by Jose Marcano of Puerto Rico. Non-communist youth organizations were bitterly attacked as agents of the American State Department. The Soviet organizers of the congress stressed not only anti-Americanism and anti-colonialism but also the necessity of creating a new united front of world youth. They appealed to the rank and file membership of non-communist national student unions throughout the world over the heads of their leaders, and, as at the 1962 Helsinki Youth Festival, sought to convey the impression that Moscow represents the interests of all right-minded youth everywhere, regardless of present organizational affiliation.

Of all the Soviet-organized Youth Festivals to date, the 1962 Helsinki assemblage appears to have given Moscow the greatest cause for concern, and perhaps even for chagrin. It was apparently poorly organized and ineptly conducted, and competition by American, Swiss, and other anti-communist delegates was more effective than at any previous Soviet-organized youth assembly. As one might expect, a comparison of Soviet and western news sources, including, on the Soviet side, *Pravda, Izvestiya,* and *Komsomolskaya pravda,* and among western newspapers, the *New York Times, Le Monde,* and the *Manchester Guardian,* revealed an extreme lack of agreement on the achievements of the Helsinki Festival. *Komsomolskaya pravda* for August 7, 1962 quoted Claude Gatinion, General Secretary of the WFDY, to the effect that the Helsinki Festival marked "a great step in the international movement of youth." The same paper for August 8 carried a pronouncement by Jean Garcia, President of the International Preparation Committee for the Festival according to which it was "an enormous success." These estimates were supported by such communist newspapers in western Europe as *Unita* in Italy and *L'Humanité* in France. On the other hand, the *Manchester Guardian* apparently thought that the

Festival had been a complete failure, while the *New York Times* regarded it as more a failure than a success, and *Le Monde*, more cautious than the British and American press, reported that some of the non-communist Festival participants had been disillusioned or disappointed by the conduct and results of the Festival.

While it is impossible to arrive at anything approaching a definitive evaluation of the success, from the point of view of its organizers, of the Helsinki Festival, at least two major kinds of frustration or irritation seem to have bulked large in Soviet eyes. One of these was the obvious hostility of many, probably most Finns. The Soviet press indirectly admitted this by publishing items attributing anti-Festival riots to "provocateurs, many of whom were talking with a Washington or Bonn accent," to cite the words of Komsomol leader and Soviet Festival delegation chairman Sergei Pavlov in *Komsomolskaya pravda* for August 8, 1962.

The other main source of Soviet concern about the results of the Festival was the apparent failure to achieve the desired impact upon the youth of the underdeveloped countries. Some of these countries were represented by extremely small delegations, a fact indicated by failure of the Soviet press to give any figures on the size of delegations from India, Indonesia, and other important countries. Figures gathered from the Soviet press indicated that the largest delegations were from Finland—apparently mostly communists, France, Italy, the Soviet Union, West Germany, East Germany, the United States, and Cuba, all of which sent 400 or more delegates. According to Soviet figures, Japan was represented by 200 delegates and Algeria by 150. *Pravda* for July 29, 1962, reported that a total of 18,000 delegates attended the Helsinki Festival. This figure was the same as that given for the Vienna Festival of 1959 and was much smaller than the participation in the 1957 Moscow Festival and all previous Festivals since 1949. On the other hand, the same source claimed that while

131 countries had been represented at Moscow, and 112 had been represented at Vienna, 137 countries had sent delegations to Helsinki and that the 1,500 organizations represented by these delegations were by far the largest number ever to have sent delegates to one of these gatherings.

Apparently, if one disregards Cuba, Latin America was represented by only about 200 delegates. Africa was very sparsely represented and one of the most important African countries, Ghana, did not send any delegation. Moreover, the delegations of Uganda and Nigeria withdrew from the Festival while it was in progress.

The failure of the Soviet press to report more than a very few statements by delegates of African, Asian, or Latin American countries may indicate that in the opinion of the Soviet leadership the impact of the Festival on the delegations from those continents was not outstanding. However, *Komsomolskaya pravda* for August 2, 1962 was able to report a fairly enthusiastic statement by the General Secretary of the Afro-Asian Solidarity Conference who was chosen at a conference in Conakry by representatives of 27 African countries. Apparently the reference was to a meeting held in 1960. The General Secretary praised the understanding displayed by Soviet youth toward African aspirations for peace, and assistance in "the struggle against imperialism, colonialism, and neo-colonialism."

Such sensational events as the departure of some disgusted delegates while the Festival was in progress—including apparently about half of the Ceylonese delegation—were of course widely reported in the western press. A more subtle indication of the failure of the Festival to achieve a very powerful impact upon delegates from Africa, Asia, and Latin America was the report in *Le Monde* for August 8, 1962 that 43 delegates from those continents had preferred to accept invitations from western student organizations to travel in Europe, rather than accept similar offers by the Soviet youth authorities to travel in the USSR. Western newspapers also reported considerable irritation among non-communist delegates because of suppression by the Festival organizers of their points of view. For example, a demonstration against Soviet nuclear tests by 100 delegates from 10 countries was forbidden by the Festival organizers.

We may conclude that the Helsinki Festival was something of a disappointment to the Russians. However, it was part of a continuing effort and the mistakes made at Helsinki will probably be avoided in future Soviet efforts. One of these mistakes was the choice of Helsinki as the host city in the face of Finnish hostility. This hostility may have been underestimated. Another error—as at Vienna—may have been to hold the Festival outside the protective shield of the Iron Curtain. However, if the USSR wishes to avoid the vulnerabilities associated with allowing non-communist youths to spend several weeks on communist-controlled territory it must run certain other risks, such as those involved in forcing the Festival upon the Finns.

Non-communists have little reason to feel complacent about the efforts made by Stalin's successors to turn to communist purposes the desire of the world's youth for peace, prosperity, and progress. Despite its mistakes the Soviet campaign remains formidable. Thus far the west has not succeeded either in discrediting the Soviet youth drive to any significant degree or in mounting an adequate alternative program of persuasion. Commendable efforts by small private student groups, such as the "Young America Presents" exhibition organized by students from Yale and other American universities in competition with the Helsinki Festival are all to the good. But a more massive, systematic effort is needed if Moscow is not to win by default the struggle for the minds of the future leaders of men. Such an effort of course is not mainly a matter of organization. It is largely a matter of imaginative statecraft by which democracy would demonstrate that it is not merely the ideological façade of plutocracy, but is a meaningful doctrine for mobilizing minds and wills to put the great modern resources of scientific knowledge at the service of the idealism of youth.

The other Soviet international propaganda front organizations are similar in their style of operations to those already described. This style is characterized by extreme conformity to Moscow-approved views, achieved by manipulation, pressure, intimidation, and even by violence. To the extent that those non-communist individuals, groups, or organizations that participate in Soviet-sponsored world youth gatherings express unorthodox opinions, they are likely to be ignored or slandered. Non-communist participation, if skillful, can be effective, and in connection with the 1957, 1959, and 1962 Youth Festivals, probably did much to bring new ideas to the attention of Soviet young people, but the difficulties attendant upon such efforts to break into the closed circuit of communist communications channels should not be underestimated.

No comprehensive descriptive or analytical study of international communist front organizations is available.[15] In spite of the elaborate efforts made by these organizations to mask communist control, often including frequent changes of name and the establishment of front groups as covers for the activities of other front groups, their character is usually not difficult to discern. This is true because of the usually patent similarities, or even identity, between the decisions, positions, resolutions, and slogans of the front groups and those of the CPSU. Other international communist fronts or front-type organizations are the World Federation of Teachers Unions, an affiliate of the WFTU which held its Third World Conference of Teachers in Conakry, Guinea, in July 1960, the World Federation of Scientific Workers, and the International Organization

[15] See, however, the works of Seton-Watson, Selznick, Neal Wood, and others cited in this study, as well as the pamphlet by Robert Orth, *Hilfsorganisationen des Weltkommunismus* (Bonn, n.d., probably 1958).

of Journalists.[16] This brief survey of international front organizations will be concluded with mention of recent developments in the activities of Soviet friendship societies.

The present era in the activities of the friendship societies
began with the abolition of VOKS, the All-Union Society for
Cultural Relations with Foreign Countries, in 1958, and its
replacement by a system of foreign friendship societies and
Soviet counterpart societies. While signaling an expansion of
Soviet foreign cultural relations and exchanges of persons, this
reorganization in effect represented little more than a change
of name. It was followed, however, by a steady increase in the
numbers of Soviet friendship societies and the conclusion of
cultural exchange agreements and treaties with an increasing
number of foreign countries, especially in Africa.

Of special interest to Americans was the establishment on
August 31, 1961 of an Institute of Soviet-American Relations
in Moscow. The birth of this new friendship organization was
reported in release No. 196, dated September 12, 1961, put out
by the press department of the Soviet Embassy in Washington. The first paragraph of the release described this organization as a "voluntary, non-governmental organization." It stated
that the purpose of the Institute was to "develop and
strengthen, in every way possible, mutual understanding, trust
and friendship between the peoples of the Soviet Union and
the United States in the interest of lasting peace." The constituent assembly which established the new organization "on
the initiative of forty-two Soviet organizations" issued an
appeal "to the citizens and public and cultural organizations
of the USA."

The establishment of this new institute may well have been
an important step in Soviet propaganda. Certain aspects of

[16] On the activities of the World Federation of Teachers, see address
by Lyman B. Kirkpatrick, Jr., Inspector General of the Central Intelligence Agency, delivered April 12, 1961, and reprinted in the Congressional Record for May 4, 1961.

this move are worthy of comment. Every attempt was made in the above press release to create the impression that the formation of the institute was a spontaneous action on the part of individual Soviet citizens and private organizations. Among the organizations that, according to the above press release, took the initiative in establishing the Institute of Soviet-American Relations, was the All-Union Society for the Dissemination of Political and Scientific Knowledge. The Soviet publication, *Problems of Ideological Work*, previously cited in this study, contained on pages 137-143 a decree of the Central Committee of the CPSU, dated August 27, 1959, entitled "Concerning Measures for the Improvement of the Work of the All-Union Society for the Dissemination of Political and Scientific Knowledge." This decree, which had not been published prior to the appearance of the above book, indicates the limitations of the Soviet concept of a "voluntary" organization. It severely criticized various activities of the All-Union Society. However, more pertinent for our purposes is the fact that the central committee decree devoted four full pages to issuing the most detailed instructions to the society regarding its obligations and activities. The contrast between the above Soviet Embassy press release and the central committee decree is illuminating. Comparison between the language of the press release, directed to the American public, and that of the central committee decree, directed to the Soviet communist bureaucracy, underscores the fact that when Soviet sources use the word "voluntary" with regard to propaganda organizations, they use it in a fashion peculiar to themselves.

In concluding these observations on front organizations, it should perhaps be noted that communists cannot always use such organizational devices as fronts solely for their own purposes and to the disadvantage of their competitiors. Summing up their well-documented chapter on "Fronts and Fellow Travelers," in India, Overstreet and Windmiller conclude that the front is a double-edged weapon which may even "provide a means by which those who are not Communists, or not even sympathetic to Communism, can influence Communist policy."[17]

An important and growing aspect of the Soviet foreign propaganda effort consists in the provision of opportunities for higher education to students from non-communist countries. The most arresting development in this field in recent years was the establishment of the Patrice Lumumba Peoples Friendship University in 1960, mentioned in Chapter V. Friendship University began its second academic year in September 1961. Five hundred and forty-two foreign students, who had devoted the previous academic year mainly to the study of the Russian language, began a four-year course that included physics and mathematics, natural sciences, engineering, agriculture, medicine, history, philology, economics, and law. Sixty Soviet students were also admitted to the second year. In October, 700 new students enrolled in the preparatory faculty, and of these 520 came from 50 countries of Asia, Africa, and Latin America. The remainder were either Soviet students or foreign students transferred from other Soviet institutions of higher education. By 1965 the enrollment at Friendship University is expected to mount to between three and four thousand.[18] Friendship University differs from all other educational institutions presently operating in the world in that it is an international institution for general higher education. It constitutes a significant part of the Soviet and Soviet bloc program for international elite recruitment. If its efforts are successful, it will produce cadres of a Soviet-oriented technical intelligentsia for underdeveloped countries. An interesting propaganda aspect of Friendship University is the fact that its governing council includes representatives from the Soviet affiliate of the Afro-Asian Solidarity Committee, the

[17] Overstreet and Windmiller, *op.cit.*, pp. 444-445.
[18] David Burg in *Problems of Communism*, *op.cit.*, p. 50.

Union of Soviet Societies for Friendship with Foreign Countries, the All-Union Central Council of Trade Unions, and the Komsomol.

In addition to foreign students at Friendship University there were, by 1960, 1,757 students from free world countries in the Soviet Union. This represented an increase from a figure of 1,113 in 1959. The Soviet student program had approximately quadrupled in size since it began in 1956. One major cause for the above increase, of course, was the establishment of Friendship University. It might be useful to indicate here also the number of free world students studying in the entire Sino-Soviet bloc in 1960. The largest increases in this area had come from Latin America and Africa. The number of students from Latin America increased from 167 in 1959 to 496 in 1960, while African student numbers increased from 694 to 1,166. Countries of the Middle East accounted for 1,281 students in 1960, compared with 993 in 1959.[19] According to information compiled in 1962 by the United States Information Agency, by the end of 1961, 6,625 "technical students" had been trained in the Sino-Soviet bloc between that date and January 1956. Of these, 4,325 received their training in the USSR. It is not clear whether these figures include Cubans sent to communist countries to be trained as farm machinery operators, factory technicians, etc. In 1962 the United States Information Agency reported that as of 1961, a total of 3,494 Latin American students were enrolled in educational institutions of communist-ruled countries. These were sub-divided into 1,634 "academic" students, and 1,860 "technical" students. In both categories, Cuba was overwhelmingly predominant, although the figures included 60 Bolivians, 55 Mexicans, 26 Brazilians, and 19 Venezuelans.

The numbers of students from underdeveloped countries in the Soviet bloc countries were apparently still increasing

[19] Unclassified Intelligence Report No. 8401, entitled "Sino-Soviet Bloc Exchanges with the Free World in 1960," Bureau of Intelligence and Research (Washington, D.C., 1961), p. 9.

rapidly in 1962. This was the impression gained by members of a Yale student group which spent two weeks in the USSR in March of that year. A member of this group reported that he was told by a Cuban student at Kiev University that there were 600 students at that university from Cuba alone. Moreover, the same Yale student reportedly heard that 4,000 Cuban youths, some of them students, were about to come to Russia for various kinds of technical training.

According to a United States Information Agency report, as of March, 1962, 3,064 African students were enrolled in educational institutions of all kinds in communist-ruled countries, with the USSR in first place in numbers. Unclassified Department of State Intelligence Report No. 8182, dated December 21, 1959, states that over 90 per cent of the free world students in the Soviet bloc came at that time from underdeveloped countries of Asia and Africa. As of that date, about 1,800 free world students were enrolled in universities of the Soviet bloc as a whole. East Germany and Czechoslovakia were, next to the Soviet Union, the most important participants in this educational effort. As far as student and faculty exchanges between the USSR and western countries were concerned, the most substantial were those with France, Great Britain, and the United States.

It seems clear that the major motivation of Soviet academic and scholarly exchanges with advanced western countries is to obtain technical information. Exchanges with underdeveloped countries are apparently motivated mainly by both short-term and long-term propaganda considerations. In the short run, an impression is made by associating the USSR with educational opportunity. In this connection, it should be mentioned that the IUS, as well as the Soviet government directly, offer scholarships to many Asians, Africans, and Latin Americans, particularly Cubans. Some of this recruitment activity has led to friction between the Soviet Union and Asian and African governments. The latter are concerned about the possible dangers of political exploitation of their nationals. It is significant that some of the African students who have left Russia and other communist-controlled countries in disillusionment over their treatment—a striking episode was the exodus from Bulgaria in early 1963—have complained about political indoctrination efforts. The long-run propaganda implication of Soviet educational and training programs consists, as has already been suggested, in a possible contribution to the formation of a pro-Soviet or even a communist-oriented professional elite in the developing nations. In this area, such Soviet activities as the construction of a polytechnical institute in Guinea are significant. The extreme caution displayed by the Soviet authorities in handling student and other exchange programs with the advanced western nations indicates that for the foreseeable future Moscow entertains little hope of utilizing them to exert substantial political influence. Such exchanges can, however, make a modest contribution to Soviet peace and friendship propaganda. Also, they provide training opportunities for future Soviet experts on western Europe and the United States.

A word should perhaps be said here about the various Soviet programs of the 1920's and 1930's for the training of foreign communists. The institutions involved included the Lenin School, devoted mainly to training communist functionaries from western countries, the Sun Yat-sen University, the Communist University of the Toilers of the East (known as Kutv), named after Stalin, and a Communist University of the Peoples of the West, named after Markhlevski, a founder of the Polish Communist Party.[20] Apparently a considerable number of individuals who today serve as middle-rank functionaries of the Indonesian, Chinese, Indian, or Vietnamese communist parties were graduated from those of the above institutions that specialized in training Asians.[21] Many of the graduates

[20] "Friendship University—The Early Versions," *Survey*, No. 37, July-September, 1961, pp. 17-23.
[21] *Ibid.*, pp. 20-22.

of these schools, however, later defected from communism. One of the best known Americans in this category is Joseph Zack Kornfeder, who, as a member of the Central Executive Committee of the Communist Party of the USA was sent to receive training in the Lenin School in 1928-1929.[22]

While somewhat incidental to our main concern here, the conversion of some African, Asian, and Latin American students to communism during periods of study in western European or American universities should be mentioned. In contemporary Africa, in particular, students who returned from the west as radical anti-western nationalists or in some cases even as communists and now occupy positions of leadership in governments and in the labor movement, have played a part in fostering the world-wide Soviet propaganda effort. Some African trade union leaders were trained, following World War II, in WFTU schools.

For long-term potential impact the educational and training programs discussed above probably are the most significant aspect of the Soviet exchange of persons effort. However, a significant role in Soviet international propaganda is also played, particularly in terms of immediate propaganda dividends, by the steady growth of cultural, athletic, tourist, and other exchanges. While not without its risks to the Soviet side, as we have already pointed out, this traffic has the advantage of fostering the image of the legitimacy and the respectability of the Soviet regime sought by the Kremlin.[23] The growth of the Soviet exchange program can perhaps best be indicated by

[22] *The Revival of the Communist International and Its Significance for the United States,* Staff Study by the Subcommittee To Investigate the Administration of the Internal Security Act and Other Internal Security Laws to the Committee on the Judiciary, United States Senate, 86th Cong., 1st Sess. (Washington, U.S. Government Printing Office, 1959), p. 20.

[23] Some astute comment on the extremely self-centered political calculations underlying the Soviet exchange program, particularly the sending of Soviet citizens as well-briefed "tourists" to foreign countries, is contained in Chap. ix of Joseph Novak, *The Future Is Ours, Comrade* (New York, 1960).

the fact that in 1960 more than 40,000 Soviet tourists visited free world countries. Sudan, Tunisia, Guinea, Thailand, and Nepal were new countries added to the list in that year and as 1960 closed, the first Soviet tourists arrived in Cuba. About 500 came to the United States.[24] More than 100,000 free world tourists visited the USSR in 1960, including some 12,000 to 13,000 from the United States. These figures are impressive when it is considered that in 1953 only 42 private travelers "were enjoying Soviet hospitality."[25]

The geographical and topical pattern of the over-all Soviet exchanges of persons program, except for tourism, has remained remarkably stable since 1954. According to information compiled by a United States government source, and based upon statistics gathered over the period 1954-1960, the most impressive feature of the program was its consistency both in types of exchanges and in geographical emphasis. Technical, scientific, and professional delegations have always dominated the Soviet side of the exchange program. Western Europe, the United States, and Canada have consistently had a majority of the exchanges with the USSR. This includes both delegations going into the USSR and those sent out from the USSR. Further, there has been a consistent ratio of two to one in exchanges, with two delegations going to the USSR for every one leaving, and this has been true regardless of geographic area. In terms of total numbers involved, the Soviet exchange program surged upward rapidly from 1954 to 1958. At that point, the rate of growth began to flatten out. However, the rate of receipt by the USSR of foreign tourists continued to grow rather rapidly.

While, as indicated by the above data, the Soviets have obviously regarded the advanced western countries as the main sources of concern for their exchanges of persons pro-

[24] U.S. Department of State, Bureau of Intelligence and Research, Unclassified Report No. 8401, February 1, 1961, pp. 6-7.
[25] F. Bowen Evans, *op.cit.*, p. 89.

gram, their emphasis in terms of publicity given to exchanges has been on the Afro-Asian area. In exchanges with the west, the Soviets are primarily concerned with obtaining information. In exchanges with underdeveloped countries, they are primarily concerned with propaganda. In all of their exchanges of persons programs they seek to import information and to export propaganda. Despite quantitative and qualitative changes in Soviet policy toward exchanges of persons with non-communist countries, the interpretation of this policy made by F. Bowen Evans in 1955 remains valid. "The government makes no effort really to widen the paths of understanding between the peoples of the East and West. Instead, while professing for propaganda purposes that cultural exchange is a valued instrument in easing tensions between the people, internally the Soviet press keeps up its bitter denunciations of the culture and peoples of the West. It feeds its people interviews and favorable comments of visiting delegates from the West regarding their impressions of the Soviet Union, but provides them with no basis for getting a broader understanding of these visitors.

"In short, the Soviet cultural program is not a true exchange program, but strictly an export program. The visitors into the Soviet Union are there to see the advancements and progress under communism and are expected to go back and relate their impressions. The people the Soviet Union sends out are expected to expound the advantages of life under communism."[26]

Ronald Hingley, in his article "Britain Today in Soviet Writing," which appeared in *Survey* for October 1962 came to conclusions similar to those reached by Evans seven years earlier. Hingley compared the "widely differing stories" about Russia published by western visitors with five representative published Soviet impressions of visits to Britain—in which, he observed, there was "something approaching uniformity." There was also, Hingley noted, uniformity of omission, in

[26] *Ibid.*, pp. 88-89.

Soviet accounts, of the fact that in "capitalist" Britain university students are largely supported by the state or by local authorities, that free medical service is available, etc. Hingley concluded his survey with the observation that Soviet readers "may well come to the erroneous conclusion that life in Britain must be a kind of paradise on earth if it is necessary to misrepresent it at such length and with such persistency."

The propaganda-conscious Soviet leadership early appreciated the unique advantages of radio as an instrument of international communication. Radio has the greatest potential for reaching the largest audiences. It can leap over political boundaries. It can reach illiterates. All those who are within range of a receiving transmitter belong to its potential audience. Those who hear broadcasts can and do pass the word on to others. Provided a radio broadcast is not jammed, and that natural conditions make its reception possible, it has the advantage of not being subject to the distortions which may be involved in editorializing of foreign communications transmitted in printed form.

Lenin is said to have called the radio a newspaper "without paper and without distances."[27] The Soviets began in 1933 on a small scale with German-language broadcasts by long-wave, and started short-wave broadcasts in 1934. By 1942, Soviet short-wave broadcasting had reached a figure of approximately 400 hours per week, in 17 foreign languages.[28] By 1952, Russia was first among 68 nations engaged in international radio broadcasting, with a total of almost 700 hours of the world total of about 7,000 broadcast hours a week. As of 1953, the Soviet Union broadcast 78 hours a week to the United States, for example, while Voice of America broadcasts to the USSR amounted to 52½ hours.[29] Cut back as a result of World War

[27] Quoted in Simon Costikyan, *Twelve Years of Communist Broadcasting, 1948-1959* (U.S. Information Agency, Washington, D.C., n.d., probably 1960), p. 3.
[28] *Ibid.*, p. 7.
[29] Martin, *op.cit.*, p. 47.

II, Soviet foreign radio broadcasting amounted in 1948 to 334 hours per week, or 55 per cent of the total communist effort. The primary target was western Europe, which received 40 per cent of total Soviet radio propaganda. The Near East, South Asia, and Africa area, and the Far East area received, respectively, 14 and 17 per cent of the Soviet broadcast hours. Very little attention was devoted to the Americas. By 1959, while total Soviet broadcasting had greatly increased, along with the increased output of the entire Sino-Soviet bloc, western Europe had dropped to second place among Soviet radio targets, with 27 per cent of the total. The Near East, South Asia, and Africa area had by that year attained first place in the Soviet effort. The hours of radio propaganda devoted to the Near East, South Asia, and Africa rose between 1948 and 1959 from 14 to 30 per cent of the total Soviet output, and the number of languages used increased from six to thirteen. Soviet broadcasts to the Far East, on the other hand, accounted for only 12 per cent of the total USSR output in 1959, as compared with 17 per cent in 1948. Output to Latin America remained at a low level, but broadcasts to North America more than doubled, increasing from 5 per cent to 11 per cent of the total Soviet effort. Broadcasts to Soviet refugees abroad also greatly increased during this period.

Soviet propaganda by short-wave radio has displayed the same sensitivity to emerging opportunities as has been characteristic of other Soviet propaganda media over the years. For example, Africa has lately, and with startling suddenness, become an important target for Soviet broadcasting. Beginning in 1956, the Chinese communists began broadcasts in English for "Egypt and Central Africa." These broadcasts were dropped in February 1958, but in April 1958 the USSR inaugurated its first broadcasts to Africa in English and French, announcing also that programs in native languages and dialects would also be transmitted soon. In February 1960, Radio Moscow started broadcasting regularly in Swahili, a language first used by it in the fall of 1958. In recent years, the communist countries have offered technical assistance to African countries in setting up radio stations, gifts of radio transmitters and sets, training of Africans as technicians and announcers, etc.[30] Communist radio broadcasting to Africa almost doubled in the first half of 1960.[31] According to a report issued by the United States Information Agency on August 25, 1961, the highest rate of expansion of communist broadcasting in the first half of 1961 was to Africa. Among other things, broadcasts in Amharic to Ethiopia began during that period. During the year 1961, Moscow Radio's Swahili broadcasts quintupled, and Portuguese-language broadcasts to Portuguese Africa were initiated. In 1961, the USSR exceeded 1,000 hours of broadcasting per week for the first time, while the eastern European communist states, taken as a group, broadcast 1,100 hours per week. Broadcasts to the Near East and South Asia, to the Far East, and to Latin America were also increased substantially. Sino-Soviet bloc broadcasts to Latin America increased in 1961 from 167 hours to 218 hours, while the share of Moscow in this effort increased from 56 to 63 hours.

Illustrative of both the continued steady growth of Soviet foreign radio broadcasting and of its ceaseless probing for vulnerabilities in the non-communist world were the increases in the first half of 1962 in total USSR broadcast hours from 1,067 in 1961 to a rate of 1,129 in 1962, and the beginning of USSR broadcasting to Africa in the Hausa and Somali languages. According to official American sources the Soviet Union in the first six months of 1962 increased its African output by 33 per cent. The USSR and other communist countries greatly increased their broadcasts in this period to Vietnam and other Southeast Asian countries, pointing to the heightened significance of this area of acute tension and flaming guerrilla warfare. Also indicative of the increasing role of

[30] Costikyan, *op.cit.*, p. 28.
[31] *Ibid.*, p. 29.

radio propaganda and of heightened international tension was a substantial increase in communist clandestine broadcasts, with three new stations, attacking, respectively, the governments of Portugal, South Vietnam and Thailand, and all coming on the air in the first half of 1962. In this connection, it is significant that communist clandestine broadcasts, according to United States official sources, have steadily increased in volume, rising from 125 hours a week in 1951 to 244 hours in 1961.

An interesting aspect of Soviet and Soviet bloc radio propaganda consists of the activities of the International Radio and Television Organization (OIRT). This organization was formed in 1946 in Brussels. Many countries participated at first, with the notable exception of the BBC, which in 1950 took the initiative in setting up a rival body, the European Broadcasting Union (EBU). All the leading non-communist countries have left the OIRT, which like a number of other international front organizations, has its headquarters in Prague. In recent years, the OIRT has conducted a campaign designed to bring about "cooperation" with the EBU. However, its efforts in this direction have been largely unsuccessful, due in part at least to its persistence in disseminating militantly anti-American and anti-British propaganda.[32] Among the broadcast activities of OIRT is the "Science in the Service of Peace" series, inaugurated in 1957. The first lecture in this series was delivered by Professor John Bernal, the eminent British physicist and vice-president of the World Federation of Scientific Workers and also of the British Peace Committee.[33]

Other devices used by Soviet and other communist radio programs include language lessons, radio contests, quizzes, and the celebration of holidays and anniversaries. As has already been noted, Soviet and other communist radio efforts include extensive broadcasting of covert propaganda over

[32] *Ibid.*, pp. 45-47.
[33] *Ibid.*, p. 35.

282

clandestine stations. These communist clandestine stations attack "unfriendly" governments in violent language and on occasion advocate revolt.[34]

An analysis of Radio Moscow broadcasts in English to North America covering three weeks, in February and March 1960, led to the conclusion that the tasks of the broadcasts were: to present the Soviet foreign policy in the most favorable light possible; to reveal the "true" motives of western foreign policy; to present Soviet domestic life favorably, connecting its benefits with "socialism"; and, finally, to present socialism, communism, and the socialist state persuasively.[35] It was found that the staff of the North American Service spoke excellent English, with a good command of American idiom, mixed, however, with occasional British expressions. The two main categories of the broadcasts were music, especially Russian classical music, and various kinds of news items. There were also special features such as "Moscow Mailbag," which had the purpose of "answering its listeners' questions about the Soviet Union and playing their musical requests." Other features included interviews with "average" Soviet citizens about matters of everyday life, "travelogue" programs, and such ideological programs as "What Is Communism." The results of this study tended to confirm the impression of United States government experts on Soviet propaganda that Radio Moscow was not likely to achieve much impact, at least on Americans. The effort expended on Radio Moscow's North American service is somewhat puzzling. One wonders whether or not it is intended mainly for communists and fellow travelers, although certainly such groups can follow the Soviet point of view in English or Russian-language Soviet magazines and newspapers that are readily available in the United States and Canada.

The content of Radio Moscow North American service

---

[34] *Ibid.*, pp. 2, 4, 77.
[35] This study was made by Mr. John Peterson, on the basis of monitoring with a short-wave radio set.

broadcasts, as indicated by the above study and by subsequent reading of monitored reports on it, did not, at least until very recently, appear to be of a character calculated to persuade anyone not already strongly sympathetic to the Soviet cause. For example, during the February-March 1960 period, the anti-American statements of Fidel Castro were frequently quoted. Also, while the Soviet Union was officially neutral in the French-Algerian conflict, Moscow Radio about once a week reported the casualty list of French soldiers as published by the rebels. Over the years, this service of Radio Moscow has presented the same denunciations of "Fascists" in West Germany as could be found in *Pravda*. With regard to disarmament, western arguments were always refuted, but the western side was not allowed to speak for itself. In other words, on Radio Moscow the listener heard what the Soviet Union said the west said.

However, it might be premature to write off as crude and hence ineffective even that portion of Radio Moscow's output which is beamed to North America. The most recent available study of the Soviet North American service stressed the increasing sophistication of its broadcasts, and noted both the care with which they are now being prepared—despite "an illusion of casual spontaneity"—and also the "frankly experimental approach" displayed in their subject matter and in answering the most difficult questions on matters formerly dodged by Soviet broadcasters.[36]

According to United States government sources interviewed by this writer, the world-wide audience of Radio Moscow is smaller than that of either the Voice of America or the BBC. It seems certain that Radio Moscow does not enjoy anything like the reputation for objectivity possessed by the BBC. It does, nevertheless, have certain advantages over western radio

[36] W. S. Howell and E. W. Ziebarth, "The Soviet Airwaves," Ch. 8 of *Soviet Union*, ed. by Robert T. Holt and John E. Turner (New York, 1963).

programs. Because it is not subject to such controls as those exercised in the United States by Congress over the Voice of America, it can proceed with great quickness to shift its attention to areas and events thought to be susceptible of propaganda exploitation. It has immense financial and personnel resources at its disposal. Certainly in terms of weekly broadcast hours, the Soviet effort in the use of radio as an international propaganda instrument is the largest in the world. It also has the most powerful transmitting equipment of any international radio system. The advantages enjoyed by Radio Moscow in terms of numbers of hours, strength of signal, and ability to exploit developing situations may at times be of considerable political importance.

Such a view was expressed, for example, by C. L. Sulzberger in the *New York Times* for August 7, 1961. Referring to United States efforts to strengthen American propaganda in the Middle East, Mr. Sulzberger noted that in numbers of languages, numbers of hours broadcast, and strength of transmissions in the Afro-Asian area the United States lagged far behind Russia, Communist China, and the United Arab Republic. The United States had even ceased Persian programs to Iran in October 1960 because the American radio signal was too weak. In evaluating such a situation it must be kept in mind that Soviet and satellite radio programs are coordinated. This division of labor permits the Soviet Union to devote more attention to the Far East, for example, with a given amount of resources, than would otherwise be the case.

Although television is of far more limited international propaganda use than is radio, both the Soviet Union and the United States are employing it on a considerable scale for the purposes of international political and cultural communication. The greatest penetration of a non-communist audience by communist television is achieved by Soviet orbit countries that have arranged a number of exchanges of television films with western countries. As of 1956, the BBC had an exchange agreement with Moscow Television, which furnished the BBC 66 newsreels and shorts over a six-month period.[37] In 1961 the Eurofilm television network disseminated all over western Europe broadcasts on Soviet astronauts Gagarin's and Titov's feats and also broadcast the Moscow May Day parade. However, in terms of comparative propaganda gains, as far as television exploitation of space activity is concerned, it seems likely that the openness with which American space flights have been conducted conferred compensatory benefits for television and radio coverage that may have more than made up for Soviet priority in time and superiority in numbers of orbits.

In terms of capacity for exerting long-run influence, the export of printed matter may well rank second in significance only to student exchange, and may even be a more potent channel of influence in certain respects and under certain conditions. The Soviet Union has for many years made use of the export of books, magazines, and newspapers, in Russian and in foreign languages, as instruments of agitation, propaganda, and indoctrination. Soviet publications are exported by the International Book Company, or Mezhkniga (its Russian abbreviation). This organization, which is a branch of the Ministry of Foreign Trade of the USSR, was founded in 1923. It exports books, periodicals, music, and records. Other Soviet export agencies such as Artkino Pictures, Inc., which distributes Soviet films, and institutions such as the Academy of Sciences of the USSR, or the major Soviet libraries, particularly the Lenin Library in Moscow, disseminate Soviet publications, as well as artistic and musical materials, throughout the world. It should also be noted that, large as the program of export of books in foreign languages published inside the USSR and other communist countries is, it accounts for but a fraction of the total of books published under Soviet bloc

[37] Kirkpatrick, *Year of Crisis*, pp. 316-317.

auspices. According to United States government sources, by far the largest percentage of such publications are issued outside of the Sino-Soviet bloc by pro-communist presses under contract with such firms as Mezhkniga or the Chinese Communist International Bookstore of Peking.

As of 1958, the International Book Company had reportedly concluded contracts with 840 firms in 68 foreign countries for the export of books and periodicals. It was sending to these firms more than 1,000 newspapers and magazines, and 16,000 titles of books for distribution. There were over 200 publishing houses engaged in supplying this material.[38] While it is extremely difficult to obtain total figures on Soviet publications exports, partly because the USSR prints a large number of books and pamphlets for free distribution, on which no figures are available, it is obvious that the Soviet publications export program is large and is growing rapidly.[39] In 1961, according to a Government report, some 150,000,000 copies of books in foreign languages were produced by the USSR for distribution abroad. One important aspect of the dissemination of Soviet influence by means of printed matter is the translation, in foreign countries and by foreign publishing houses, of Soviet books. As the author of one recent study notes: "Soviet spokesmen have frequently complained that there is but little interest in the West for Soviet books, whereas so many Western writers have been translated in recent years in the Soviet Union. But the published figures do not seem to bear out this complaint. In comparison with about twelve hundred books by non-Soviet authors published in Russia in 1959 around nine thousand Soviet books have been published abroad each year since 1957. It is an impressive figure, even

[38] The above information was obtained from an unclassified U.S. Information Agency Report entitled "Book Publishing Program of the Sino-Soviet Bloc," issued in 1959.

[39] United States government sources estimate that the number of copies of Soviet publications handed out at the Soviet Pavilion at the Brussels Fair in 1958 may have run into the millions.

if one takes into account that probably the great majority of these books and booklets were sponsored by Soviet representatives abroad and local Communist parties rather than published through ordinary commercial channels."[40]

Soviet publications are distributed throughout the free world by such large, well-stocked outlets as the Four Continent Bookstore in New York, Collet's Holdings Ltd., in London, the Maison du Livre Étranger, in Paris, and the network operated in India by the People's Publishing House. Indicative of the scope of Soviet distribution of publications in India is the fact that in 1958 the People's Publishing House expanded its thirty-page 1957 English-language catalogue to one hundred and eleven pages.[41] The material distributed through such outlets is generally sold at a very low price. In fact, Soviet books are often priced at a level so low that the only apparent reason for charging for them at all is to avoid the accusation of distributing free propaganda. At the same time, however, the sale of material originating in the Sino-Soviet bloc is a source of revenue to foreign communist parties. According to Overstreet and Windmiller, "The Indian Communist Party receives, free of charge, a flood of books from the Communist countries, and these are distributed through its regular channels at very low prices. The foreign Communist material is supplemented by the publications of the Soviet news agency TASS; its New Delhi office not only issues official press releases to Indian newspapers, but also produces occasional pamphlets for general circulation."[42]

According to an official U.S. government source, the Soviet Union shipped about 4,000,000 copies of books to India in 1958, compared with 2,900,000 copies in 1957, 79,000 in 1956,

[40] The above quotation was the concluding paragraph of an article "Foreign Books in the USSR," in *Survey*, No. 31, January-March, 1960, p. 19.

[41] *Communist Propaganda: A Fact Book* (U.S. Information Agency, Washington, D.C., n.d.), p. 74.

[42] Overstreet and Windmiller, *Communism in India*, p. 457.

and only 17,000 in 1955. A letter, dated September 12, 1958, and entitled "An Electric Light in India," written by the editor of the Indian weekly tabloid *Current* to the editor of the *Washington Post*, stated that the Russians were taking advantage of the desperate desire of Indians to learn by making reading available for the Indian masses at ridiculously low prices. The Indian editor observed that "Soon a whole generation through no fault of its own will grow up believing there are virtues in communism under the light India has installed with the aid of the democracies." During the same year, the Soviet Union and other communist countries began a campaign to saturate the Latin American countries with books. The catalogues of communist publishing houses in Montevideo and Mexico City for 1958 and 1959 listed hundreds of titles of Soviet books in Spanish. In Japan, as long ago as 1956, 146 Soviet books were translated, according to U.S. Government information, and 885,000 copies were published.

In 1960 the Soviet Union inaugurated a large-scale program for the publication of textbooks in foreign languages for underdeveloped countries. The books ranged from objective texts on scientific subjects to such topics as Marxism-Leninism or the history of the CPSU that had a heavy load of indoctrination. English, Spanish, and French editions ran from 20,000 to 40,000 while Arabic editions ran to about 5,000 copies. The 1961 schedule of this expanding textbook publication program called for the publication of more than 30 textbooks in the English language alone. According to Soviet sources, the textbooks were destined mainly for students of secondary schools and higher educational institutions in underdeveloped countries. The *New York Times* for April 1, 1962, on the basis of material supplied by the chairman of the board of the McGraw-Hill Book Company, reported that the USSR was exporting about half again as many books as the United States. Publishing circles in the United States apparently believe, however, that such factors as the already well established position of

American textbooks together with American promotional skills, will enable the United States to compete effectively with the Soviet Union in meeting the rising demand of the underdeveloped countries for books of all kinds.

The Soviet export program of publications in foreign languages is accompanied by promotion of study of the Russian language abroad. For example, the 100,000 subscribers of *Moscow News*—published in English, with a version also in French—received free of charge, in 1960, a copy of a textbook entitled *Learning Russian.* In 1961, textbooks for the study of Russian were published by Soviet presses in at least ten languages, including Afghan, Hindi, Arabic, and modern Greek.[43]

The Soviet venture into large-scale textbook distribution added an important new category to a program which had long featured such major areas as Russian classical literature, Soviet fiction and drama, the "classics" of Marxism-Leninism (until 1953 dominated by the works of Joseph Stalin), children's books, etc. A survey based on the *UNESCO Index of Translations,* for 1960, indicated that out of 4,456 titles translated by Soviet publishing houses either from Russian to a foreign language, or the reverse, in 1959, 13.3 per cent of these translations were to or from English, 3.5 per cent to or from either Hindi or Urdu, 1.5 per cent to or from Spanish, 1 per cent to or from Arabic, and .02 per cent to or from Japanese. The largest category of such translations in 1959 was literature. The second was law and social science. In all of these languages except for English, these two categories far outweighed the exact and applied sciences. In English, however, the exact and applied sciences bulked fairly large and, judging from the material presented above, there has in recent years been a growing tendency for the Soviet Union to export Soviet-

[43] The above material is drawn from an unclassified U.S. Information Agency Report entitled "Growth of Book Publishing in the Sino-Soviet Bloc," distributed in 1961.

originated scientific textbooks in the English language. During 1961, the USSR greatly increased its publication of Spanish-language publications, especially in such "action" subjects as organization of demonstrations, anti-government revolts, and guerrilla warfare.

Some indication of the missionary spirit in which the Soviet Union approaches the export of printed matter may perhaps be gained from a book published in 1958 by the State Publishing House for Political Literature.[44] The chapter titles of this book such as "The Word of Truth," or "The Hope of Peace and the Bulwark of the Universe," reflect an evangelistic spirit. The author, for example, quotes the well-known Chilean communist poet Pablo Neruda, as saying of the USSR, "Your achievements are the happiness of our life."[45] This publication also quotes Indian, Indonesian, Italian, and other writers and critics extolling the virtues of Soviet books. It asserts that during the period 1955-1958 more than 900 Soviet writers had been published abroad in about 100,000,000 copies and in 45 languages, and that this program was spreading the ideas of communism. Japanese students were quoted as having told Soviet publishers that Soviet books showed them the path they must follow in their struggle for "freedom and peace."[46] A Ceylonese was quoted to the effect that his people wanted to base agriculture on the model of Soviet collective farms.[47] The famous Mexican muralist, the late Diego Rivera, was reported to have said that the Soviet poet Mayakovski had exerted a powerful and still persisting influence in his country.[48] Considerable satisfaction was expressed regarding the translation into Portuguese of Boris Polevoi's *Story of a Real Man.*[49]

On a more prosaic level is a statement made by K. Bogolyubov in the magazine *Sovetskaya pechat*, No. 5, 1959. Bogolyubov asserted that "the broadening of the cultural ties of the

[44] G. Filippovich, *Kniga idet po svetu* (Moscow, 1958).
[45] *Ibid.*, p. 92.   [46] *Ibid.*, p. 10.   [47] *Ibid.*, p. 15.
[48] *Ibid.*, p. 32.   [49] *Ibid.*, p. 77.

Soviet Union with foreign countries makes it necessary to increase the output of literature in foreign languages, and in particular of technical and scientific books and also newspapers, magazines, albums, catalogues, prospectuses, and descriptions of equipment for export abroad."

In addition to the channels already described, the Soviet Union and other communist countries bring communist publications to the attention of foreign audiences by a variety of other means. These include book fairs, gifts, and library exchanges. The Soviet Union, for example, in 1959 held book fairs in Stockholm, Tokyo, New Delhi, Colombo, Addis Ababa, Phnom Penh, Luxemburg, and Montevideo. Also, the Soviet Union includes book exhibits in international trade fairs and industrial exhibitions. The Soviet library exchange program, too, is a large one. According to Soviet sources, the Library of the Academy of Sciences of the USSR in Leningrad, for example, has agreements with more than 2,100 institutions in 87 countries. In an article in the official Soviet English-language magazine *USSR* for August 1960, Vladimir Orlov, chief librarian of the Lenin Library, stated that his Library was conducting a book exchange with 2,500 institutions in 73 countries, including 180 in the United States. The Lenin Library, according to Orlov, also had book-loan arrangements with 200 libraries in 30 countries. Orlov noted, among other things, that the Lenin Library had prepared, for a library in Pakistan, a bibliography on "The Culture of Tea and Its Cultivation in the USSR," an example he cited of services it performed for various foreign individuals and agencies.

Mention of book fairs leads to consideration of the propaganda role of Soviet exhibitions in foreign countries, including Soviet participation in international trade fairs. The main Soviet governmental agency directing these activities appears to be the All-Union Chamber of Commerce of the USSR, which, to mention an example, represented the Soviet side in negotiating the 1959 United States-Soviet exchange of exhibitions. Commenting on this type of activity, F. Bowen Evans pointed out in 1955 that the communist nations generally greatly increased their effort after 1950. In 1950 and 1951 combined, the total Soviet bloc participation at free world international trade fairs was 15, while, at a minimum, it was 45 in 1954.[50] Although Evans felt that the success of this effort was debatable, he believed it possible that the viewers of communist products in some areas were "probably impressed." A favorable impression might be heightened by explanations of communism's late start in the industrial race and by claims of rapid technological advances in the past and still more rapid progress to come.[51] It seems probable that exaggerated impressions of Russian backwardness played some part in fostering the success of Soviet exhibitions of scientific-technological achievements. The contrast between preconceived stereotype and actual display tended to shatter faith in the assertions of non-Soviet communications media, as well as to build up the kind of image desired by the Russians. In this connection it is well to remember that the unique virtue of international exhibitions as communications devices is that they directly present to the viewer evidence about foreign civilizations, permitting him to form, to a greater degree than would otherwise be possible, his own opinions rather than simply accepting or rejecting the statements of others. For this reason such events as the Soviet-American exchange of exhibitions, beginning in 1959 and continued, with three specialized exhibitions, in 1961-1962, were significant. The American exhibitions were in the fields of plastics, transportation, and medicine, while the Soviets exhibited in the fields of children's books, medicine, and education.

At some fairs and exhibits the communists have won the communications contest by default.[52] According to United

[50] Evans, *Worldwide Communist Propaganda Activities*, p. 104.
[51] *Ibid.*, p. 105.
[52] Apparently, one such case was the Damascus Fair in 1954 and another area where for a considerable time the Soviets made a powerful

States government sources, communist countries participated in 93 international trade fairs and industrial exhibitions in 1956. This appears to have been the high point of such participation in terms of numbers. By 1960, Sino-Soviet bloc representation had dropped to 40, but communist countries staged more than 30 unilateral trade or industrial exhibitions abroad in 1960. In 1961, the communist-controlled countries exhibited their wares at some 60 international trade fairs. A growing trend in Soviet practice in recent years has been participation in special exhibitions on a reciprocal and bilateral basis. The already-mentioned United States-Soviet exchanges, and the Franco-Soviet exhibition exchanges of 1961 are good examples of this.

Perhaps the high point of Soviet use of exhibitions for propaganda purposes was at the Brussels Universal and International Exposition in 1958. At that exhibition, the massive Soviet display of heavy machinery and other evidences of technological prowess apparently made a considerable impression on many viewers, especially on the Flemish farmers who flocked to the fair, although sophisticated intellectuals were repelled by what appeared to them to be the relative crudity of parts of the Soviet display. It should, however, be noted that even from a strictly cultural point of view, the Soviet pavilion at Brussels had many strong points, including an excellent book exhibition. In general, the communist countries in their exhibition policy have sought to create an image of overwhelming power combined with cultural development and humanitarian concern for the individual. Particularly in underdeveloped countries, they have also sought to create the impression that the standard of living under communism was higher than under capitalism. They have done this by emphasizing consumer goods and social welfare services, especially in the fields of public health and education.

---

impression by exhibitions and other propaganda devices, in the absence of effective western competition, was Iceland.

The vast and systematic organized propaganda effort described in this chapter rests upon a solid foundation of financial support, language instruction, and research on the cultures, history, and contemporary conditions of foreign societies. Important developments during the last two or three years have further strengthened the logistics of the Soviet foreign propaganda program. In the field of African studies, for example, it was announced in December 1959 that an African institute had been organized within the Department of Historical Sciences of the Academy of Sciences of the USSR. Previously, the Institute of Ethnography had been the coordinating center of Soviet-African studies. Professor I. I. Potekhin was appointed director of the new African Institute. Potekhin has been active in the formulation as well as the implementation of Soviet policy toward Africa in recent years.[53] On a more purely propagandistic level, in April 1959, a Soviet Association of Friendship with African Peoples was established, also under the chairmanship of Potekhin. As we have indicated in Chapter V, an important feature of the political strategy for Africa worked out by Potekhin, D. A. Olderogge, and other Soviet Africanists appears to be the idea that at least some African nations can, with the help of the Soviet Union and local communist movements, proceed directly from a pre-capitalist stage of development to socialism, without experiencing an intermediate period of capitalist evolution. An interesting view of Soviet strategy toward African cultures, which emphasizes the role of social science in Soviet propaganda to that continent, is that of the anthropologist Christopher Bird of the University of Hawaii. Writing in 1960, Bird argued that the Soviet anthropologically-based strategy was one of undermining the system of African political units based upon former colonial boundaries, by activating tribal ties.[54]

[53] "Russia Looks at Africa," pp. 10-15.
[54] An article by Bird, entitled "Soviet Ethnography: A Base for Applied Study of and Operations in Africa," was published in *Human Organization*, Vol. xix, No. 3 (Fall, 1960).

Like some other scholars disturbed by growing evidence of Soviet political interest in Africa, Christopher Bird has expressed the view that Soviet universities were well ahead of the United States in teaching African languages. He pointed out in an article published in 1962 that when in 1959 Haile Selassie visited the Soviet Union, several Soviet guides were available who could speak the Emperor's native language, Amharic. Bird also stated that a western orientalist found during a visit to Leningrad University in 1958 that Soviet scholars were translating medieval Arabic and Hausa texts, not available in London or Paris, into Russian.[55]

Whether or not Soviet Africanists are doing a better job than their western colleagues and competitors, there is abundant evidence that the teaching of African languages has been developing rapidly in the USSR in recent years. For example, an Ethiopian who spent several years working as an announcer in the Amharic language on Moscow radio was quoted in the *New York Times* for January 27, 1962 to the effect that Amharic was being taught at Moscow and Leningrad universities and in other higher educational institutions. According to the same source, other African languages offered in Soviet higher educational institutions included Swahili, Hausa, and Zulu. He added that two Ethiopian students were working as translators in the Moscow Foreign Languages Publishing House.

Like African studies, Latin American studies were relatively neglected in the USSR until about 1958 or 1959. Alexander Dallin noted in 1961 that a bibliography of Soviet writings on Latin America published in 1959 revealed that "the growth of Soviet interest in Latin America is mirrored in the increase from forty titles published in 1945 to three hundred and sixty-one in 1958." He added, correctly, that "undoubtedly the trend has continued since 1958."[56]

[55] Christopher Bird, "Scholarship and Propaganda," *Problems of Communism*, Vol. IX, No. 2 (March-April, 1962), pp. 32-38. Material cited is on p. 32.

[56] *American Slavic and East European Review*, Vol. XX, No. 1 (February, 1961), pp. 148-149.

In the autumn of 1961, the Academy of Sciences of the USSR established an Institute of the Peoples of Hispanic America, under the direction of S. S. Mikhailov, an historian with considerable experience in the Soviet diplomatic establishment. This important event in the development of Soviet Latin American study climaxed a number of prior steps, including the founding in 1953 of a Section for the Modern and Contemporary History of the Countries of the Americas, in the Academy's Institute of History, and, in 1960, the formation of the Soviet-Hispanic American Friendship Society. As P. Urban points out in a heavily-documented survey published in 1962, an impressive volume of historical and political studies on Latin America has flowed from Soviet presses in the last three or four years. Most of this literature is highly tendentious. Its major themes include "colonialism," "imperialism," and "the national liberation movement." In a word, as Urban notes, this research and publication effort constitutes an elaboration of Soviet tactics in relation to the countries of Latin America. Soviet publications on Latin America—like those dealing with Asia and Africa—are intended both for the instruction of Soviet diplomats and intelligence agents, and for export, in translation, for foreign communists and also for Latin American students, especially those enrolled in Friendship University.[57]

With regard to the general area of foreign language teaching in the USSR, it is of interest that *Pravda* and *Izvestiya* for June 4, 1961 reported that the Council of Ministers of the USSR had adopted a resolution on measures to improve the teaching of foreign languages. The resolution instructed the councils of ministers of the various Soviet republics, as well as the Minister of Higher and Specialized Secondary Education to improve the curricula, syllabi, textbooks, etc., utilized

[57] P. Urban, "Los Estudios Iberoamericanos en la URSS," *Estudios sobre la Union Sovietica*, Vol. II, No. 3 (July, 1962), pp. 27-40. The above journal is published by the Institute for the Study of the USSR, in Munich.

for this purpose. Another indication of Soviet concern with foreign languages was an article in the publication of the above ministry in February 1960, arguing that foreign languages were the "specialists' tool."[58] An announcement in *Komsomolskaya pravda* for July 22, 1960, inserted by Moscow State University, made it known that the university was enrolling graduate students in fields including Oriental languages and literatures, African languages, as well as in the history of Hungary, the history of England, the history of Latin America, the history of the international labor movement, and the history of religion and atheism, etc.

Foreign scholars who attended the Twenty-fifth International Congress of Orientalists in Moscow in 1960 were impressed by the evidence afforded there of Soviet intentions to utilize Oriental studies "to influence the intellectual leaders of the rising new nations of Asia and Africa."[59] The Soviet organizers of this congress made a studied effort to belittle western scholarship on Afro-Asian nations and to flatter their academic guests from those continents. Professor William B. Ballis, a participant, concluded the article from which the above quotation was taken by expressing the view that at the next congress, scheduled for 1963 in New Delhi, "The Soviets will be able to continue their very impressive campaign to influence Oriental studies and the relations between the USSR and the new nations of Asia and Africa." While this is undoubtedly true, it should also be recalled that the Chinese communist delegation which had been invited to the Orientalists' Congress failed to put in an appearance. This embarrassing absence may perhaps be indicative of complications which in the future may increasingly plague Soviet cultural propaganda efforts in Asia, Africa, and Latin America, as the Sino-Soviet rivalry among the peoples of those continents is

[58] *Vestnik vysshei shkoly*, No. 2 (February, 1960), pp. 51-54.
[59] William B. Ballis, "The Soviets Conduct a Congress," *Michigan Alumni Quarterly Review*, May, 1961, pp. 161-166. Quotation is on pp. 165-166.

intensified. It should also be noted that Soviet graduate students and young scholars sent to the United States in the graduate exchange program which began in 1959-1960 have on the whole been considerably inferior in their language preparation to their United States counterparts sent to the Soviet Union. In language and area studies, as in most of the other enterprises discussed in this chapter, Soviet efforts are impressive and improving, but by no means overwhelmingly successful.

CHAPTER IX

EFFECTIVENESS AND LIMITATIONS

OF SOVIET PROPAGANDA

WHAT is signified, after all, by the sound and fury of Soviet foreign propaganda? How effective is it? Can it create political parties, topple governments, subvert the social order? Or does it have merely a nuisance value for the Kremlin, the capability of influencing or even converting some alienated intellectuals, who may then become either cogs in the Soviet espionage machine, or rather ineffectual and probably temporary propagandists for the Soviet "line"? Or, finally, is it a significant but supplementary instrument of Soviet foreign policy, which reinforces and is congruent with military, economic, and diplomatic instruments?

A qualifiedly affirmative answer would appear to be appropriate for most of the above questions. With the possible exception of Russia itself, in 1917-1918, when Lenin's promises of bread, peace, land, and national self-determination proved overwhelmingly persuasive, propaganda has probably not played the decisive role in communist seizures of power. It has, however, been an important or even crucial Soviet instrument of power. It has made, or helped to make, converts to communism. It has pushed many individuals far enough along the road to conversion to win at least their benevolent neutrality toward Soviet policies and designs. Others, basically hostile to Marxist-Leninist ideology, have either naively believed Soviet promises or have thought, mistakenly, that they could use the communists rather than be used by them in alliances against "capitalists" or "imperialists."

Most important of all, Soviet propaganda has succeeded in intensifying and channeling in directions desirable to the

Kremlin attitudes such as fear of war, anti-colonialism, and anti-western nationalism. Soviet propaganda, as Paul Kecskemeti has noted, has been most successful when it has been in a position to project an image of the Soviet Union as being bent on combatting a "manifest evil." In such situations, it has made a significant impact, and has been able to win helpers or at least benevolent neutrality toward Soviet policy.[1] Kecskemeti has identified four historical situations in which the Soviets were able to employ what he called the "universalistic argument." These were: (1) the First World War; (2) the rise of Nazi Germany; (3) the fear of war in the late 1940's; (4) the decline of colonialism in Asia and Africa. It will be noted that three of the four situations identified by Kecskemeti as exceptionally favorable to the success of Soviet foreign propaganda were concerned with the effects or the fear of war.

Kecskemeti's analysis is useful both because it indicates the difficulties confronting Soviet propagandists and points to some of the major factors influencing the effects of Soviet propaganda efforts. Kecskemeti correctly emphasized the essentially negative character of Soviet foreign propaganda. However, he wrote before the full development of certain major features of post-Stalin foreign propaganda which we have sought to analyze in this study. In recent years, the Soviet leadership has made increasingly successful efforts to project important positive propaganda themes, especially to the peoples of the less-developed countries and the newly emerging nations of the world. As Dyer noted, in commenting on Soviet propaganda handling of the launching in 1957 of Soviet artificial earth satellites, the Soviet Union "proclaimed a right to leadership on the ground that its knowledge was superior."[2] Soviet propaganda regarding such matters as educational and scientific progress, economic development, and the alleged

[1] Paul Kecskemeti, "The Soviet Approach to International Political Communication," *Public Opinion Quarterly*, Vol. xx (Spring, 1956), No. 1, pp. 299-308. Quoted material on p. 305.

[2] Dyer, *op.cit.*, p. 3.

Soviet solution of the "nationality problem" has told the peoples of the developing areas that by following the Soviet path of economic, social, and political development, they could most effectively realize their own legitimate aspirations.

"Positive" and affirmative Soviet propaganda, while often resting in part on a foundation of facts—as in the case of Soviet scientific achievements—can be in its way as demagogic as the negative propaganda identified by Kecskemeti.[3] Soviet propagandists as we pointed out in Chapter IV, frequently offer solutions to urgent problems, such as disarmament, which seem plausible but which in the opinion of western experts cannot be implemented and which they themselves would refuse to put into effect were their propaganda bluff to be called.

In many economically underdeveloped countries Soviet propaganda has guided and reinforced the efforts of local communist parties to exploit peasant poverty and land hunger. As in Russia, peasants have often supported leaders who have promised to give the land to those who till it. But the leaders conceal from their followers their Marxist-Leninist goal of collectivizing farming and turning the farmer into a cog in a state-directed economic machine. Cuba, Vietnam, and many other examples come readily to mind. Soviet propaganda has inspired moods or generated pressures within foreign states which have tended to lessen the ability of their governments to oppose Soviet policies. Soviet "ban the bomb" propaganda, for example, probably was an important factor in enabling the USSR to simultaneously pursue an expansionist foreign policy

[3] However, propaganda about Soviet scientific and economic achievements serves as a powerful instrument of psychological pressure upon the non-Soviet world. Needless to say, the impact of this pressure depends not only upon the material realities involved, but also upon the accuracy of information and maturity of judgment of the publics to whom Soviet claims regarding material achievements are directed. For this reason, among others, such studies as Nicholas DeWitt's monumental work, *Education and Professional Employment in the USSR*, Washington, D.C., 1961, are useful.

and limit the effectiveness of western countermeasures during the years when the United States had a monopoly of atomic weapons. Also, Soviet anti-western propaganda may have played a sufficient part in shaping the attitudes of individuals in "neutralist" countries to influence the policies of their governments in a pro-Soviet, anti-western direction. Of course, the Suez crisis, the Algerian conflict, the situations in the Congo and Angola, among many, were exploitable and Moscow did its best to fan the flames.

However, the effectiveness of Soviet propaganda regarding, for example, Algeria or Angola, may have been limited because while Moscow talked it did little to aid the groups it professed to support. One wonders whether many a Latin-American radical did not feel at least temporarily let down or even betrayed when Khrushchev in October 1962 agreed to remove Soviet "offensive" ballistic missiles from Cuba. Moreover, the Soviets have usually been remarkably parsimonious in offering positive programs for the correction of the evils they decry and denounce. The self-seeking line followed by the Russians could not fail, one would think, in the long run, to be disappointing to all but communists. However, we must recognize the fact that many intellectuals and would-be intellectuals in underdeveloped countries feel that Soviet policy, because it is "socialist" must be constructive. Soviet propaganda in the last few years, despite improvement in the quantity and quality of its informational support, as well as increased use of promotional devices, such as radio quiz shows, a philately department in the magazine *USSR*, and, recently the placing of advertisements in major American newspapers, has not been strikingly original or imaginative. For example, the Kremlin seems to have neglected to exploit propaganda opportunities inherent in differences of emphasis among the western allies on such matters as the degree and kind of inspection necessary for a workable agreement banning nuclear weapons tests.

It should be borne in mind, nevertheless, that in terms of

careful briefing and coordinated action for the purpose of quickly marshalling data necessary to support their government's policy line, Soviet UN personnel—and Soviet participants in international scientific and other kinds of conferences and organizations—are probably at an advantage, and operate more effectively, than their British or American counterparts. In part, these observations are prompted by conversations with American and African diplomats serving at the UN.

There is increasing evidence that with the growth in Soviet self-confidence occasioned by the expanding world role of the USSR, and, perhaps also reflecting the relatively relaxed post-Stalin domestic situation, Soviet personnel serving abroad, especially at the United Nations, are less reluctant than formerly to participate in various social activities on a more or less informal basis, especially with nationals of the less-developed countries. But, in connection with Africa, it is worth remembering that no African state has yet become communist, and even in leftist-oriented Guinea the Soviets, in 1961, failed dismally in their efforts to organize an actively subversive movement, and have apparently been losing rather than gaining influence ever since.

It appears that Soviet communicators, like others, have found face-to-face contact a more effective instrument of influence than the printed page or the radio broadcast. It is probably in connection with this superiority of "primary contact" as a propaganda tool that Moscow derives the greatest benefit from the existence of a network of foreign communist parties that present the Soviet line as fellow-countrymen of those to whom they speak.

The success of Khrushchev in projecting his personality and using himself as an instrument of propaganda access has been considerable, and the same can probably be said, though to a far lesser degree, about Mikoyan, Kozlov, Mukhitdinov, Brezhnev, and other leading Soviet agitator-politicians. However, the nature of Soviet totalitarianism imposes limits on Soviet use of face-to-face communication. Many instances have been reported to this writer, and he has personally observed some, in which the inflexible, phonograph-like presentation of the official Soviet foreign policy position by Soviet representatives, either at home or abroad, has proved to be a source of irritation rather than persuasion. In addition, Soviet fear of easy intimacy and informality often interposes barriers to easy communication. Generally speaking, Soviet successes in the area of cultural diplomacy and exchanges of persons are more likely to occur when carefully staged spectacles and regimented masses—as in youth and sports festivals—can be employed, than in the smaller, more intimate type of gathering, where communist aversion to spontaneity is likely to strike a jarring note.

Also, Moscow achieves an impact with some its dramatic propaganda spectacles, such as the youth and students' festivals, partly because of the failure of the United States and other free nations to develop positive programs to demonstrate the values of democracy. Why not a democratic world youth festival? In connection with the 1962 communist youth festival in Helsinki, the American State Department had no clear policy regarding its attitude toward participation by American youth—and participation by some curious, idealistic, and in some instances highly competent American young people was inevitable, with or without official encouragement or discouragement. It is to be hoped that the efforts of various groups of young Americans to exploit for democratic purposes this Soviet-organized propaganda spectacle did not go unappreciated by American policy-makers. A noncommittal, evasive attitude such as the United States Government has sometimes taken toward communist efforts to exploit the idealism of youth or the legitimate grievances of peasants and workers furnishes no basis for countering Soviet propaganda, let alone for developing an effective positive program of democratic action. The same can be said about the tendency of

American officials serving in many countries to associate mainly, sometimes solely, with members of the entrenched local elites, and to neglect contacts with leaders of reform movements and even with artists, scientists, and other persons outside of government. In addition, the American image has of course suffered from the ethnocentrism, cultural parochialism, and ignorance—for example, of foreign languages—still too often displayed by otherwise well educated Americans. Obviously, we cannot cultivate whatever favorable predispositions exist toward democracy if we lack knowledge of them and are unable to establish rapport with those who possess them.

Some characteristics of the Soviet foreign propaganda effort stand out with particular clarity. The hostility and aggressiveness underlying it, though relatively mild in comparison with Peking's output, are patent. However, the road to world domination is not necessarily paved with craving for power. It is certain that the Soviet effort is a big and an expensive one. It is not, perhaps, as big an effort, in terms of financial support, as some of us, including this writer, have in the past been inclined to believe. Still, it is large and growing. According to information received by the author from a well-informed United States government source, in March 1962 it was estimated that as of 1957 the total communist bloc foreign propaganda effort amounted, in terms of American dollars, to something between four hundred and seventy-five million and seven hundred million. As of 1962, the range of estimates was between something under a billion and something more than one hundred million. The Soviet part of this total effort was estimated to be about forty per cent. A reflection of communist fear of free communication can be seen from the estimate the USSR alone was spending about one hundred and fifteen million dollars a year, as of 1961, for the jamming of foreign radio broadcasts. This figure was in excess of the estimated Soviet expenditure for transmitting radio broadcasts to foreign countries.[4]

The questions posed at the beginning of this chapter could be better answered if the government agencies concerned, as well as private scholars, undertook, on a much bigger scale than at present, to produce the necessary descriptive, historical, analytical, and statistical studies of the impact of Soviet propaganda on different geographic regions and social strata. The most sophisticated and balanced study of communist influence which has so far been published is Gabriel A. Almond's *The Appeals of Communism*. This study, however, deals primarily with the activities of four major western communist parties, namely, the American, British, French, and Italian parties, rather than with the foreign political activity of the Soviet Union. A difficult problem, only partially explored as yet in the literature on the Soviet Union or on foreign communist parties, is that of distinguishing between the influence of Soviet propaganda and that of the various national communist parties. Of course, even with an abundance of good case studies, the evaluation of the effectiveness of Soviet propaganda would remain formidably difficult. It is often impossible to perceive accurately or fully the relationship between a particular political act and a given, identifiable propaganda stimulus. As Lerner has indicated, the four main types of evidence of propaganda effectiveness— responsive action, participant reports, observer commentaries, and indirect indicators—are all difficult to obtain and require caution and subtlety of interpretation to be useful.[5]

It is well to strike a cautious note in any general appraisal

[4] The figures on Soviet foreign propaganda expenditures given in this author's *Soviet Cultural Offensive*, *op.cit.*, p. 158, may have been somewhat inflated. For additional data on the logistics of the Soviet program, see the already-cited works of F. Bowen Evans and Evron Kirkpatrick, as well as the 1957-1958 *Fact Book*, distributed by the United States Information Agency.

[5] Daniel Lerner, "Effective Propaganda: Conditions and Evaluation," in Schramm, *op.cit.*, pp. 485-487.

of the effectiveness of Soviet propaganda. The tendency of the American public is to attribute almost superhuman cunning, skill, and effectiveness to Soviet propaganda. This is indicated, for example, by such typical press items as the headline in the *New York Herald Tribune* for January 31, 1962, "Gallup Poll Gives Reds Four-Three Edge in War of Ideas." The public tendency, as well as that of some experts on communism, is to attribute the growth of communist power exclusively to communist cunning, and to ignore the complex situations which predispose individuals, groups, and sometimes nations to respond to the appeals of communism. It is useful to have the warnings about the effectiveness of Soviet propaganda produced by Suzanne Labin and Stefan T. Possony.[6] Labin argues that Soviet and French communist propaganda was responsible for the defeat of EDC in France in 1954. She also asserts that "European universities are so contaminated that the Communist and para-Communist movements of Asia and Africa can be said to have been nurtured in them."[7]

There is a grain of truth in such assertions, but of course they represent gross exaggerations. The danger in being guided exclusively by estimates of Soviet propaganda influence such as the foregoing, is two-fold. On the one hand, excessive emphasis on the role of propaganda in Soviet policy can blind one to the importance of such factors as education and scientific research that enable the USSR to build the power which makes its propaganda impressive. Perhaps more important, the alarmist view of Soviet propaganda may lead us to think that all that is required to combat communist influence is American counter-propaganda.

[6] Madame Labin's study, "The Technique of Soviet Propaganda," was distributed in a pamphlet under that title by the Subcommittee to Investigate the Administration of the Internal Security Act and Other Internal Security Laws, of the Committee on the Judiciary, U.S. Senate, 86th Cong., 2nd Sess., Washington, D.C., 1960; see also Stefan T. Possony, "Language as a Communist Weapon, " distributed by the House Committee on Un-American Activities, under date of March 2, 1959.

[7] Labin, *op.cit.*, p. 7.

We must constantly keep reminding ourselves that ours is an era of disturbing and puzzling social and cultural change. The unsettling effects of rapid social change have been compounded by the destruction and disillusionment resulting from wars. Add to all this the anxieties induced by the existence of nuclear weapons and there is a situation pregnant with potential for propaganda manipulation. Unfortunately for Moscow, however, the extremism of the Chinese communists may have rendered it difficult for the international communist movement to exploit the "peace" theme as effectively as Khrushchev might desire. This is indicated, for example, by the fact that in his already-cited speech of December 12, 1962, in which he defended Soviet Cuban policy against the "Trotskyite" policy of his "Albanian"—a thinly veiled reference to Chinese—critics, Khrushchev said that their willingness to risk the "destruction of millions of human beings" could "repel millions and millions of people from the communist movement."

Emphasis on the factors in the international environment which foster susceptibility to the appeals of communism is in no sense defeatist. If we are to limit the effectiveness of these appeals, we must first perceive their dimensions as clearly as possible. In some situations, awareness of the predispositions which favor communist influence may stimulate action designed to alter the circumstances which foster pro-communist attitudes. It may also prevent us from falling into the trap of indiscriminately labeling all social protest movements as "communist." Finally, it may facilitate refutation of communist propaganda by enabling us to point to incompatibilities between standard communist operating procedures and the promises communists often make to persons unaware of the gulf between Soviet propaganda and the reality of Soviet international practices.

The main purpose of this study has been to demonstrate the energy with which Soviet propaganda has exploited both the negative and the positive sentiments generated by the revolutionary social-political and psycho-cultural developments of the twentieth century. It is sensible to assume that continued existence of the favorable predispositions toward Soviet claims and promises of some strata of the contemporary world propaganda audience combined with systematic, intensive Soviet cultivation of these attitudes will tend to foster Soviet influence. This will be particularly true in the absence of effective free world concern. However, direct evidence of Soviet propaganda effectiveness is extremely scanty. There have been, of course, a few studies which strongly suggest that Soviet achievements in outer space, for example, have had a powerful impact on many sectors of world opinion.[8] However, it is a real question to what extent the impact of Soviet achievements in this or other fields can be considered evidence of the effectiveness of Soviet propaganda exploitation of these achievements and to what extent it is merely a reflection of the fact that they occurred. Perhaps it is not irrelevant to remind ourselves here that if the positive example of Soviet achievements can influence world opinion, so also can knowledge of western shortcomings, such as unjust treatment of ethnic minorities.

Khrushchev evidently regards Soviet scientific and technical progress as one of the main instruments for the victory of communism in the world today. Beginning in 1956, he has increasingly emphasized the crucial significance of victory in the "battle of production" for the world triumph of communism. This conviction is also indicated by current stress, in Soviet articles regarding propaganda and ideology, on the priority of the propaganda of production.[9]

[8] See the already-cited study by Gabriel A. Almond, "Public Opinion and the Development of Space Technology," and the analysis by Donald Puchala, also mentioned in Chapter VI.
[9] It is significant that the first, in order of listing, of the duties prescribed for members of the CPSU by the statutes adopted at the Twenty-second Congress is to "work for the creation of the material and technical basis of communism," etc., and that both Khrushchev's

The Soviet leadership has displayed unusual sensitivity to the potential propaganda effect of science, technology, and economic development. An apt illustration is furnished by the decision made by Moscow to utilize the development of powerful rocket boosters for a propaganda effect which achieved a stunning impact in 1957. Of course, the necessary decisions were made long before the dramatic launching of the first Soviet artificial earth satellite in October of that year. Soviet policy in this sphere contrasted sharply with the indifference to psychological factors inherent in the cautious American policy of restricting effort to "purely scientific" activities. There was a sharp contrast between the propaganda sensitivity displayed by the Kremlin, and the view of certain American officials that the first Soviet sputnik was nothing but "a hunk of iron in the sky." Other examples of Soviet sensitivity to the capacity of a wide range of achievements and activities to influence world opinion include the use of the Soviet Merchant Marine and of civil aviation personnel as agencies of propaganda in underdeveloped countries, and the unremitting efforts made by Soviet propaganda to cultivate the international scientific community. It is also interesting to note the speed with which Moscow shifts propaganda and cultural personnel from one area to another as world conditions change. One is reminded of this Soviet capability by the United States Information Agency report of April 1962, noting that Soviet radio broadcasts to Africa doubled in 1961, as compared with 1960.

However, these activities relate more to the prerequisites

---

major speech of December 12, 1962, and the foreign policy declaration published in *Pravda* for January 7, 1963 emphasized the centrality, for the world victory of communism, of victory in the US-Soviet production contest. Also, a decree of the CPSU issued in 1957 prescribed that Soviet trade unions should disseminate, among foreign trade unionists, information regarding the economic-scientific achievements of the Soviet Union. The text of this decree is available on pp. 160-176 of *Spravochnik sekretarya pervichnoi partiinoi organizatsii* (Moscow, 1960).

for Soviet propaganda success than to direct evidence thereof. They underscore the fact that the Kremlin is determined to make energetic use of its army of professional propagandists to enhance its own power and weaken that of the west. A few years ago Ralph K. White noted that "There is a curiously widespread assumption in the United States that the cunning Communists are past masters at the propaganda game and that we innocent democrats are rank amateurs. Actually the reverse of this assumption would be at least as easy to defend."[10] Dr. White's observation would appear to be approximately as correct today as it was in 1954, although the Soviets have introduced a number of presentational devices designed to enhance the appeal, for example, of their foreign radio broadcasts. Similarly, they have improved the format, paper, and printing of propaganda publications such as *USSR*, in which an almost dramatic change for the better occurred in the summer of 1960. In the economically advanced western countries at least, the effectiveness of Soviet propaganda, especially if measured in terms of the strength and ideological vitality of communist parties, appears to be gradually diminishing. This is indicated, among other things, by the increasing inability of the British, French and Italian communist parties to attract youth. In spite of Khrushchev's flexibility, propaganda emanating directly from Moscow, also, seems to be of diminishing effectiveness in western Europe.

The effects of Khrushchev's own 1956 "secret speech," of Soviet actions in Hungary, and of Soviet intransigence regarding testing of nuclear weapons, Berlin, Cuba, and other issues are involved in this complex picture. The ability of the Soviet Union to influence the west depends less and less upon Moscow's critique of the western social order, and more and more upon possession of hydrogen bombs and ballistic missiles. As White notes, "When it comes to evaluating communist

[10] Ralph K. White, "The New Resistance to International Propaganda," in Schramm, *op.cit.*, pp. 180-190; quoted material on p. 181.

propaganda techniques as illustrated in the communist press and radio, the verdict of the typical reader or listener in either eastern or western Europe seems to be that they are boringly repetitious, obviously 'propagandistic,' and therefore dull."[11] Comparative evaluations of the effectiveness of Soviet *versus* British and American radio broadcasts cited by White, as well as more recent ones, indicate that, as far as western Europeans are concerned, the Soviet radio comes off second or third best.

It would be a mistake, nevertheless, to dismiss as insignificant the Soviet propaganda effort, even in western Europe or the United States. This is of course obvious in the case of such countries as France and Italy, where the communist parties can still count on receiving approximately a quarter of the total vote cast in national and municipal elections. It should also be kept in mind that Soviet propaganda is a very useful instrument to the Kremlin if it can generate sufficient pressure to inhibit or slow up responses to aggressive Soviet moves. It is in this area of weakening the western world's will to resist Soviet pressures that Soviet propaganda on peace and war is probably a potent political instrument. As John Keep observed in an article in the January 1962 issue of *Survey,* "the Soviet Union enjoys considerable advantages in a psychological warfare operation of this kind, since . . . in an open society even organs of 'bourgeois' opinion can be expected to spread, if not actual sympathy for, then at least an understanding awareness of the Soviet viewpoint." But as Keep also observes, Soviet efforts to exploit western war fears amount, in the last analysis, only to "a gigantic piece of bluff."

Even in the advanced industrial countries of the west, of course, many pressing social problems remain unresolved. The Kremlin may well still believe that a new major economic depression might exacerbate social tensions in Europe and the United States and thus create golden opportunities for exploitation by Soviet propaganda. Perhaps with hope of such an

[11] *Ibid.*, p. 182.

outcome, Moscow strives to build the broadest possible "fronts" and "blocs," while continuing to "unmask" trade union leaders, socialists, and others who reject its overtures.

As for the underdeveloped countries, there the situation is more favorable from the Soviet point of view, despite the fact that even in these exceptionally susceptible regions Soviet propaganda has continued to be somewhat handicapped by the insistence of Soviet ideologists on the use, in describing the revolutionary ferment of those areas, of an only partly applicable Marxist terminology. It is an interesting—and sobering—thought that Castro's victory in Cuba was won partly because Castro, though of course Marxist-oriented, was pragmatic enough to speak a language that he sensed was appealing to a society where, as Theodore Draper's writings point out, discontented intellectuals, unemployed semi-proletarians, poverty-stricken peasants, and agricultural laborers—rather than the "proletariat" as Marx would have defined the term—constituted the raw material of revolution.

Particularly in Latin America, increasing unrest, for example in Colombia or Venezuela, or even in the key countries of Argentina and Brazil, appears to be accompanied by increasing support for communist-oriented groups and movements. The communists have been particularly successful in penetrating student movements in Latin America. Energetic Soviet, Castro, and local communist propaganda undoubtedly play some part in generating increasing communist influence. The greatest stimulus to increased communist influence in recent years in Latin America was of course the rise of Castro, whose example, with modifications perhaps, and apparently not without trepidation, Moscow hopes to see other Latin lands emulate. With particular drama, Moscow flashed to the Latin American lands its association with Castro, "the national hero of the Cuban people," during the Cuban leader's Soviet visit in April and May 1963. Soviet activities, particularly the bringing of Latin American students and intellectuals on free or heavily subsidized trips to the Soviet Union, and the recognition accorded by Moscow to such Latin American literary figures as the poet Neruda or the poetess Mistral by awarding them well-publicized honors, also have played a part. At the same time growing training programs for Cubans and other Latin Americans in the USSR have contributed to this propaganda effort. Insofar as these activities have harnessed to Soviet purposes the explosive forces of Latin American "anti-Yankeeism," frustrated aspirations for social justice, and the desire of Latin American peoples to achieve on the international scene a satisfactory status of group identity and dignity, they have, in recent years, fostered the growth of Soviet influence.

Even in traditionally anti-Russian Turkey, the Soviet call for a return to the relatively friendly pattern of Soviet-Turkish relations, which were at their most cordial during the years when both Lenin and Mustafa Kemal were at the helm of their respective regimes, may have had some effect.

Aspects of Soviet and Soviet orbit propaganda in the underdeveloped countries that might achieve particularly significant impact in the emerging future include the following: an expanding program of technical education for selected youths from these areas; the publication and export by Iron Curtain countries, at low prices, of textbooks, in local languages; assistance to the new nations of Africa, and to Cuba, in developing radio and television networks, and other communications systems, as well as in supplying equipment and personnel for airlines; perhaps most significant of all, the increasing Soviet tendency, mentioned at the end of Chapter VII, to study and apply empirical social science techniques developed in the west. Then too, the steady growth of Soviet and Soviet bloc propaganda output to the developing areas should warn us against complacency in evaluating its present and possible future effectiveness.

Finally, John H. Kautsky, Bernard S. Morris, and Morris Watnick have emphasized that the "multi-class bloc" strategy, perhaps borrowed by the Soviets from the Chinese communists, and increasingly elaborated since the early 1950's, has enabled Moscow and the communist parties of the underdeveloped countries to make more effective use of such sentiments and aspirations as anti-westernism and the desire for rapid modernization, regardless of cost or consequences.[12]

But if the Soviet foreign propaganda effort is a massive and energetic one, it is also plagued by weaknesses which may in the long run ensure its failure. The major weaknesses of Soviet propaganda arise from the increasing theoretical obsolescence of Marxism-Leninism and from the conspiratorial, totalitarian structure of Soviet communism. It is likely that to all but the least sophisticated intellectuals, at least in the west, Marxism-Leninism appears today to be not much more than a set of ritualistic phrases masking the power-drive of a totalitarian political movement. Even after the death of Stalin, the Soviet communists did not appear to become fully aware that the clichés which presented a more or less accurate picture of the evils of capitalism in the 1840's had little relevance to the welfare-state society of western Europe or the United States in the 1960's. Although increased Soviet power, and the doctrinal revisions noted above, imparted unprecedented flexibility to Soviet propaganda by giving it a wider choice of means, they could not free it from the necessity of proclaiming adherence to an allegedly infallible doctrine, nor release its ties to a centralized, conspiratorial political leadership.

In this situation, Soviet and other communists are forced to choose between such radical reforms as, for example, the repudiation of a manipulative style of political discourse,

[12] John H. Kautsky, *Political Change in Underdeveloped Countries, op.cit.* See the essays by the above-named authors, on pp. 57-89 and 282-303. Overstreet and Windmiller in their study on communism in India, cited earlier, regard this "neo-Maoist" strategy as, essentially, a contemporary version of the "anti-imperialist" line advocated by Lenin at the 1920 Comintern congress, and later, but they do not reject the general framework of Kautsky's analysis.

which might destroy communism as a messianic, though opportunistic semi-religious movement, and continued adherence to their traditional tactics of secrecy and deception. Thus far, they have obviously preferred the latter, which from their point of view represents the lesser evil. It may be doubted if in some parts of the world, where freedom of opinion, and other kinds of individual freedom, rank low on the order of value priorities of some of the most politically discontented groups, Soviet orthodoxy and secrecy are a great liability, or even, perhaps, a liability at all. Still, as William H. Stringer indicated in the *Christian Science Monitor* for September 13, 1961, the Egyptian press expressed surprise that the Soviet people had not been told that their government had detonated five nuclear test explosions—a pattern of "maintained ignorance" preserved, it may be noted, throughout the 1961, and also the 1962 Soviet nuclear test series.

Perhaps even more striking and possibly more damaging to the credibility of Soviet communications media was their handling of the acute stage of the Cuban crisis in October 1962. After the Soviet press had for days ridiculed United States revelations about Soviet offensive missile bases in Cuba, Mr. Khrushchev in his message to President Kennedy, published in *Pravda* for October 29 and broadcast throughout the world, expressed his "understanding" regarding Kennedy's concern over "weapons which you consider to be offensive." No mention was made of missiles, and, even if slyly, Khrushchev admitted by implication the falsity of previous Soviet assertions and the dishonesty of Soviet policy toward Cuba. It should also be remembered, as Edward Crankshaw stressed in his article, "Case History of an Unfree Press," in the *New York Times* Magazine for December 2, 1962, that the Soviet people were never given the text of President Kennedy's statement of October 22, regarding Soviet rockets on Cuba, and that subsequent United States actions were denounced as "piracy" and "aggression" by the Soviet press. Thus, in the "mirror image" style so characteristic of Soviet political communication, Soviet aggression was depicted as defense against an alleged American plot to attack Cuba, and of course, as in his speech to the Supreme Soviet on December 12, Khrushchev was to credit himself with having, by his wise handling of the Cuban crisis, saved the peace of the world. In part, it would appear, the communists have been able to successfully practice deception and secrecy because the west has thus far not made a realistic and systematic effort to expose the backwardness of Soviet secrecy. "What are you hiding?" and "What are you afraid of?" are questions the free world should more often put to the rulers of communist states. Above all, we should do more, with tact and skill, to make clear to the intellectuals of uncommitted countries the nature and scope of Soviet secrecy and other repressive aspects of communism.

The west today is in a better position on the whole than is the Soviet Union to employ its own version of the tactics of "exposure." A government which is afraid to permit its citizens to have free access to the supposedly "decadent" products of modern western civilization can scarcely claim to have achieved full success in modernizing itself. On the contrary, it should not be too difficult to prove that a backward, neo-medieval, culture pattern still prevails under Soviet communism. Is this the wave of the future, or the wave of the past?

A program of carefully calculated pressure on communist states to "open up" their societies to observation and study and to disclose the data which would make possible a critical examination of their claims to have achieved progress not merely in rocketry and space technology, but also in social welfare and personal freedom, might help to diminish the attractiveness of the Soviet model for the discontented intellectuals of underdeveloped countries. Along the same lines, comparison between the utopian, libertarian, and humanitarian values present in the writings of Marx, and even to some degree in those of Lenin, with realities of everyday life in communist-dominated societies can play its part in effective western counter-propaganda. At the same time, we must, as Urie Bronfennbrenner pointed out in a perceptive article in the *New York Times* magazine for April 22, 1962, exercise patience in our efforts to reduce Soviet secrecy and repressiveness, lest we do more harm than good by increasing, rather than allaying, the fear and anxiety which give rise to this constrictive pattern. Brashness in such delicate matters may backfire, both in its effect on the communist state, and in its possibly harmful effects on underdeveloped countries, which, suffering from manifold insecurities, cannot be expected to fully share the preferences of western liberals for publicity and fullness of disclosure of information about governmental activities.

The most important tool of the free world in the struggle against communist propaganda, however, is not propaganda or counter-propaganda at all, but a series of programs designed to mitigate or eliminate the conditions which foster susceptibility to Soviet propaganda. There is obviously no single formula by which this effort can be guided. In a world which sometimes seems to be falling apart at the seams, the task is a difficult one. The policies designed to deal with it must be selective. If there are areas where situations are so chaotic that any early achievement of a well-integrated society is impossible, perhaps these unfortunate lands must be permitted to pass, for a time, through a period of chaos. With regard to susceptibility to the appeals of communist propaganda, much of the world today is in a situation somewhat similar to that through which western Europe and the United States passed during the depression-ridden years of the 1930's. It is not entirely utopian to hope that many of the more disturbed lands will gradually achieve a degree of integration and national purpose which will render them less and less susceptible to the influence of Soviet promises and threats.

In the meantime, the west can intensify and systematize its efforts to achieve effective, sympathetic, and honest communication with the peoples of the developing countries. The problem is only partly one of economic development. More important, perhaps, is the effort, by exchanges of persons, by assistance to local educational institutions in the form, for example, of appropriate printed matter and cultural materials, and on terms within the means of the emerging, modernizing intelligentsias of the less-industrialized lands, to achieve greater mutual understanding and respect.

A prime necessity for a successful western effort in the struggle to contain Soviet influence is increased cooperation on all levels among the western nations. Such a program of voluntary cooperation, employing the strategies referred to above, and many others, would be within the framework of the pluralistic western tradition. It would set an example to the "neutralist" nations of a model by which common goals are achieved through cooperation rather than through constraint and coercion.

Finally, the citizens and the governments of the free societies must constantly remind themselves that the survival and extension of free institutions in a revolutionary era require proof that a system based upon a broad exercise of individual initiative and responsibility can serve better than the conformist collectivism of communism to assist the peoples of the world in the realization of aspirations which are common to all men but which are expressed in a variety of ways.

A more effective American, and perhaps a common western, international information effort will result from the skillful and tactful projection of an example worthy of respect. This is especially true if the peoples of the western democracies can combine a readiness to explain their purposes in the world with eagerness to understand the problems and aspirations of men in other situations and settings, whose aspirations, moods and modes of expression may require much study to achieve the sympathetic understanding essential for mutually satisfactory communication.

320

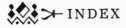